GREAT VACATIONS for YOU & YOUR DOG, USA

Martin Management Books

ISBN 1-878500-07-4 1997-98 edition

Library of Congress LC 96-95138

Editor/Publisher
MARTIN MANAGEMENT BOOKS
2108 Kahekili Highway
Wailuku, Hawaii 96793
808-244-4187

CONTENTS

INTRODUCTION

So, your dog is going on vacation with you! He deserves it and will be delighted to share this fun aspect of your life with you. But where to go? This book will help. It identifies some great vacation destination accommodations in 49 States, that welcome dogs with guests, have some recreational facilities on-site, or in the immediate area, that can make it a GREAT VACATION for you, family, friends, AND your DOG.

HOW TO USE THIS BOOK

We suggest you read the listings carefully. They differ from one another, offer different types of vacations, and charge a variety of rates...most lower-moderate to upscale. Some charge fees for your dog, others do not. Some charge for activities on-site, others do not. Rates given, where available, are standard rates. Use your travel agent or ask for packages yourself to get the lowest rates.

There are five categories in this guide:
RANCHES: Dude, Guest, Resort, and Working
A DOG CAMP
RESORTS, HOTELS, LODGES, INNS, B&B'S
CAMPING; Parks, Forests, Wilderness
CITIES: Boston, Chicago, New York City, San Francisco, Washington DC

Within each category, the States are listed alphabetically. Within the State, the accommodation is listed by location. Detailed descriptions of the accommodation and what they offer guests is noted where available, the minimum standard rate is given, and the dog policy. Also, geographic information in surrounding area is given.

After you have selected several accommodations that interest you in your state, region, or across the country, telephone for a brochure with details and rates. Ask questions now and tell reservations you are vacationing with your dog along. Then ask your travel agent to MAKE ADVANCE RESERVATIONS EARLY. Space for dog owners is sometimes limited. Reconfirm in writing to be safe.

NOTE:

A listing in this travel guide does not constitute a rating or an endorsement of any kind by our company. We provide this information as a public service. We believe the information to be accurate at the time of publication. However, since rates and policies change, be sure to check all details for yourself to avoid problems.

HAVING A SUCCESSFUL VACATION

To have a great vacation with your dog depends on several aspects. He must be healthy and in good shape...up to additional exercise if planned. Do not take an old dog or one with medical problems. Your dog must be sufficiently socialized. He must be able to tolerate strange people, different situations, and other dogs and animals, without getting overly excited, biting, or barking excessively. If you have serious doubts about his behavior, plan to take him next year and work on this problems during the year, starting immediately. He must be completely housebroken, and free of fleas.

If he meets the criteria fairly well, take him along.

TIPS ON TRAVELING WITH A DOG

PLANNING THE TRIP

Make a list of supplies needed by your family, and by your dog, such as:

his regular dog food and dish, to prevent stomach upset.

his water dish, water container, blanket, dog towel, favorite toy.

a first aid kit , extra leash, "pooper scooper" if needed.

dog brush and comb, flea preparations.

He should be wearing his dog license and ID tag with owner name, address and telephone number

His vaccinations should be up-to-date. Carry the "papers" with you indicating he is free of rabies, distemper etc.

Be sure to walk and exercise him before leaving on the trip.

TRAVELING BY CAR

A station wagon, large car, or other vehicle is the best way to transport vacationers with a dog. Since you are in the car too, you will know when it is too hot, too cold, time to make a pit stop, stretch your legs, eat, or drink water. Be sure your dog is used to riding in the car without getting car sick. Consider traveling at night if you know the route and have faith in your vehicle. The kids and the dog may sleep, there is less traffic, and it is cooler.

Never leave a dog in a closed car at all. Even if you have the windows open and park in the shade, don't leave him for more than a few minutes. Ideally, confine him in a large carrier on the shady side of the vehicle, or with a harness or leash. Make frequent stops, every 2 hours is good. Don't let dog hang out of window. He may jump out or injure his eyes with dust. If you use a carrier, be sure it is large enough for him to stand and turn around easily, is strong, leak proof, and has ventilation on at least 2 sides. Pad with paper on the bottom.

TRAVELING BY AIRPLANE

Be warned, there may be a problem taking your dog by air. On the plus side, airlines usually allow a limited number of very small dogs in a carrier in the plane cabin with owner. Reserve early.

On the negative side, most major airlines treat dogs as baggage, and require that they fly in the cargo compartment. You can buy or rent the required flight crate. However, be aware that the dog may be bounced around on the conveyor belt and not hand-carried to the plane, will be subjected to loud noise, and may wait for many minutes in hot sun or bitter cold with the "other baggage" on the runway. Ventilation and air pressure may be inadequate in cargo compartment. There may be toxic fumes that will harm or even kill your pet. You don't want this kind of stress for him.

To have a "safe" trip it is essential that you investigate specific alternative airline procedures in handling dogs. Crate should be large enough and have water, strong enough to withstand pressure and not cave in. It should have handles for carrying and ventilation on at least 2 sides, with the words LIVE ANIMAL labeled on 2 sides with arrows pointing up. MOST IMPORTANT, keep your eyes on what is happening with your dog. INSIST that he get prompt loading and unloading attention at both ends of the trip. DON'T BE TIMID. Insist on the best fast attention for your pet. He relies on you.

It will help to reserve a flight midweek when airline not as busy. Take a direct flight so there is no baggage transfer. Travel in the evening for coolness. There will be some stress. Healthy dog only.

AT THE LODGING

As owner, you are legally responsible for any damage your dog does. Know managment expectations and follow policy or you may be asked to leave. To minimize damage, set up carrier and feed on non-carpeted area, or cover furniture with his own sheet . Cooperate with housekeeping policy. You may be expected to keep dog exercise area clean by using "pooper scooper". Also, there may be a leash requirement at resort, park, forest, city you visit. Know how much freedom your dog can expect to have at your resort. If he needs lots of running space, this should be a criteria of selecting the resort which best fits your needs.

OUTSIDE THE LODGING

There will always be owners who violate the leash law. They may or may not be discovered and fined. But, use your good judgement to protect your dog. Don't let dog chase cattle and horses at a ranch. Don't let dog chase and fight with wild animals. Leash him near road or bridle path. When hiking where hunters are, put a bright strip of red or orange on neck. Carry fresh water. Don't let him drink from rivers or streams or eat anything. Keep him cool, rest in the shade. Don't load him down with backpacks. Beware of cliffs and fast rushing water...leash him. When hiking in winter or across rough ground, he needs boots. Do not go out on frozen lakes, it is easy to fall into freezing water.

FIRST AID TIPS FOR DOGS

Cut feet or legs, need hydrogen peroxide, gauze, adhesive.
Mosquitos and flies, use your own repellant lightly all over dog.
Carry a snake bite kit in some areas. Burn, apply cold water.
Nearly drowns? Open mouth, pull tongue forwd, lift hind quarters and let water drain. For bleeding, apply tournequet and pressure to wound. In all cases of injury, rush to veterinarian.

RANCHES

DUDE, GUEST, RESORT AND WORKING

Called by many the unique American vacation, ranches offer a one of a kind experience to individuals and families. The larger ranches listed here range from rustic to ritzy, with chuckwagon style food to gourmet cuisine. All emphasize horseback riding and the various aspects of ranch life, and some also offer a full range of recreational activities.

Most ranches have dogs of their own and it is important that your dog be well-behaved and not chase ranch animals. You must be able to control your dog at all times. Aside from this aspect, your pet will enjoy the almost unlimited space a ranch has to offer.

See the "resorts" etc. section of this book for smaller ranches, or lodges and even B & B's offering horseback riding at the accommodation or available nearby.

NORTHLAND RANCH RESORT

P.O. Box 2376, Kodiak , Alaska 99615 907-486-5578

This lodge on Kodiak island offers a unique Alaskan working ranch experience. Guests horseback ride along mountains and streams, and enjoy fishing. You can enjoy Kodiak, birdwatch, relax, hike, beachcomb, photograph wildlife on sandy beaches. Lots of space. Fine riding program. RATE: inquire. special packages available. Accommodations are comfortable but not plush at this working ranch. DOG: well-behaved dog welcome.

SAN YSIDRO RANCH

900 San Ysidro Lane, Montecito, California 93108
800-368-6788, 805- 969-5046

A legendary hideaway, this 540-acre Ranch has charming cottages sequestered throughout...overlooking gardens, creek, or the Pacific Ocean. Each cottage has its own individual charm, with wood-burning fireplace, private sundeck and more. Thirteen cottages are complemented by private whirlpools. There is also Camp SYR for younger guests. Activities include tennis, hiking, mt.biking, indoor and outdoor fitness center, personal body and beauty services, horseback riding, and helicopter tours of the Channel Islands. Santa Barbara is nearby. Named by Conde Nast Traveler as "One of the Top 50 Restaurants in the Country" the Stonehouse offers superb American Regional cuisine, while the historic Plow & Angle serves dinner nightly, and offers live jazz Thursday and Friday evenings.
RATE: Standard room minimum $305, cottage suite $495, Charge for dog $75. DOG: Dogs welcome in self-standing cottage. Must be kept on leash, and owners must "withdraw deposits" left by the dog. They may not swim in pool, whirlpool, or bathtub. No barking. Otherwise "have fun and come back soon" is the message. Privileged Pet gifts and menu are provided. Grooming available.

BEAVER MEADOWS RANCH RESORT

P.O. Box 178, Red Feather Lakes, Colorado 80545
970-881-2450, 800-462-5870 open all year

Described as more than a dude ranch, this ranch resort is nestled in a high mountain meadow at 8,400' on the North Fork of the Cache La Poudre River. There is an excellent western restaurant, and many ways to enjoy the beauty and serenity of the Colorado Rocky Mountains. Activities include horseback riding, daily trail rides, breakfast rides, and steakfry rides. Rates charged extra. Mountain biking trails available for all ability levels. Ranch rents bikes or bring your own. Hiking is popular around ponds and wildflower meadows, or along marked trails in Colorado back-country. National Forest trails to explore within 20 minutes of resort. Fishing is excellent in area with trout stocked ponds and streams. Also, 4 public lakes nearby. Permit required.

RATE: Cabin minimum First night (dbl) $60, addtl ngt $48
Rate includes central heat, linens, firewood, kitchen facilities. Inquire about campgrounds and group rates.

DOG: allowed in cabin, or campground. One x cleaning charge $20, regardless of length of stay. Local leash laws apply. Dogs welcome on hiking and biking trails and ranch on leash, but not on horseback rides or ski trails in winter.

LANE GUEST RANCH

P.O. Box 1766, Estes Park, Colorado 80517 303-747-2493
Host: Lloyd C. Lane, Owner

Located near Estes Park, the Ranch and resort is a treasure nestled high in a secluded forest, spaning 20 acres of forest and meadow bordering the magnificent Rocky Mt National Park. There are thousands of acres for hiking in pine and aspen forests, and streams and lakes that guests and their dogs would enjoy. Activities include horseback riding, whitewater rafting, fishing, 4-wheel drives, photography, nature hikes, tennis, golf, shopping, gold mine tours, and swimming in a heated pool. Overall, this ranch offers a fine level level of food, activities, guides, trips, horses, personal services to guests...a full-service all inclusive summer resort for families.

For an all inclusive package price, visitors enjoy 3 meals a day, lodging in one of 25 modern cabins, a host of recreational and sightseeing activities, live nightly entertainment, and supervised children's events.
RATE: $230 per person per day. Single $260. Child 8-11 $160 per day, under 8 $80. (7 day package rate $190 per day)
DOG: No charge on package plan. No specific restrictions.

DIAMOND D RANCH

P.O. Box 1555 Boise, Idaho 83702 Summer: Box 35, Stanley 83278
208-336-9772
Host: Tom & Linda Demorest
This delightful ranch for the adventurous is in the heart of the Salmon River Mountains, and the federally designated Wilderness Area. Activities offered include: horseback riding through unequaled scenic trails, fishing at our private lake or mountain lakes, boating, swimming at a sparkling swimming pool, two saunas, hiking and photography through miles of trails, pan for gold, western B-B-Q, games. RATES: Include 3 meals a day served in lodge or cookouts, lodging, activities, horseback riding. Accommodations consist of 2-bedroom cabins or larger, and lodge rooms.
Weekly rate per person: Cabin $895, Lodge room $800.
DOG: Will permit a dog by advance arrangements only. Must be well-behaved.

BAR Y 7 RANCH

HC 60, Box 10, Brusett, Montana 59318 406-557-6150
Host: Claude and Meredith Saylor
This is a working cattle ranch, not a dude ranch. The Saylor's offer a great ranch vacation on this 10,000 acre property located in the Missouri River Breaks. Guests see cows, horses, chickens, sheep, and 1800 acres of wheat, barley, and oats. Activities available include horseback riding, going on a covered wagon ride for a day or longer, hiking, fossil viewing, fishing, hunting, and viewing wild life in the area such as deer and buffalo. Guests can bring

their own horses if they wish. Guests can ride and help move cattle and check the fence line. Special deer hunts and fishing trips can be arranged. There are rustic cabins and a modern log cabin for guests. The ranch provides 3 meals a day and family style living. RATE: Include lodging and meals,$100 per day adults, $75 per day children 12 and under.

MEADOW VIEW RANCH

HC 91, Box 29, Gordon, Nebraska 69343
308-282-0679, 308-282-1359 Host: Clyde & Billie Lefler
Open: March-October

This is a working cattle ranch in Northwest Nebraska, surrounded by sandhills and lush meadows. The ranch offfers a quiet and restful scenic retreat. Activities to enjoy include: horseback riding, fishing, a sandhills drive, and scenic walks. Cattle drive also . Accommodations are in a ranch bunkhouse with comfortable antique decor with bath, shower, TV, and a kitchenette. The Gordon area nearby has attractions including: cowboy museum, rodeo, country fair, festival, canoeing, Niobrara River, Chadron State Park, Fort Robinson, art show, La Creek National Wildlife Refuge, Gateway to the Badlands and Black Hills of South Dakota.

RATE: single daily minimum $45, dbl $60.

DOG: $5 per day or $10 stay. Dogs have freedom to roam anywhere with owner supervision.

FLYING M RANCH

23029 N.W. Flying M Road, Yamhill, Oregon 97148
503-662-3222

The Flying M Ranch embodies the spirit of the Oregon frontier. A massive Douglas fir lodge, scrumptious steak-fry trail rides, and glimpses of elk and beaver await you year around.

The Ranch is located in the Oregon Coast Range near the base of the 3,500 Ft Trask Mountain, near No Yamhill River. Facilities include cozy cabins, a bunkhouse motel, and campgrounds. Barbeques are a specialty. Restaurant seats 180 people. Guided horseback rides may last from hourly to several days for both

novices and advanced riders. There are pony rides for children. Rides are charged by the hour ($17.00) Other amenities include a swimming pond as long as a city block, tennis, volleyball, basketball, live entertainment. Also, fishing, hiking, wildlife viewing, and country western dancing.
RATE: cabins, minimum dbl $75 per night. Motel minimum dbl $50 & $60 per night.
DOG: Housebroken dog welcome at no charge in lodge or cabins. They must be leashed in main areas but can be turned loose in outlying areas. There is lots of space on this ranch, but dog should respond to voice commands.

BAR H DUDE RANCH

Box 1191, Clarendon, Texas 79226 800-627-9871, 806-874-2634
Host: Frank and Terri Hommel open all year
This working Dude Ranch is in the rugged and scenic heart of the Texas Panhandle. It has been owned by the Hommel family for three generations. Activities are tailored to suit your interests and budget. Guests can watch cowboys work cattle, feed livestock, move herds, or climb in the saddle and join the work. To relax, take a leisurely ride across the prarie, take a stroll, swim, pitch horseshoes, play volleyball, fish. Tours of the ranch can be made by horse or in wagon. Chuckwagon mesquite-grilled steak offered, with homemade cobbler. There is square dancing and live entertainment. A climate controlled bunkhouse awaits guests at night. The ranch is also a game preserve and is licensed for bird hunting on 5,500 acres of rangeland. RATE: One night minimum stay includes lodging, 3 meals, 2 horseback rides and all other ranch activities.
Minimum single daily $70, weekly $450
double daily $60, weekly $385. Special group rates.

Y.O. RANCH

Hwy 41 W., Mt Home, Texas 78058 512-640-3222
Host: Schreiner family, owners since 1880
"No visit to Texas is complete without a trip to this 40,000 acre working ranch". Cowboys, longhorns, and rustic charm abound.

In addition to longhorns, the Y.O. pioneered the ranching of exotic wildlife, now a booming Texas industry. Today, it houses the country's largest collection of roaming exotic animals, such as the Zebra, Ibex, Giraffe, and more. Activities at this ranch include: photo safaris (addtl charge), horseback riding (addtl charge), tour of exotic game pastures and ranch, swimming. Special activities on request. Inquire. Hearty Texas-size meals served. RATE: 9 cabins available. One night minimum stay. Minimum per adult per day, Sun-Thurs $75, Fri-Sat $85. Age 15 and under $50. Infant free. Ask about incentive programs and group rates. DOG: welcome with guests. Must be under control. There is lots of space for dog fun.

CIRCLE H HOLIDAY RANCH

810 Watt Canyon Road, Thorp , Washington 98946 509-964-2000
Host: Betsy and son Jamie Ogden

This ranch is located in a lush oasis skirting the cascade foothills and overlooking the Kittitas Valley and the rugged Stewart mountain range. Cabins are available with sitting room, kitchenette, bedroom, and bath. Horseback riding is the main activity. You can explore 100,000 acres of beautiful wilderness. Horses are proven mountain trail riders, gentle and dependable. You can also hike, bike, swim, explore, or just relax or help do ranch chores. Children will enjot the enclosed play area and the corral of small critters. You can bring your own horse to clean, secure stalls. Close by is fishing on the Yakima River, rafting, skiing, an elk feeding station, and Mt Rainier. RATE: Minimum rate $125, includes all meals. Horseback riding hourly rate $15.
DOG: well-behaved dogs welcome. No fee.

WOODSIDE RANCH

Mauston, Wisconsin 53948 800-626-4275, 608-847-4275
Open: 7 days a week summer; weekends in fall, winter, spring

This 1000 acre operating ranch is situated on a high wooded hillside in the famous Upper Dells Region. Guests welcome all year and can observe ranching and farming. Riding leads the field of interest with guests. Excellent horses canter over trails or down country roads. Horse shows are also held. Ponies are available for children. Covered wagon rides and hayrides also.

In addition, the ranch has a new private swimming pool, fishing pond for boaters, and sauna. Square dancing and campfires make evenings enjoyable. Other sports offered include tennis, hiking, badminton, canoeing, and miniature golf with public courses near. Winter sports include skiing and ice skating. Food is home-cooked wholesome, and plentiful, and is served family style...all you can eat...during the summer season. The rest of the year a "bunk & breakfast program". RATE: fireplace cabin (2 person min.) adult weekly summer $575, weekend $252. Fall & spring is $199 weekend, winter $99 weekend.

DOG: welcome in fireplace cabins only. Guests may also bring their own horse at variable charge. Dog must be kept on leash on main resort grounds, but can run free in open fields and woods, and may swim in the large fishing pond. Charge: per dog $8 per night

BRETECHE CREEK

P.O. Box 596, Cody, Wyoming 82414 307-587-3844

Host: Louis "Bo" Polk, Amy Sheppard

Open June 7 to Sept 14

This is an educational foundation dedicated to using the natural wilderness environment as a learning stimulus. It is accessible by car and air. Breteche Creek is surrounded by a 7,000 acre working cattle and horse-breeding ranch, on which guests can participate in wrangling horses, breeding cattle, and horse training. Nestled in a high, mountainous valley above the No. Fork of the Shoshone Nat. Forest, part of the 18 million acres of Greater Yellowstone Ecosystem, haven to bear, elk, coyote, and more.

Seven day sessions include food, lodging, lectures, workshops, guided rides and hikes, fishing, creek swimming, evening programs, and a Yellowstone National Park tour. Addtl charge for horsemanship private lessons, whitewater rafting trips, rodeo and museum. Accommodations are comfortable and rustic, consisting of tent-cabins. There is a central lodge. Elegant country fare served indoors or around the campfire.

RATE: Seven day session: $975 per adult, child $825 (under 12) Nightly, (3 ngt minimum) $175 per adult, child $125
DOG: No charge. Dogs must get along with guests, children, and must not be a barker. Must be able to respond to simple commands Limit 2 dogs per guest. Only one set of dogs at a time. There is lots of space for fun and exercise. Dog can participate with owner in most things. Your horse welcome also.

DEER FORKS RANCH

Rte 6, 1200 Poison Lake Road, Douglas , Wyoming 82633
307-358-2033 Host: Benny & Pauline Middleton
Located in eastern Wyoming, this is a fourth generation working ranch with about 6,000 acres. There are 2 guest cabins, with bath and kitchens. Activities include riding cattle round-ups, trail rides, nature study, hiking, fishing. Meals can be in your cabin or with hosts. RATE: inquire DOG: Welcome, but must be carefully controlled so not injured by cattle.

4 W RANCH RECREATION

1162 Lynch Road, New Castle, Wyoming 82701 307-746-2815
Host: Bob & Jean Harshbarger
This is a working cattle ranch with lots of wildlife and 20,000 acres to explore. Ranch provides a good place to sleep, good food, clean air, and beautiful scenery. No structured entertainment. Not a dude ranch. RATE: Inquire DOG: allowed.

A DOG CAMP

If you are LESS interested in vacation activities for yourself and MORE interested in focusing on your dog with fun filled days and many dog training activities, plus discussions about dogs with other owners ... then a dog camp might be for you.

The camp presented here is a good one, and is popular with those who have attended. Many return more than once, leaving little free space. Therefore, very early reservations are mandatory.

CAMP GONE TO THE DOGS

R.R. #1, Box 958, Putney, Vermont 05346 802-387-5673
Host: Honey Loring, owner OPEN: 1 week camps in June and October, plus 2-day weekend training

At this unique dog camp you will have lots of fun, meet other owners with canine buddies, and can concentrate on obedience and agility with top instructors, try dozens of activities, or just relax... walk the countryside and swim with your pet. All this togetherness is great for socializing your pet further. However, he must be friendly to begin with. Aggressive pets cannot register.

The camp is located near Brattleboro. It is held on the grounds of a 500 acre private boarding school in Putney. The mountains, meadows and fields in this area are spectacular. There are many miles of wooded trails for walking with your dog, a pond for swimming, and some horseback riding. Your dog sleeps with you in dorms. There are also 3 motels off-site available for those who want more privacy and their own bathroom. Also a nearby KOA. The food is delicious. Bring the dog food the pet is used to eating to avoid stomach upset.

Formal activities include: show obedience, novice through utility, motivational retrieving, puppy kindergarten, free style obedience, behavorial problem counseling, agility, tricks, swimming, hunting, herding, weight pulling, and more.

Camp rules are sensible. They are:
. owners must clean-up after dog.
. dogs are leashed in training and heavy traffic areas. They can run off lead in fields and woods.
. dog cannot be left unattended in rooms. Use crate or your car.
. no smoking allowed in buildings.

Other fun activities include leash making, doggie softball, costume parade, doggie line dancing and steeplechase.

Proof of freedom from disease and current rabies innoculation is required. There is a veterinarian close by camp. Owners are responsible for their own dog and are asked to sign a liability waiver.

RATE: All dogs welcome including puppies and mixed breeds. There are two 1-week sessions in June and the Fall @ $800 per person. There is also 2-day weekend training. Inq uire about dates and rates for this. Register early in the year since space is limited.

This camp is liability insured.

RESORTS, HOTELS, LODGES, CABINS, INNS, AND B&B's

This section contains a wide variety of resorts and other accommodations that make very appealing vacation destinations for travelers on vacation with their dog.

Facilities are either self-contained, or are within a resort or recreational destination area that vacationers will enjoy. Once you arrive there, travel will be minimal.

Descriptions are geographic, by State alphabetically. The standard rates given range from confortable lower-moderate to upscale and lavish.

We urge you to telephone the reservations manager if there is a problem about your dog or his size. Frequently a "small dog only" policy can be modified as an "exception" to allow your well-behaved pet .

In all cases there is lots of activity available and opportunities for everyone to have fun with the family dog, either on-site or in the immediate geographic area.

Birmingham is the largest city; Montgomery is the capital. Gulf Shores is a family-oriented beach area with hotels. Northeast, Lookout Mountain Parkway is a 100 mile scenic drive. There are 22 State parks.

• BIRMINGHAM
THE TUTWILER
2021 Park Place N, 35203 800-845-1787, 205-322-2100
Elegant hotel with charm and hospitality. Restaurant, pool.
RATE: min. $109 DOG: small dog allowed

BEST SUITES OF AMERICA
140 State Farm Pkwy 35209 800-237-8466, 205-940-9990
Pool, free hot breakfast, sauna
RATE; min. $81 DOG: allowed

MOUNTAIN BROOK INN
2800 US 280 35223 205-870-3100, 800-523-7771
Oriental ambiance in hotel at foot of Red Mountain. 180 rooms, pool
RATE: Min. $99 DOG: allowed under 15 lbs; fee $15.

• ANDALUSIA AREA has Conecut National Forest with a 20 mile scenic hiking trail, lakes, recreation area.
CHARTER HOUSE INN
US 84 Bypass E, Andalisia 36420 800-443-9110, 334-222-7511
62 units, swimming pool, restaurant.
RATE: min $49 DOG: allowed if smaller with $25 deposit.

• DAUPHIN ISLAND boasts an 850 ft deep water fishing pier. and the Audubon Bird Sanctuary, 164 acres of forest, dunes, and beach, 45 acre lake, 2 miles of walking trails.
GULF BREEZE MOTEL
800-286-0296, 334-861-7344
RATE: inquire DOG: Dog $5 per night, no puppies allowed.

DOTHAN

OLYMPIA SPA GOLF/TENNIS RESORT

P.O. Box 6108, Dothan 36302 205-677-3321

The golf course here has been described as the finest in the South, designed by Bob Simmons. Instruction available. If tennis is your game there are eight lighted courts available.

You will also enjoy the jogging trail, swimming in olympic-size pool. Other health facilities are a natural hot mineral spring, steam and sauna rooms. Elegant dining room.

Local attractions include an amusement park, greyhound racing.

RATE; min about $40. DOG: $2.50 per day charge. No restrictions.

EUFAULA AREA

Excellent fishing, boating on Lake Eufalu and Chattahoochee Trace with picturesque lakes and antebellum homes.

HOLIDAY INN EUFAULA

PO Box 725 (US hwy 82 & Riverside Dr) 36027

800-HOLIDAY, 334-687-2021

96 rooms, pool, restaurant. RATE: min. $50 DOG: allowed.

GULF SHORES

the best of sun & surf on miles of white sand.

RAMADA LTD

610 W. Beach Blvd, Gulf Shores 36542 334-948-8141

100 rooms, pool, TV. RATE: min about $40. DOG: $10 non-refundable

YOUNG'S BY THE SEA

401 E Beach Blvd, Gulf Shores 36547 800-245-0032, 334-948-4181

offers 98 units, kitchens, pool, TV

RATE: min about $35 DOG: $25 non-refundable 1x fee

BEACH RENTALS

- Anchor Management, 500 West Beach Blvd, Gulf Shores, 36547 334-948-6680 houses and apts; some allow dogs.
- Wade Ward Rentals & Real Estate, 1709 Gulf Shores Pkwy 36542 800-634-1429, 334-968-8425
  60 units, golf, pool. Dog allowed.

- Rentals on ORANGE BEACH contact:
  Island Management & Rentals, 26021 Perdido Beach Blvd
  Orange Beach 36561 334-981-2909

Alaska has more land in national parks, wilderness areas and national wildlife refuges, than all other States combined. Capitol is Juneau.

- ANCHORAGE
REGAL ALASKAN HOTEL

4800 Spenard Road, Anchorage, Alaska 99517 800-544-0553, 907-243-2300

Lovely hotel located along eastern shore of Lake Spenard, a mile from airport and 10 min. from downtown Anchorage. Good service. Good base to explore natural wonders in area. 248 rooms, health club, spa, rental bikes, jogging paths around lake, floating plane dock for sportfishing or sightseeing. RATES: Inquire DOG: allowed, $50 deposit

- DUTCH HARBOR
GRAND ALEUTIAN HOTEL

Pouch 503, PO Box 921169, Dutch Harbor 99692
800-891-1194, 907-581-3844

A luxury hotel in the magnificent Aleutian Islands. 112 luxurious rooms and suites, restaurants. Wild beauty, sport fishing, bird watching, volcanic tundra, land and sea tours, guides, hike and bike. RATE:min. $135 DOG: allowed with deposit, against damages.

- KODIAK
BUSKIN RIVER INN, INC

1395 Airport Way, Kodiak 99615 907-487-2700, 800-544-2202

Inn is Kodiak's newest full service hotel, with a fine restaurant and view of Buskin River. Free freezer storage for your fish and game, a refrigerator in every room, color TV, washer/dryer, free parking. Inn is within walking distance of Kodiak National Wildlife Refuge. Air tours available to see the bears.

Activities include a golf course, ski chalet, mountain hiking, bike rental. Fishing is a favorite recreational sport. Guests can charter boats, planes, or drive. Hoseback riding available at Kodiak Cattle Co, a 21,000 acre ranch. RATE: min. $105 off-season,
DOG: Large dog: $25 per night; small dog: $15 per night.

LAKE MINCHUMINA
DENALI WEST LODGE

Lake Minchumina, Alaska 99757 907-674-3112

Hosts: Jack & Sherri Hayden, owners

This is a great place to come if you love nature and want to see Alaska's "Last Frontier" wilderness...100 miles from the nearest highway on the border of Denali National Park and Preserve. A true frontier lifestyle, resort affords you the intimacy of Alaskan wilderness in 1st class comfort. Resort has lodge and log cabins with wood stoves, set near birch and cedar saunas. Hearty meals served. Resort has bush planes, knowledgeable guides, fishing, canoeing, hiking, exploring, photography.

Dog mushing is popular. Lodge has 50 resident dogs.

RATE: Friday-Monday $1290. Monday-Friday $1700 per person, includes free float plane service. Children under 12 half-price.

DOG: Your dog welcome. Can be flown in by bush plane with advance arrangements.

SITKA
BARANOF WILDERNESS LODGE

PO Box 2187, Sitka, Alaska 99835 916-582-8132

(During year write for info: PO Box 42, Norden, CA 95724)

Host: Mike Trotter

Open June - September at Warm Springs Bay, 20 miles from Sitka, located on one of the largest and most pristine islands in Alaska, Baranof Island. Accessible by boat or float plane, it boasts waterfalls, lakes, snow-capped peaks, forests, teaming with fish and wildlife. Staff is experienced, certified and licensed. Base camp cabins and lodge are comfortable, meals excellent, selection of wines. Fishing is abundant, hiking, photography, beach combing, canoes and boats available, Gear provided.

RATE: example of packages:

3 day, 2 night, per person $985 guided, $485 unguided.

DOG: allows dog. Host has a dog himself.

Arizona boasts the Grand Canyon National Park and state parks, including Lake Havasu. Phoenix is the largest city; Tucson second.

- CAREFREE
THE BOULDERS

PO Box 2090, 34631 No. Tom Darlington Drive, Carefree 85377
602-488-9009, 800-553-1717

Rated America's top resort by many people, The Boulders offers the enchantment of a dramatic location created by time. This world-famous resort blends easily with nature. It features two top golf courses built into the desert, a tennis court, fitness center, desert trail hikes, llama treks, nature walks. Also, horseback riding, hot air ballooning, jeep tours, swimming, spa, shopping.

There is no typical guest room, but 160 guest casitas individually shaped into the natural terrain, with fireplace and patios.

RATE: European Plan (no meals) Minimum sgl about $200 offseason. Packages available. DOG: Small dog allowed, with $50 deposit.

- CASA GRANDE
FRANCISCO GRANDE RESORT & GOLF CLUB

26000 Gila Bend Highway, Casa Grande 85222
800-237-4238, 520-836-6444

Called a "friendly legend" for 25 years, this resort has been a favorite of some of the world's top golfers and celebraties. It has championship golf, lighted tennis courts, swimming pool, 112 spacious guest rooms and suites, and a full service restaurant.

RATE: min. single $49 , special packages available
DOG: Permitted with a $25 pet fee.

- LAKE HAVASU CITY
LONDON BRIDGE RESORT

1477 Queen's Bay Road, Lake Havasu City 86403
800-624-7939, 520-855-9209

Highlighting this resort is the distinctive London Bridge built over 160 years ago and transported from England to Arizona in 1968.

This resort seeks to fulfill all your needs with world-class service: dining, cocktails, dancing, a full-scale off-track betting facility, exercise choices that include swimming, boating, tennis, golf, jogging, dancing, a fitness facility. Nearby, jet ski's, paddle boats, canoes, Leisure choices include whirlpool, massage, tanning salon, sauna, lake cruises, a stroll through the British Village or along a mile of beautiful beach on the shores of Lake Havasu. Also, cruises, shopping, restaurants, nightclubs, movie theater.

Accommodations include 50 impressive suites, each with a separate living area, bedroom, and fully-equipped kitchen.

RATE: Min. room mid-week, dbl $75. Suites start at $175.

DOG: permitted in hotel rooms. Can be walked around resort property and in the English Village on a leash. $10 non-refundable fee per night.

LAKESIDE
LAKE OF THE WOODS

P.O. Box 777, Lakeside 85929 520-368-5353

This is a family resort with large and small cabins, with heat, fireplaces, kitchen, deck, color TV, microwave. 23 cabins, 4 houses. Resort has a private 12 acre lake, stocked with trout, bass, and more. Fish from boats or shore. No license required. There is also a playground, spa, sauna, games. Nearby, horseback riding, hiking, golf, ski areas, stores, and restaurants.

RATE: vary according to season. Minimum small cabin about $56.

DOG: Dog under control is welcome. Not allowed on furniture and are to be leashed at all times on property, so do not disturb other guests. Wooded area with great dog hiking possibilities.

LAKE POWELL
HOLIDAY INN PAGE/LAKE POWELL

287 N Lake Powell Blvd, Lake Powell 86040 520-645-8851

Full service hotel in good location with views, adjacent 18-hole golf course, pool, picnic area. In area, water sports and golf.

RATE: Min. sgl $64. DOG: no charge, owner responsible damages

• LITCHFIELD PARK
THE WIGWAM RESORT

300 Indian School Road, Lichfield Park 85340
602-935-3811 800-327-0396
An excellent resort, 25 minutes from Phoenix, set in a 75 acre oasis of palm trees. Offers a year around recreational paradise... 3 championship golf courses, 9 tennis courts, horseback riding, biking, hiking, health club, and more. Three dining rooms with various cuisines, lounge, dancing. The 331 guest casitas are unique, decorated in style with surrounding desert landscape.
RATE; Offseason (summer, May-Sept) min. sgl. $105; winter $250.
DOG: any size dog welcome. Walk them anywhere on property. $50 security deposit required, of which $25 is refundable.

• MESA
ARIZONA GOLF RESORT

425 South Power Road, Mesa 85206 602-832-3202, 800-528-8282
This is a full-service destination resort with it's own 18 hole PGA championship golf course on premises. Guests come for a vacation and/or golf packages. Pleasant atmosphere combined with outstanding facilities. Activities include, golf and instruction, tennis, swimming spas, on 150 lush acres that invite a walk or bike ride. Dinner at Annabelle's provides excellent food. Sunrise Cafe and Anna's Lounge & Grill for lighter fare, entertainment.
Nearby attractions include rafting on the Salt River, sailing, moonlight trail rides through desert foothills, Wild West rodeos and other spectator sports, plus shops, theatres, factory outlets, and more.
RATE; Delux room(Dbl)$120 min. Suites available. No charge children under 12. Special golf packages.
DOG: Welcome at resort. Owner liable for damages. Can be walked in designated areas. Also, state park off-site for walking.

• PAYSON
KOHL'S RANCH LODGE

East Highway 260, Payson 85541 800-331-KOHL, 520-271-9731
Lodge located on the banks of Tonto Creek, in the largest ponderosa pine forest in the world. Famous for western hospitality in "Zane

Grey Country". Guests enjoy horseback riding, swimming, trout fishing, hiking, exploring forest trails for a perfect weekend or family week vacation. Offers 41 Main Lodge rooms and 8 2-bedroom cabins. Features fireplaces, color TV, restaurant, pool, sauna.
RATE: min off-season(dbl) about $55; cabin $115.
DOG: allowed at $10 per night, and $50 deposit against damage.

• PINETOP

MOONRIDGE LODGE & CABINS

596 W. White Mountain, Pinetop 85935 (PO Box 1058)
520-367-1906
This resort offers knotty pine cabins in the pines with cable TV, fireplaces, and kitchens. Accommodate 2-10 persons. Activities in White Mountains include fishing, skiing, hiking, golf, hunting, and more outdoor activities.
RATE: summer minimum 2-person cabin $76 daily
Children 4 and under free. DOG: $5 charge, $50 refundable deposit.

• SCOTTSDALE

MARRIOTT'S CAMELBACK INN RESORT, GOLF CLUB

5402 E. Lincoln Drive, Scottsdale 85253
602-948-1700, 800-242-2635
This award winning resort in spectacular desert setting offers 423 casitas, 7 with private pools. Has world-class European Health spa, shopping, 36 holes of golf, tennis, swimming, biking. Nearby is horseback riding, hiking, jeep tours.
RATE: min. dbl $245. DOG: small dog allowed; owner responsible for damages.

THE PHOENICIAN

6000 East Camelback Road, Scottsdale 85251 602-941-8200
This is a luxury hotel nestled against the beauty of Camelback Mountain, amidst 250 acres of lush landscaping. Offers 580 luxury guest rooms and suites, 7 magnificent swimming pools, 12 tennis courts, 18-hole golf course, spa services at Centre for Well-Being. Variety of dining choices.
RATE: Min sgl $170 in summer. Special packages.
DOG: 20 lbs and under only

- SEDONA

SKY RANCH LODGE

PO Box 2579, Sedona 86339 520-282-6400

Hosts: Sheri & Gary Graham, John & Isabel Joynt

This Lodge is located atop Table Mountain, in the heart of Sedona and Red Rock Country, on 6 acres. Offers beautiful gardens, a stream, ponds, 75-mile views, spa, pool. Convenient to restaurants, shopping. Cottages and 94 rooms available, TV, phones, some fireplaces or kitchenette.

RATE: cottages $145 per day dbl, room min. summer $75 dbl.

DOG: Dog allowed at $7 per dog per night. Max, in one room is 2. Do not leave unattended in room. Must be on leash outside on property.

- TUCSON

SHERATON EL CONQUISTADOR RESORT AND COUNTRY CLUB

10000 No. Oracle Road, Tucson 85737

520-544-5000, 800-325-3535

Lovely resort in southern Arizona. Fresh air, inspiring views, lots of recreation. Mexican-Spanish ambiance. Offers 434 guest rooms with patio, some fireplaces, two 18-hole golf courses, restaurants, 31 tennis courts, racquetball, fitness, pool, horseback riding, jeep tours, western cookouts, and hike through the Santa Catalinas.

RATE: min, $190 double

Inquire about special packages

DOG: allowed.

- WICKENBURG

BEST WESTERN RANCHO GRANDE

293 E. Wickenburg Way, Wickenburg 85358 520-684-5445, 800-854-7235

Offers 80 rooms, suites, kitchenettes, pool, spa, tennis court, playground, restaurant.

RATE; Min sgl $55, DOG: allowed, no charge

This State has 18 million acres of forests, lots of beautiful foliage and an emphasis on outdoor sports. Little Rock, the major city, lies in the center of the State. Northwest Arkansas has sparkling lakes and forests is popular with visitors, especially the Ozarks and Eureka Springs. In the West, Hot Springs is a favorite.

BULL SHOALS
DOGWOOD LODGE

505 Shorecrest Drive, Bull Shoals 72619 800-883-4311, 501-445-4311
This Lodge offers 1-2 bedroom housekeeping units, TV, microwave, decks, swimming pool, boat rental.
RATE: Inquire DOG: allows small dogs

HOT SPRINGS
LADY HAMILTON RESORT

2803 Albert Pike, US 270 W., Box 2070 Hot Springs 71913
800-426-3184, 501-767-5511
Thia is an all-suite luxury resort on a peninsula on Lake Hamilton. Ouachita Mountains nearby. Offers swimming pools, marina, boat rentals, tennis courts, restaurant
RATE: Inquire DOG: allowed. No charge, no restrictions.

LAKEVIEW
GASTON'S WHITE RIVER RESORT

#1 River Road, Lakeview 72642 501-431-5202
Host: Jim Gaston, owner
Gaston's calls itself "America's #1 Trout Fishing Resort". A first-class resort, it has everything you need for a complete relaxing vacation...kids playground, swimming pool, tennis court, game room, nearby golf course. There is a 1.7 mile nature trail along river for hikers, meeting room holds 150. Restaurant, large and complete on White River banks. Various cottages available, air conditioned, comfortable, and clean. Some fireplaces and decks. One 20 ft John Boat furnished with each cottage. Main pastime is trout fishing. Experienced and licensed guides are handy with boats.. Scenery is breathtaking RATE: Housekeeping cottage $73 (2 guests)
Bedroom accommodation (no kitchen) 2 dbl beds $58. Winter season offer, inquire. DOG: Welcome. No charge, no restrictions.

- ## LAKEVIEW
TWIN FIN RESORT

PO Box 218T, Lakeview 72643 501-431-5377, 800-622-6291
Offers cabins, condos, pool, dock, free boat, on beautiful Bull Shoals Lake. Complete fishing and family resort.
RATE: Inquire DOG: Allowed in Fall and Spring, not in Summer.

- ## MOUNTAIN HOME
SCOTT VALLEY RESORT & GUEST RANCH

PO Box 1447 ATG, Mountain Home 72653 501-425-5136
Experience the beauty of the Ozarks and the comfort of Scott Valley. World-class fishing, horseback riding, heated pool, spa, canoeing, tennis, hayrides and more. Meals available. Maid service.
RATE: Inquire
DOG: allows dog at resort owner discretion. Inquire.

- ## MOUNT IDA
MOUNTAIN HARBOR RESORT (on Lake Ouachita)

PO Box 807, Mount Ida 71957 501-867-2191 800-832-2276
This lovely dog-friendly resort is on the shore of the largest and most beautiful lake in Arkansas, nestled into the mountains on 600 acres of green forest.
Accommodations include 76 guest rooms, cabins, cabanas, and condos. There is a large marina, swimming pools, tennis courts, walking areas, horseback riding on forest trails, parasailing, back road hiking. Restaurant on premises.
There are a number of much loved resident pets, dogs and cats, so all must get along. RATE: min. weekend room $85.
DOG: $12.50 per night. No dog can be left unattended at any time.

SHANGRI-LA RESORT

Star Route 1, Box 257, Mount Ida 71957 501-867-2011
Resort offers cottages and a lodge and restaurant on Lake Ouachita. Swimming pool, tennis courts, boat dock.
RATE: Inquire DOG: allowed at $2 charge

California has many places of interest to the visitor or vacationer with a dog. From Yosemite National Park, San Francisco, and Napa Valley and Lake Tahoe in the North, to the delightful central coast near Monterey, to the ethnically diverse Los Angeles, to San Diego and Palm Springs desert playground.

BIG BEAR LAKE
SHORE ACRES LODGE

40090 Lakeview Drive, Big Bear Lake 92315 800-524-6600; 909-866-8200

Lakefront lodge, surrounded by towering pine trees, sits on one of best fishing spots on Big Bear Lake. 11 units offered. Activities include swimming, golf, boating, hiking, horseback riding, games, fishing, and bar-b-ques. In winter, add skiing, ice skating, sledding. There is a children's playground.

RATE: Housekeeping cabins vary by season and size. Min sgl $65 per day. Returnable security/cleaning deposit required.

DOG: Welcome in most units. Small per night charge. There is lots of space surrounding the Lodge for hiking and fun with your dog.

CARMEL
CYPRESS INN

Lincoln & 7th Street, PO Box Y, Carmel-by-the-Sea 93921 800-443-7443, 408-624-3871

This charming Spanish-Meditteranean style Inn is owned in part by Actress Doris Day, whose fondness for animals is well known. Enjoy your continental breakfast in front of the fireplace in our living room lobby, in the garden courtyard, or in the "Library Lounge". Rooms include a decanter of cream sherry, daily paper, basket of fruit, fresh flowers and bottled drinking water. Just steps away from all of the shops, restaurants and galleries that the picturesque Village of Carmel-by-the Sea is so well known for.

RATE: min. dbl $98 DOG: Dog welcome. Charge $17; each additional dog $10. DOG POLICY: Dog must be leashed in Carmel and the Inn. Dog must not be left alone in room; pet sitters available. Cleanup after dog required. Dry off after beach. Owner will be billed for damage or mishaps.

INNS BY THE SEA

. WAYSIDE INN, Carmel

Offers spacious rooms and suites, many with full kitchens and wood burning fireplaces. Pet rooms available. Carmel is quaint and charming to explore. RATE: min sgl $109 DOG: allowed

.CYPRESS GARDENS INN

1150 Munras St, Monterey
Inn has a nice garden setting with a waterfall, heated pool, hot tub. Guests can see Cannery Row, Monterey Bay, hike, sightsee.
Pet rooms available.
RATE; Minimum rate $64, townhouse $175.
DOG: allowed

EL ADOBE INN

936 Munras Street, Monterey
This Inn offers best value rooms, simple and tasteful. Hot tub.
Pet rooms available. RATE: Minimum $59 DOG: allowed

INNS BY THE SEA RESERVATIONS NUMBER 800-433-4732

QUAIL LODGE Resort & Golf Club

8205 Valley Greens Drive, Carmel 93923
800-538-9516, 408-624-1581
This excellent dog friendly resort is located on 10 beautifully landscaped acres with small sparkling lakes. There are 100 luxury guest accommodations of various sizes. There is an 18-hole golf course, nature walks, jogging trails, swimming pool, tennis courts, and shops, all on a beautiful 800 acre preserve. The elegant Covey Restaurant on the lake serves a refined European cuisine.
Five minutes away is Carmel-by-the Sea with white sandy beaches galleries and Village. The Big Sur coastline, old Monterey's Fisherman's Wharf and famous 17-mile drive are easily reached.
RATE: Delux min sgl $275 DOG: Any size dog welcome. No charge. Dog can walk anywhere but must clean-up after dog.

VALLEY LODGE

P.O. Box 93, Carmel Valley 93924 408-659-2261
Hosts: Peter & Sherry Coakley

Lodge is a quiet, charming, country inn tucked into the rolling hills of sunny Carmel Valley, 12 miles from Carmel-by-the-Sea and within minutes of beaches. It is a peaceful retreat for visitors to historic Monterey Peninsula who want to be away from crowds, but near the action. Available are privacy, nature, hiking, golf, tennis, swimming, and riding. There is a heated pool, hot tub, and game area. Nearby, championship golf courses, tennis, quaint shops, restaurants within walking distance in Carmel Valley Village.
Dog welcome in any units which range from standard queen and king bedrooms to 1-2 bedroom fireplace cottages. Units have color cable TV, phone, garden patio or deck. Some have kitchens and hibachi's on patio, complimentary breakfast, and newspaper.
RATE: min $99 DOG: allowed at $10 per day. Dog must never be left alone in room and must be on a leash or under voice control on the grounds. Your dog will enjoy picnics and hiking in a park nestled in a lovely meadow alongside the Carmel River. Hiking trails wend their way up the face of Santa Lucia Mountains, and beaches are easily reached. Area leash laws apply.

• COALINGA
THE INN AT HARRIS RANCH

Route 1, Box 777, Coalinga 93210 800-942-2333

The Inn features western charm and hometown hospitality, with 123 comfortable guest rooms and 27 luxurious suites available. There is an olympic style pool, jacuzzis, and a fitness facility. This Inn is located midway between San Francisco and Los Angeles, perfect for a stop-over or short vacation. There are different dining rooms, each featuring Harris Ranch Beef specialties.
RATE: Min sgl $80. Children under 12 stay free.
DOG: Dogs welcome in designated pet rooms. $10 fee for cleaning.

• CORONADO
LOEWS CORONADO BAY RESORT

4000 Coronado Bay Road, Coronado 92118
800-23-LOEWS, 619-424-4000

This exquisite and unique resort occupies a private peninsula in San Diego Bay, just a stroll from the Pacific shore. The resort is entirely surrounded by water, thus welcoming guests into an extraordinary world of recreation, swimming, sailing, sunning, surfing, tennis, and nearby golf. There are 3 pools, 2 spas, and a large sun deck, 5 tennis courts, and a complete fitness center. Rooms offer custom furnishings, an entertainment center, 2 phones, an oversized bath with steeping tub, and exemplary guest services. RATE: Inquire DOG: small dog accepted. No charge

• DEL MAR

DEL MAR HILTON North San Diego

15575 Jimmy Durante Blvd, Del Mar 92014
619-792-5200, 800-445-8667

Casual elegance in San Diego's North Country, less than a mile from magnificent beaches and near a racetrack. Hotel offers 245 beautifully appointed guest rooms, tennis, golf, spas, health facilities and restaurant and lounge. RATE: certain rooms designated for guests with a dog; inquire about rates. DOG: Welcome. Charge $10 per stay. Must not be left alone when outside room. Must be leashed. Cannot go on furniture. $200 refundable deposit if no damage.

• GROVELAND

THE GROVELAND HOTEL

P.O. Box 481, Groveland 95321 800-273-3314, 209-962-4000

This charming historic hotel in Yosemite Park area was built in 1849 and restored in 1992. Offers 17 elegant rooms and suites. Dine in casual elegance. Fresh seasonal cuisine. Activities include Yosemite National Park 23 mi away, where dogs are welcome on leash, and other public lands including rivers, creeks, hiking trails. Golf, tennis at Pine Mt Lake. Beach, swimming pool. Hotel also offers you a Wilderness Survival Course and a Fly Fishing School You can bring dog at no extra charge. RATE: min. $95 DOG: Welcome. Hotel will give him a bone on arrival.

• HOPE VALLEY
SORENSEN'S

14255 Hwy 88, Hope Valley 96120 916-694-2203, 800-423-9949
This is a beautiful, rustic, all seasons resort in the Sierra Nevada. Activities include swimming, hiking, fishing, backpacking, biking, skiing. Close to mineral hot springs, horseback riding, river rafting, Lake Tahoe, Carson River, high mountain meadows. Located near highway.

Resort offers 22 housekeeping cabins of various sizes. Four cabins allow a dog. RATE: moderate, Inquire. DOG: allowed in a few cabins, must be leashed on property, not allowed on furniture, and cannot be left alone in cabin. Pooper-scooper must be used.

• LAKE TAHOE
HOLIDAY HOUSE on Lake Tahoe

PO Box 229, Tahoe Vista 96148 800-2-WINDSURF, 916-546-2369
Resort features lakefront suites, kitchenettes, queen beds, TV, barbeque, hot tub. There are mooring buoys for your boat. Walk to the marina and famous restaurants Captain Jon's and Le Petit Pier. Activities include skiing, snowmobiling, swimming, golf, tennis, bike, hike, fish, horseback ride, sail, and more. 10 minutes to Nevada gambling and nightlife. RATE: min. $85 DOG: cannot be left alone in room; should be on leash outside; must clean-up after dog. Security deposit required of $40 per dog. Charge for dog is $25, or $5 per day if staying more than 5 days.

NOTE: This management also has LAKESIDE CHALETS available at Carnelian Bay. RATE: $95 min. Information phone: 916-546-5857

• HEAVENLY, ALPINE MEADOWS, KIRKWOOD, NORTHSTAR, SQUAW VALLEY SKI LODGES

Five large ski areas are open as resorts during the summer. Cabins, houses, chalets, lodges, some lakeside, are available to vacationers with a dog. Call for information and reservations at: 800-824-6348, 800-544-3234, at Squaw Valley 800-545-4350

LA QUINTA
LA QUINTA RESORT & CLUB

49-499 Eisenhower Dr, PO Box 69, La Quinta 92253
619-564-4111, 800-598-3828
A legendary hideway, this resort is distinctive in the Palm Springs area. Accommodations include 640 quaint casitas (Spanish-style cottage) on 45 acres of flowering gardens. Historic Spanish architecture. Some rooms have fireplace, patios, poolside setting. Suites designed for royalty and celebrities are elaborate. Activities include pools and spas, golf, tennis, shops, dining facilities. There are paths, park benches, waterfalls, live music and flowers. Nearby horseback riding, jeep tours, polo. RATE: min summer $109, fall $190 DOG: welcome at $25 pet fee per stay, nonrefundable.

LOS ANGELES
HOTEL BEL-AIR

701 Stone Canyon Road, Los Angeles 90077
310-472-1211, 800-648-4097
This is an elegant, luxurious, and classic hotel on 12 acres. Offers 92 rooms and 40 suites in Mediterranean-style villas and bungalows surrounded by lush landscapes and lawn, terraces, jacuzzis. French-California cuisine. Bar with piano entertainment. Swimming pool, fitness center. Located in Bel-Air Estates within a heavily wooded canyon. RATE: min room $315, Suite $550. DOG: Welcome at charge of $250 cleaning fee, non-refundable.

FOUR SEASONS HOTEL at Beverly Hills

300 South Doheny Dr, Los Angeles 90048
310-273-2222, 800-332-3442
This award winning hotel is known for exceptional service. Offers 179 rooms, 106 suites, in tropical landscapes. Located in a residential area blocks from Rodeo Drive. Gourmet cuisine and informal dining cafe. Exercise area, swimming pool, complimentary limousine. RATE: min $265 DOG: small dog allowed.

MAMMOTH LAKES

AUSTRIA HOF LODGE

PO Box 607, Mammoth Lakes 93546 800-922-2966,619-934-2764

Great skiing on Mammoth Mountain here. This newly decorated accommodation offers rooms, spa, and sun deck. The Austria Hof Restaurant is known for its delicious German-American food. There is also a cocktail lounge. Mammoth Lakes is a year 'round recreational area...great in summer also. Lots of space.

RATE: min $78 in winter, $50 in summer.

DOG: allowed, no restrictions.

THRIFTLODGE

PO Box 353, Mammoth Lakes 93546

619-934-8576, 800-578-7878, 800-525-9055

Affordable lodge in an excellent location, Mammoth Lakes resort town in the Eastern Sierras. Hundreds of backcountry trails and many lakes in area. Trails allow dogs as long as they are on leash or respond to voice command. Ski, hike, horseback ride, fish, bike, and more. Lodge has cabin apartments. RATE: summer $65, winter $70. DOG: pet rooms must be reserved in advance and a pet agreement signed. $50 pet deposit required agst damages, refundable. Dog cannot disturb other guests and cannot be left unattended in room.

MENDOCINO

THE STANFORD INN BY THE SEA

Coast Highway One & Comptche-Ukiah Road, PO Box 487, Mendocino 95460 707-937-5025

Host: Joan & Jeff Stanford

This Inn offers luxurious lodging on the rugged and dramatic Mendocino Coast...a coastline nestled against giant redwood forests and bounded by the Pacific. They offer superior accommodations, personal service, a greenhouse enclosed pool, spa, sauna, lush tropical plants and gardens with a variety of fruits and vegetables. Activities nearby include Big River canoeing, bicycling on back roads. The Inn has llamas, cats, dogs, horses, and a family of deer and swans. There are some trails where dogs are not allowed, but there are many good walking areas and some beaches dogs are welcome.

Chasing a stick in Big River is a popular dog activity.
RATE: Min. $175 (2 persons) rooms have fireplaces, TV, champagne breakfast. No smoking.
DOG: $15 for entire stay for 1 dog, and $5 for each additional dog. Must be walked on leash in appropriate areas and not left in room unattended.

• NEWPORT BEACH
FOUR SEASONS HOTEL at Newport Beach

690 Newport Center Drive, Newport Beach 92660
714-759-0808, 800-332-3442
An excellent hotel that will exceed your highest expectations. It has many resort amenities...tennis, a 3,000 sq ft pool, spa, jacuzzi, and fitness club. Golf is at Pelican Hill Golf Club. Bikes available. Luxurious rooms are large with water views. Pavilion restaurant offers cuisine of Italy and Mediterranean. Lounge for tea; piano bar. Location convenient to shops, theater, beaches, other area attractions.
RATE: min. $245. No charge for children under 18.
DOG: Any size welcome. Must be house-trained and on leash.

• PALM SPRINGS
CASA CODY COUNTRY INN

175 South Cahuilla Road, Palm Springs 92262 (619)320-9346
Host: Frank Tysen
Ready for a beautiful Palm Springs vacation? Casa Cody is a friendly, quiet hotel reminiscent of the original Palm Springs. Founded in the 1920's it is nestled against the spectacular San Jacinto Mountains in the heart of Palm Springs Village.
There are 2 pools, a tree-shaped spa. Rooms and suites are available. Suites with patios, fireplaces and kitchens. Complimentary continental breakfast is served. The hotel is located near some of the best hiking trails, stables, tennis courts, golf courses, shops, and fine restaurants in Palm Springs. RATE: minimum summer $49
DOG: well-behaved dog welcome. $10 charge.

HILTON RESORT at Palm Springs

400 E. Tahquitz Canyon Way, Palm Springs 92262
800-541-3129, 619-320-6868

This 13 acre resort offers 260 spacious rooms and suites, each with a shady terrace. There is a terrace reataurant, poolside cafe, and piano bar. The resort has a 1 1/2 acre pool area, 6 lighted tennis courts, golf membership privileges at nearby championship courses, shops, and entertainment at galleries, cafes, theaters, and clubs, plus horseback riding, hiking, and bike trails. There is also a spa, fitness center, and kids game room. RATE: about $200 min. DOG: any size welcome. $300 deposit required against damages, fully refundable. (credit charge accepted).

MARRIOTT'S RANCHO LAS PALMAS

41000 Bob Hope Drive, Rancho Mirage, 92270
800-458-8786, 619-568-2727

This is a relaxing desert escape with 240 acres of Spanish-style charm, tranquil lakes, brillant gardens, swaying palms. 450 rooms and 22 suites are available in tile-roofed casitas. Lush golf holes wander through the grounds and 25 tennis courts invite your play, followed by an inviting dip in 2 swimming pools. There are also 2 whirlpools, a fitness center, and jogging trails. Nearby Palm Springs has jeep tours, hot air balloon rides, horseback riding, theater, shops. RATE: Jan-April about $170, summer $80. DOG: small dog under 20 lbs allowed. Must sign waiver against damage and guarantee with credit card.

PT. REYES

THIRTY-NINE CYPRESS BED & BREAKFAST

Box 176, Pt Reyes Stn, 94956 415-663-1709
Host: Julia Bartlett

This delightful small B & B on 1 1/2 acres is on a bluff above Tomales Bay, located one hour drive from San Francisco. There are 3 guest rooms, fireplace, in a separate cottage. Red Wing, another little garden cottage, is also available. Owner lives in another home on property. Substantial breakfast served. Delightful wild setting... cliffs, crashing waves, flowers, deer, cattle. Inn at the edge of Pt Reyes National Seashore. RATE: $110 (2- ngt min. on weekends) DOG: owner, Julia, is a professional dog trainer and loves it when guests bring well-behaved dogs. Dog paradise with beach and trails. No "problem" dogs allowed. Charge $10 per night.

RANCHO SANTA FE

THE INN AT RANCHO SANTA FE

5951 Linea Del Cielo, Rancho Santa Fe 92067
619-756-1131, 800-654-2928
Host: Duncan Royce Hadden
This elegant small Inn, family run, is a complete service hotel surrounded by rolling hills, eucalyptus, citrus groves, and sunshine. Most accommodations are in cottages of 4-10 rooms with baths, some private patios, wet bars, and fireplaces. There are 3 tennis courts, a large heated swimming pool, and a beach cottage on the ocean for day use. Championship golf course about 1 mile away. Massage and fitness available by appointment.; small gym. The Inn offers relaxation, warmth, and tranquility any season of the year. Area offers shops, restaurants, a Wild Animal Park, Sea World, San Diego Zoo, and Scripps Institute of Oceanography.
RATE: min. sgl $95. Also suites and cottages.
DOG: Well-behaved and house-broken dogs welcome. There are over 20 miles of trails through Inn property on which to walk or jog with a pet dog. At Inn's beach cottage in Del Mar, dog is allowed on beach if on leash. San Diego County has a leash law.

RANCHO VALENCIA RESORT

Box 9126, Rancho Santa Fe 92067 619-756-1123
This luxury resort is located on 40 lovely acres in the foothills, 30 minutes north of San Diego. It offers 43 suites. The resort is close to the beach and features 18 tennis courts, bicycling, and spa facilities. Nearby, golf, polo, fishing, shopping.
RATE: Sgl min. $315 DOG: allowed at $75 per night

SACRAMENTO

RADISSON HOTEL

500 Leisure Lane, Sacramento 95815 916-922-2020,800-333-3333
This hotel has unique resort surroundings...lakeside pool and spa, paddle boats, golf, bike trail, 18 acres of lush landscape to walk, gourmet and casual dining, entertainment, Located 5 minutes from State Capitol. RATE: min $90 DOG: $50 refundable deposit

SAN DIEGO

CARMEL HIGHLANDS DOUBLETREE GOLF & TENNIS RESORT

14455 Penasquitos Drive, San Diego 92129 800-622-9223, 619-672-9100

This elegant world-class resort is secluded in a lush green valley and cooled by soft ocean breeses. Rooms are beautifully appointed. Activities include tennis on 6 courts, several swimming pools, decks, a spectacular golf course, a fitness center and sauna. American cuisine is served at Trent's, an elegant restaurant

RATE: min about $119 offseason. DOG: Dogs in first floor rooms only. Owner signs waiver for damage liability. Owner must be present when housekeeping comes in.

RANCHO BERNARDO INN

17550 Bernardo Oaks Drive, San Diego 92128

619-675-8500, 800-542-6096

This lovely resort offers lush surroundings, a friendly ambience, and a variety of activities. There are 287 delux rooms and 58 suites, two excellent restaurants, 108 holes of golf, 12 tennis courts, 2 swimming pools, a fitness center, 7 jacuzzis.

RATE: min sgl Sept - May $195, May - Sept $165. Packages.

DOG: allowed if 20 lbs and under with a $50 non-refundable charge.

SAN DIEGO MARRIOTT HOTEL & MARINA

333 West Harbor Drive, San Diego, CA 92101 619-234-1500

Offers dockside ambience and a resort setting, with 1355 rooms and suites, 2 outdoor pools, health club, tennis courts, jogging trail, a 446 slip marina, boat rentals, and a variety of restaurants. Nearby, beaches, golf, jogging, historic attractions, zoo, Sea World.

RATE: Min $210. Inquire about discounts. DOG: small dog allowed with non-refundable $50 deposit. Guest responsible for damage.

SAN DIEGO PRINCESS RESORT

1404 West Vacation Road, San Diego 92109

619-274-4630, 800-344-2626

This resort has been called a tropical paradise on a 44 acre island in Mission Bay. There are dazzling gardens and hundreds of tropical plants, lagoons and waterfalls. 462 rooms and suites offered, with many dining options. There are 5 pools, a mile of white sand beach, tennis, sailing, games, and exercise equipment. Nearby, San Diego offers endless recreational opportunities incl. golf, Zoo, historic towns, Wild Animal Park. RATE: summer min.$160 dbl. DOG: Welcome. Must sign a pet waiver of responsibility.

• SAN FRANCISCO - see Cities section of this book.

• SANTA BARBARA

CASA DEL MAR

18 Bath Street, Santa Barbara 93101 800-433-3097, 805-963-4418
This is a charming Mediterranean style Inn at the beach, just steps from surf and sand. Offers 20 rooms and suites, some with kitchens, around a private courtyard with gardens. Complimentary breakfast buffet served daily, eveing wine and cheese social, parking, TV, spa. At an excellent location in Santa Barbara, close to beach and city, and miles of palm-lined paths for hiking. Cruises, charter fishing, whale watching, shopping available. There is a resident cat.
RATE: min summer $84. Children under 12 free.
DOG: welcome @ $10 per night. Must not be left unattended in room. Dog enjoys mountain trails and beach. Some areas require leashes.

FESS PARKER'S RED LION RESORT

633 East Cabrillo Blvd, Santa Barbara 93103
800-879-2929, 805-564-4333
This resort is on 24 acres of prime beachfront property. At the front door lies 30 miles of shell white, pristine beach. The 360 rooms are oversized, with a balcony with sweeping view of the Pacific Ocean, Santa Ynez Mountains, or lush tropical garden. The resort is large and grand. The tone is semi-casual.Activities include tennis, golf, exercise room, pool, sauna, and ocean swimming and sunning. Miles of bicycle paths. Lucious California cuisine features aged beef and the finest seafood. Jazz entertainment at bar.
RATE: min about $190 DOG: Dog in first floor rooms only. $50 refundable deposit.

FOUR SEASONS BILTMORE

1260 Channel Drive, Santa Barbara 93108 800-332-3442, 805-969-2261

This resort is called the American Riviera's Premier Resort. Once a favored retreat for golden-era movie stars and royalty. It is now an oceanfront hideaway with legendary service. The luxury resort is nestled on Butterfly Beach in exclusive Montecito, flanked by secluded guest cottages within 20 acres of tropical paradise. There is oceanside dining, fitness options, and spa, championship golf nearby, a children's program, 2 pools, bicycles, 3 tennis courts, 4 restaurants and 2 lounges. RATE: min sgl $199. Special packages for golf, tennis, romance, spa.

SOUTH LAKE TAHOE

ALDER INN

1072 Ski Run Blvd, South Lake Tahoe 96150 800-544-0056, 916-544-4485 Hosts: Gene and Ramona Atkins

Located on beautiful South Lake Tahoe, this Inn, just renovated, has a glassed in jacuzzi, heated pool, cable TV, refrigerators. Walk to beach and restaurants. The Inn is within 1/2 mile of a national forest, 3/4 mile to Heavenly Valley Ski Area, and 3/4 mile to casinos. Transportation available. RATES Inquire. DOG: Dog welcome but absolutely cannot be left unattended. Pet sitters available. Also, owner must clean-up after dog. Charge is 1 x pet fee of $10.

TEHACHAPI

MOUNTAIN INN (Best Western)

416 W. Tehachapi Blvd, Tehachapi 93561 800-528-1234, 805-822-5591

This Inn in the mountains offers 74 rooms, swimming pool in season, restaurant, lounge. Lots of surrounding space. RATE: min $48 DOG: allowed, no charge.

TRINIDAD

BISHOP PINE LODGE

1481 Patrick's Point Drive, Trinidad 95570 707-677-3314

Nice Lodge is within minutes of Pacific coast beaches. Offers cozy

cottages of various sizes, some kitchenettes, TV, deck, garden setting surrounded by redwood trees. Children's play area. Has a snack room. Restaurants nearby. Activities include fishing in ocean, bike, hike, automobile tour, picnic, enjoy beautiful scenery.
RATE: min small cottage $60 DOG: well-behaved dog allowed with fee of $8 per pet per day. Dog must be leashed on property and kept off play area, and never left alone in room.

YOSEMITE
THE REDWOODS GUEST COTTAGES
in Yosemite National Park

PO Box 2085 Wawona Station, Yosemite National Park 95389
209-375-6666 General Manager: Joyce Koller
Guests can visit Yosemite National Park year around. Within the park is a group of privately owned mountain homes, The Redwoods, in a variety of sizes from 1-6 bedrooms, completely furnished. Activities include swimming, horseback riding, stagecoach rides, browsing the museums, art galleries, gift shops, square dancing, fishing, golf. Camera walks are popular in fall foliage time, and in winter guests ski or snowshoe. In spring, hike to high country lakes is popular. RATES: min. about $88
DOG: There are currently 12 units that allow dogs, no restrictions. However, owners must follow Natioanl Park rules:
.make sure dog is immunized for rabies, distemper etc.
.keep dog on leash. Don't leave unattended or may be attacked by wild animals.
.walk on paved paths only (no trails), no swimming; not permitted in public buildings.

MARRIOTT'S TENYA LODGE AT YOSEMITE

1122 Hwy 41, Fish Camp, Yosemite 93623 209-683-6555, 800-635-5807
Delux resort located 2 miles from park's south entrance. Offers 2 pools, aerobic and fitness center, sauna, golf, horseback riding, hiking, biking, skiing, fishing, water sports nearby. RATE: Inquire
DOG: allowed with $50 deposit. Not allowed in public areas such as pool and lobby.

YOUNTVILLE
VINTAGE INN

6541 Washington Street, Yountville 94599
800-351-1133, 707-944-1112

Located in the Napa Valley, this Inn is an hour's drive from San Francisco. It is an "exceptional country Inn". Guests can start with a California champagne breakfast, play tennis, soak up sun, swim in a heated pool, explore the walking town of Yountville adjacent to nearby vineyards, and enjoy dining at its finest.
RATE: Minimum $175 DOG: Well-behaved dog welcome. $25 1 x fee for cleaning. Inn prefers guests with dogs to select first floor accommodations.

NATIONAL PARK CABINS
in Sequoia & Kings Canyon National Parks

PO 900 Kings Canyon Park Service, Kings Canyon 93633
209-335-2314

Sequoia National Park is home of largest trees on earth. Adjacent Kings Canyon National Park has crystal clear lakes, waterfalls, meadows with wild flowers. Walking, hiking prime activities. Also motor tours, skiing, horseback riding, fishing, exploring. There are markets, gift shops, restaurants. Check with local officials on exactly where your dog can walk and hike (on roads and paved areas) He can also go with you in your car within the reaches of the park. RATES: offer rooms and cabins, some at Giant Forest allow dogs if arrangements are made.Also camp sites. Rates begin at about $35.
DOG: Park policy is that dog must be leashed. Not allowed on foot trails, public buildings, or in back country.

Colorado is a paradise for active vacationers with a dog. Among the things to see ts Rocky Mountain National Park, 40 state parks, a 20,000 Denever city park system, northwest Colorado resort areas of Estes Park, Breckenridge, Steamboat Springs, Aspen, Vail, Telluride in the southwest, Mountains, wildlife, mountain lakes, and scenic drives are all here, and lots of activities.

ASPEN
THE LITTLE NELL

675 East Durant Avenue, Aspen 81611 970-920-4600, 888-843-6355

Out among the majestic Rocky Mountains, ringed by 14,000 ft peaks, alpine meadows and snow-fed streams, The Little Nell fits snugly at the foot of Aspen Mountain. This is an intimate country inn with the service and amenities of a grand hotel. There is an elegant restaurant on site. Rooms are equipped with gas-burning fireplaces, sofa and lounge chairs, built-in bar/refrigerator unit, TV and VCR, oversized beds, and two phone lines.

Most guests are ski enthusiasts. Others visit shops, galleries, restaurants, and other cultural and athletic activities that have made Aspen a year around resort. In summer, there is a pool in a garden setting, or try hiking, fishing, or golf. RATE: min. $175. Seasonal variations in rates, as well as for various accommodations. DOG: Dog permitted. No charge. No restrictions noted. There is lots of space for hiking in this delightful area.

COLORADO SPRINGS
COLORADO SPRINGS MARRIOTT

5580 Tech Center Drive, Colorado Springs 80919 719-260-1800

Excellent location. Beautiful views and environment. Has pools, health club, golf, tennis, hiking trails, sightseeing, restaurants. RATE: min. summer $89, winter $69 DOG: allowed. requires a $250 deposit, refundable at checkout.

DENVER
HOLIDAY CHALET

1820 E. Colfax Ave, Denver 80218 303-321-9975, 800-626-4497

This is a beautifully restored brownstone mansion near downtown Denver, kitchens. Private health club. RATE: $54
DOG: allowed with $50 refundable deposit.

BURNSLEY HOTEL

1000 Grant Street, Denver 80203 303-830-1000, 800-231-3915
Offers the simple elegance of a European Inn. Tastefully furnished all-suite hotel is close to downtown. Each suite includes a kitchen, and private patio. Hotel has restaurant and bar. RATE; min $129.
DOG: allowed with $50 refundable deposit.

LOEWS GEORGIO

4150 East Mississippi Ave, Denver 80222 303-782-9300, 800-345-9172
This "European-styled" hotel in prestigious district offers 200 luxurious accommodations, lovely lounge, health club, fine cuisine. RATE: min $175 DOG: allowed on second floor, which is also the smoking floor. No charge.

DURANGO

PINE RIVER LODGE

14443 CR 501, Bayfield, Durango 81122 970-884-2563
Offers 26 housekeeping cabins overlooking Vallecito Lake, surrounded by forested mountains. Pool. playground. Near hiking, horses, marinas. RATE: min $50 DOG: allowed at $10 per ngt per pet.

ESTES PARK

AMERICAN WILDERNESS LODGE

PO Box 2387, 481 West Elkhorn Ave, Estes Park 80517
970-586-4402
A casual country lodge located on the edge of the village of Estes Park and near quaint shops. Surrounded by Roosevelt National Forest and Rocky Mt National Park with 400 sq miles of beautiful scenery, wild animals, and hiking trails. Activities in the area available include horseback riding, swimming, tennis, boating, golf, scenic tours, fishing. Offers rooms, suites, 1-4 room units, some kitchens, fireplaces, TV, heated pool, hot tub. Estes Park has 50 restaurants. RATE: summer $70 min. DOG: $5 per pet per ngt. Must not be left unattended in room.

HOBBY HORSE
(Motor Lodge)

Box 40, 800 E. Big Thompson Ave, Estes Park 80517
303-586-3336, 800-354-8253
This motor lodge offers 5 landscaped acres with large grassy areas, a picnic and barbeque area, playground, swimming pool, sun deck. Two golf courses nearby. Estes Park 1/4 mile away. Trout lake on property. Offers nice large rooms, some fireplaces and balconies, telephone, TV. RATE: min $35. DOG: allowed, no charge

MACHIN'S COTTAGES IN THE PINES

Box 2687, Estes Park 80517 303-586-4276
Hosts: the Machin family Open May-October.
Machin's is nestled in Ponderosa Pines within Rocky Mountain National Park..."a perfect vacation in the Colorado Rockies". Each delux, modern cottage has a complete kitchen, private deck, its own picnic area complete with charcoal grill, table, and lawn furniture. Also, heat, color TV, fireplaces, tub/shower in unit. Ninety percent of Machin's 14 acre property borders on federal land where guests are free to roam. Hiking trails start on property. Beaver Meadows, Moraine Park, and Rocky Mountain NationaL are nearby. Excellent photography opportunities. There is a play-ground for children. Estes Park has shopping, golf, tennis, swimming, tours, and amusements.
RATE: cottages small to extra large. Min. $73 per day, $475 per wk Most guests return year after year. Make reservations early.
DOG: small dog allowed. Two maximum per family. If in doubt call and check. There is lots of space for hiking and playing.

• GLENWOOD SPRINGS
HOTEL COLORADO

526 Pine Street, Glenwood Springs 81601 800-544-3998
Offers 127 large rooms and suites, 2 restaurants, bar, exercise room, Located adjacent to hot springs. Teddy Roosevelt stayed here.
RATE: moderate, inquire DOG: allowed

REDSTONE
AVALANCHE RANCH

12863 Highway 133, Redstone 81623 970-963-2846

Host: Sharon Boucher

Avalanche Ranch is a "Vermont picture postcard in the heart of the Rockies. It is 45 acres of lush countryside on the Crystal River... apple orchard, pond, play and picnic areas, farm animals, tree house, canoe, riverfront. National Hot Springs nearby. Accommodations are in 12 cozy log cabins, rustic but well equipped and tastefully decorated. Great for couples or families. Smoking not permitted in any building. Some woodstoves. Spectacular views. Activities can include great hiking on property or in the nearby National Forest, cross-country skiing, snowshoing, biking, horseback riding, fishing, and jeep trails. Nearby are mining towns, antique shops, the Glenwood Springs Hot Springs Pool, and more. RATE: min cabin $75 low season, $95 high season. DOG: Charge is $10 per night Horses charged $15 per night.

.owner must clean up after dog on grounds

.no barking or aggressive behavior. Never leave dog unattended.

.dog food cannot be left outside.

SILVERCREEK
THE INN AT SILVER CREEK

PO Box 4222, Silvercreek 80446 800-926-4386

This 342 room Inn is a premier resort for first-time skiers and much more. It lies in a spectacular high mountain valley at the foot of the Continental Divide between Winter Park Ski Area and Rocky Mountain National Park. The resort has extensive amenities under one roof, including an athletic club. Activities include whitewater rafting, golf, swimming in a heated pool, boating, sailing, wind-surfing, mountain biking, horseback riding, fishing, jeep tours, tennis, and hot air ballooning. In winter add skiing, snow tubing, snowmobiling, dog sled rides, ice fishing and ice skating.

RATE: min $49 dbl spring/summer/fall. DOG: Charge is $12 per dog per day; certain rooms may be restricted.

• SNOWMASS VILLAGE
SILVERTREE HOTEL

100 Elbert Lane, Box 5550 , Snowmass Village 81615
970-923-3520, 800-525-9402

This is a full service mountain resort open year 'round, ski-in, ski-out. Offers 260 rooms & suites, restaurant, nightclub, bar, 2 outdoor pools, saunas, health club, game room, airport service, shopping, golf, tennis, hiking. Horseback riding available, shops. RATE: variable, inquire. Min $115 DOG: allowed, owner must sign liability waiver. Deposit may be required.

WILDWOOD LODGE

PO Box 5037, 40 Elbert Lane, Snowmass Village 81615
970-923-3550, 800-525-9402

Mountain lodge atmosphere. Open all year. Offers 150 rooms, outdoor heated pool, hot tub, restaurant, airport shuttle. Wonderful mountain setting, wildflowers, shops and horseback riding in area. RATE: variable. min. $69 DOG: allowed. liability waiver, and deposit may be required.

• SOUTH FORK
WOLF CREEK LODGE

PO Box 283, 31042 West Highway 160, South Fork 81154
800-874-0416, 719-873-5547

This "Four Season" Lodge has 49 delux rooms, some with kitchenettes, handicap access, modem hook-up, 4 outdoor hot tubs, cable TV, Fireplace Lounge, billiards and on-site restaurant.

Winter is a skier's delight, more snow than any other Colorado resort. Enjoy cross-country skiing, snowboarding, snowmobiling or ice-fishing. In Spring, w hite water rafting will entice you. Mountain trails abound for hiking, biking, or horseback riding. Warm summer days invite you to be out-of-doors. Mother nature provides the setting, you bring along imagination.
RATE: min about $57 dbl. DOG: allowed. No charge, no restrictions.

STEAMBOAT SPRINGS
SKY VALLEY LODGE

31490 E. Highway 40, Steamboat Springs 80477
303-879-7749, 800-538-7519

Homey English country-type lodge with 24 rooms, close to town. Surrounded by wonderful scenery. Ski shuttle.

RATE: moderate DOG: $8 per day, any size dog welcome.

RENTALS OF HOUSES OR CONDOS that allow a dog:
A variety are available through:
.Big Country Management

1445 So Lincoln Ave, PO Box 5370, Steamboat Springs 80477
970-879-0763, 800-872-0763

TELLURIDE
THE PEAKS

136 Country Club Drive, PO Box 2702, Telluride 81435
800-789-2220, 970-728-6800

The Telluride region appeals to visitors and their dogs. This year 'round vacation spot is an outdoor enthusiasts dream. There are endless hiking trails, pristine lakes, streams, old mining towns, historic walking tours, and cross-country akiing in lovely scenery. The Peaks is an upscale mountain resort nestled in the beautiful San Juan Mountains, elevation 9,500 feet, with 181 delux rooms suites, and 3 penthouses. There is lots of recreational adventure... 18-hole golf course, tennis, hiking, llama trekking, jeep tours, mountain biking, horseback riding, and a luxurious Euro-American health spa. In winter, the ski area dominates, with snowmobiling and other cold weather options. Service is excellent.

RATE: May-Oct (off season) $235, winter min $320. Packages available. Inquire.

TWIN LAKES
MOUNT ELBERT LODGE

10764 Highway 82, PO Box 40, Twin Lakes 81251
719-486-0594, 800-381-4433

Older lodge and housekeeping cabins on mountain stream, surrounded by national forest. Great hiking, rafting, x-country skiing.

RATE: min cabin $72 DOG: $8 per day per pet

VAIL

ANTLERS AT VAIL

680 West Lionshead Place, Vail 81657
970-476-4146, 800-843-8245

Vail is a world class resort destination. Antlers is a condominium hotel where about 60% of owners are willing to accept a dog in their unit. Antlers is in a paradise at the base of Vail Mountain, In winter, it is a premier ski mountain for the family. Cross-country skiing, sleigh rides,, an outdoor heated pool, and hot tub are available. In summer, mild temperatures and fresh mountain air make Vail the perfect summer vacation destination. There is a swimming pool, sun deck, and convenient golf, tennis, fishing, whitewater rafting, horseback riding, mountain biking, and hot air balloon rides. RATE: winter min $205 1-2 people, summer min $115 1-2 people.

DOG: Dog welcome at additional charge of $10 per night in summer and $15 per night in winter. No restrictions, other than owner is responsible for dog actions. A credit card is required as a deposit against damages. There is a bike path behind Antlers that runs along Gore Creek and is a scenic place to exercise, plus some undeveloped ground. "Pooper scooper" provided for accidents.

LIFTHOUSE CONDOMINIUMS

555 E. Lionshead Circle, Vail 81657 800-654-0635, 970-476-2340

Vail is the acknowledged leader in the ski industry. This world-class resort provides guests with a well-rounded experience of winter sports. In summer, guests enjoy gondola rides, golf, tennis, horseback riding, jeeping, rafting, hunting, fishing, and local museums and shops. Lifthouse offers 34 condominiums, equipped with fire-places, kitchens, microwaves, whirlpool, cable and satellite TV, and a balcony. RATE: min sgl winter $127, summer $75

DOG: permitted when not too busy. If full, will not accept dog. Dog must be housebroken and not a "barker". Charge $25 per night. Cannot be left alone in the room.

The coast of this state has hiking and nature areas, and is known as a bedroom community for New York City and cities in the State. Litchfield Hills is beautiful in fall and spring. Route 169 from Norwich to No Woodstock is popular. Notable parks are the Weir Farm National Historic Site and White Memorial Foundation.

CHESTER

THE INN AT CHESTER

318 West Main St, Chester 06412 800-949-stay, 860-526-9541
Host: Deborah

This lovely country Inn is located on 12 lucious acres in the Connecticut River Valley. Offers 41 rooms and a guest house, with TV, phones, air conditioning, in a colonial decor. Elegant dining in Post & Beam; also a tavern. There is an exercise room, sauna, pool, darts, fireplace lounge, tennis, biking, hiking, and in winter skiing and ice skating. Cockaponset State Forest is adjacent with miles of woodlands for hiking, horseback riding, fishing, swimming, and sailing at Cedar Lake.

RATE: $98 dbl includes continental breakfast

DOG: The Inn has a much loved cat, Schedar, who lives inside. Guest pets are welcome but must be friendly. Your dog will love the hiking and pond swimming.

FARMINGTON

CENTENNIAL INN

5 Spring Lane, Farmington 06032 800-852-2052, 860-677-4647

This elegant all-suite hotel offers the charm of a country inn. Full kitchen, livingroom, and cable TV. There is an outdoor pool, whirlpool, exercise facility, on 12 wooded acres. Nearby, area offers a golf course 4 miles from the Inn, hot air balloons, ride the rapids, fish, horseback ride, view arts, shop, see historic places, sample fine cuisine. RATE: min 1 bedrm $105 DOG: $5 per night charge.

LAKEVILLE

INTERLAKEN INN Resort and Conference Center

74 Interlaken Road, Lakeville 06039 860-435-9878

This resort is located on 30 picturesque acres between two lakes in the foothills of the Berkshires, perfect for walking and jogging. There are 70 rooms and 8 duplex townhouses available. Guests can fish, swim, boat in rowboats, canoes, and sailboats in Lake Wononskopomuc. There is also a heated pool, tennis courts, a chip and pitch golf course and an adjoining 18-hole golf course. Also a health and fitness center, and a nearby car racing track. In winter, ice skate and ski nearby. A fine restaurant offers award winning cuisine. Culturally, there is Tanglewood, off-Broadway theater, Music Mountain, and nearly 100 shops to browse.
RATE: Midweek min sgl $99 or dbl Nov 1-April 3.
DOG: allowed @ $10 per day. No restrictions.

• LEDYARD
APPLEWOOD FARMS INN

528 Colonel Ledyard Hwy, Ledyard 06339 860-536-2022
Host: Frankee Betz, owner
Try an interesting farm vacation on a lovely historical colonial furnished with antiques fairly near Mystic. There are rose and colonial gardens on 33 acres which can be explored. 6 rooms with fireplace and bath and 1 suite. RATE: high moderate, inquire. DOG: allowed. Cannot be left alone in room. Owner responsible for damages. There is also an outside kennel on property. Lots of room for dog to run and play on farm.

• LITCHFIELD
TOLL GATE HILL INN

Route 202, Litchfield 06759 800-445-3903, 860-567-4545
A great getaway spot for people with pooches, this hansomely restored country inn is unrivaled in its mingling of relaxed country charm and quiet sophistication. Has carefully appointed guest rooms, working fireplaces, and award-winning cuisine. Guests and their dog can enjoy a walk around the parklike setting, tucked away from the road. RATE: min. about $110. DOG: well-behaved dog welcome, no restrictions.

• MYSTIC
HARBOUR INNE & COTTAGE

15 Edgemont Street, Mystic 06355 860-572-9253
This Inne has lovely views, social area with fireplace and piano, Offers 4 beautifully redecorated rooms with bath, TV, air conditioning, and a cottage with 3 rooms, fireplace and deck. There is a picnic area, gazebo, boat dock and boats on Mystic River.
It is a stroll to historic downtown area.
RATE: room min $75; cottage $175 DOG: welcome at $10 charge

• NEW MILFORD
HERITAGE INN

34 Bridge Street, New Milford 06776 860-354-8883
This Inn is a country hotel with both comforts and efficiency. Twenty rooms, 4 suites, have 20" color TV, air conditioning, phone, private bath, New York Times, and a full breakfast. At New Milford you can picnic on the green, visit shops, restauranrts, historic attractions. Litchfield County has beautiful Fall foliage, golf courses, nature centers, skiing, horseback riding, canoeing, fishing, vineyard tours and more. RATE: min sgl $69, includes hot breakfast. Children under 5 free. DOG: allowed. No charge.

• OLD LYME
OLD LYME INN

85 Lyme Street, PO Box 787, Old Lyme 06371
860-434-2600, 800-434-5352
This Inn, which has received many tributes from the Press over the years, provides fine lodging and dining. It has the warm exterior of a fine, old colonial residence, in the heart of a charming New England Village. Many acres of special historical interest. Owners and a dog would enjoy romping along the extensive trails at Devils Hopyard State Park, swimming in Uncas Lake located in Nehantic State Park and walking the expansive lawns and beach at Harkness Park. RATE: minimum sgl $86
DOG: This is a pet friendly Inn. Dog welcome but must follow rules: Cannot be left alone at any time. Not allowed on furniture. Must be

well-behaved and not bark. Kept on leash in common rooms. Dog must be curbed and taken to designated areas. Owner liable for any damage. Dry dog off before entering Inn in inclement weather.

• VOLUNTOWN
TAMARACK LODGE

10 Rod Road, Voluntown 06384 860-376-0224, 860-376-0640
Offers 22 units in 3 nonhousekeeping cabins, restaurant, lounge, sauna, outdoor pool, lake swimming, boating, private beach, and recreational areas on 20 wooded acres. Open April–October.
RATE: min $55 DOG: allowed with $50 deposit against damages.

• DELAWARE

Attractions in this state include the major city of Wilmington, the beach areas of Reboboth Beach and Dewey Beach; and Bethany Beach and Fenwick Island attract weekenders. Elsewhere in the state are estates, the duPont museum, the Delaware Bay and parks.

• REHOBOTH BEACH / DEWEY BEACH
ATLANTIC SANDS HOTEL

101 N Boardwalk, Rehoboth 800-422-0600, 302-227-2511
Oceanfront hotel offers 114 rooms, outdoor pool, restaurant,
RATE: min $145 DOG: some rooms set aside for dogs no charge.

BEST WESTERN GOLD LEAF

1400 Highway Ave, Dewey Beach 302-226-1100
Offers 75 rooms located 400 ft from beach, TV, rooftop swimming pool. RATE: offseason min $45 DOG: allowed off season

CAPE SUITES

47 Baltimore Avenue, Rehoboth 302-226-3342
Located 1 1/2 blocks from beach, 8 suites. RATE: Min. $110
DOG: allowed.

RENAGADE MOTEL

Highway One, Rehoboth 302-227-1222
20 motel rooms and 8 cabins located 3/4 mile from beach. Restaurant, swimming pool. RATE: cabin $85 DOG: allowed

FENWICK ISLAND

ISKANDER'S ISLAND INN

Route 1, Fenwick Island 302-537-1900
Offers 18 rooms and 42 efficiencies 100 yards from the beach. TV, outdoor swimming pool, restaurant RATE: min $99
DOG: allowed off-season

SANDS MOTEL & APARTMENTS

Rooute 1 & James Street, Fenwick Island 302-539-7745
16 apartments 100 yards from the beach. outdoor swimming pool. RATE: min $67 DOG: allowed.

WILMINGTON

BRANDYWINE VALLEY INN

1807 Concord Pike, Wilmington 17899 302-656-9436
Offers 98 rooms, outdoor pool, exercise facility. RATE: min $63
DOG: allowed

HOLIDAY INN DOWNTOWN

700 King Street, Wilmington 19899 302-655-0400
Offers 219 rooms, 6 suites, swimming pool, restaurant, exercise facility. RATE: min $79 DOG: allowed

SHERATON SUITES

422 Delaware Ave, Wilmington 19801 302-654-8300
800-228-9290
Offers 230 suites, restaurant, exercise facilities. RATE: min $109
DOG: allowed

With the capitol in Tallahassee, Florida has many vacation areas. Amont these are three national forests, national parks and hundreds of state parks. The Miami beach area is popular, made up of 17 islands in Biscayne Bay, and Orlando and Disney World theme parks attract many on a trip through Florida. Another visitor attraction is the Florida Keys with tropical foliage and ocean, while the Gold Coast offers Palm Beach, Vero Beach and Lake Okuchobee.

AMELIA ISLAND

BEACH RENTALS rent a beach house on this lovely resort island

contact: .Unique rentals at 800-940-3955
.All-Service rentals 800-477-8922

BAL HARBOUR

SHERATON BAL HARBOUR BEACH RESORT

9701 Collins Ave, Bal Harbour 33154 800-325-3535, 305-865-7511
This resort is located in Bal Harbour Village, mid-way between Miami and Ft Lauderdale...the best of the Gold Coast of Florida. It has 10 acres of exotic tropical oceanfront playground with an unlimited variety of leisure activities such as water sports, 2 pools and a private beach area, sailing and surfing, Also golf, tennis, health studio, shopping, and resort dining . There are 663 rooms. RATE: Min $165 between May 1 and Sept 30. DOG: allowed if 15 lbs or less, houetrained and kept on leash. May be exercised on beach and along jogging path, and may ocean swim. Pooper scopper mandatory.

BOCA RATON

RADISSON SUITE HOTEL

7920 Glades Road, Boca Raton 33434 407-483-3600, 800-333-3333
Fine services and luxurious amenities of a world-class hotel. Suites include cable TV, VCR, stereo, microwave, mini-bar, balcony. Complimentary breakfast and 2-hour cocktail reception. Recreation includes heated outdoor swimming pool, fitness center, jogging trail, nearby privileges at golf course and country club, tennis, racetracks, polo, diving, sport fishing, water sports, beaches, and shopping. RATES: Inquire DOG: Non-refundable fee of $100 for cleaning. There are established dog walking areas. Dog should be leashed when in public areas and owner present when suite is being serviced. Owner responsible for damages.

BONITA SPRINGS
SHANGRI-LA HOTEL, RESORT, & SPA

27580 Old 41 Road, Bonita Springs 34135 (PO Box 2328)
941-992-3811, 800-279-3811

Warmth, elegance and comfort offered in romantic Southwest Florida together with personalized programs for health and fitness in a tropical resort setting. Suites and cottages available. Pool, tennis, 8 1/2 acres of tropical vegetation, river, dining. RATE: cottage rate min. $125 DOG: small dog allowed in cottage only.

CAPTIVA ISLAND
'TWEEN WATERS INN

P.O. Box 249, Captiva Island 33924 800-223-5865, 813-472-5161

Captiva Island is a friendly tropical paradise of great beauty and historical lore. There is lush foliage, rare tropical birds, coconut palms, white sandy beaches, endless sea shells, beautiful sunsets, and more on the Gulf of Mexico. There is a magnificent pool complex, 3 tennis courts, bocce and shuffleboard courts. Golf course nearby. Full service marina with boat, fishing, and bike rentals. There are 137 new accommodations or quaint cottages available, restaurants and lounges. RATE: Inquire about specific accommodation DOG: Dog welcome in select cottage units and must be leashed at all times. No dog in pool, restaurant, or beaches. Charge is $10 per day per pet. Also, owner must pick up after dog.

CLEARWATER BEACH
CLEARWATER BEACH HOTEL

500 Mandalay Avenue, Clearwater Beach 34630
800-292-2295, 813-441-2425

Friendly elegant hotel on the Gulf of Mexico with pool, beach bar, lawn, tropical gardens. Nearby are fishing, sailing, tennis, golf, fine dining, and Florida attractions. Located 30 minutes from Tampa or St Petersburg airports. Hotel will meet your plane. RATE: min May-Feb $98, Feb-May $135. DOG: small dog allowed

COCOA BEACH
THE SURF STUDIO (motel)

1801 S. Atlantic Ave, Cocoa Beach 32931 407-783-7100

Attractive accommodation located on Florida's East coast, with 250 feet of ocean front, pool, and lawn in a clean and peachful surrounding. Kitchens, housekeeping services, nearby restaurants, golf, tennis, fishing, river sports, close to Disney. RATE: min. winter $70, summer $55. DOG: allowed with $10 fee.

DELRAY BEACH
THE COLONY HOTEL

525 East Atlantic Ave, PO Box 970, Delray Beach 33447
800-552-2363

Offers an elegant historic 1926 Mediterranean style landmark hotel, TV, air conditioning, phones, dining room, and the Cabana Club with heated salt water pool at a sandy beach. Open Nov 1-April 28. In area, fine beaches, residential walking areas, golf, tennis, bike rentals, theater, nightclubs, dive shop, deep sea fishing.
RATE: min sgl $55 Inquire about special packages.
DOG: well behaved dog welcome at $20 each per day.

FISHER ISLAND
FISHER ISLAND CLUB

One Fisher Island Drive, Fisher Island 33109
305-535-6000, 800-537-3708

This is an upscale world-class tropical resort seven minutes by ferry from Miami. The 216 acre private island is home to the former mansion of William K. Vanderbilt II, now the Fisher Island Club. Guests enjoy lavish accommodations in 340 suites, villas, and cottages. There are deep water marinas, swimming pools, tennis courts, championship seaside golf, one mile of soft sand beach, and an international spa. Seven restaurants serve gourmet and casual cuisine in varied ambiance. In this luxurious private community, recreation and cuisine are also world-class. RATE: min single $140. Studio cottage, 2 people, $450 May-Oct. A $25 per couple per night guest membership fee is charged guests who are not members of Fisher Island Club. Children under 12 free. DOG: dogs permitted.

INDIAN SHORES

EDGEWATER BEACH RESORT

19130 Gulf Blvd, Indian Shores 34635 813-595-4028
Offers 15 apartments on the gulf of Mexico, mostly 1 bedroom. There is a pool. Restaurants and shopping nearby. Busch Gardens a 45 minute drive. RATE: Summer May-Sept $65; winter Dec 15-April 30 weekly rate $400. Two day minimum.
DOG: small dog allowed except in summer. Prior approval and a deposit may be required.

HOLIDAY VILLAS II

19610 Gulf Blvd, Indian Shores 34635 800-428-4852, 813-596-4852
Offers 64 2-3 bedroom condos directly on beach, TV, heated pool, parking, balconies, near golf and tennis. RATE: Inquire
DOG: allowed with a $50 deposit.

ISLAMORADA

LOOKOUT LODGE RESORT

87770 Overseas hwy, Islamorada 33036 800-870-1772, 305-852-9915
"One of the finest locations in the Keys"...a crystal clear Florida Bay, minutes from the ocean. This is a small waterfront resort with 18 studios and suites, TV, phones, private beach, barbeques, and boat dock. All units have kitchenettes. Resort beach area offers swimming and sunbathing. Dive boat takes you to dive sites.
RATE: min studio $80 DOG: small dog allowed with advance arrangement in some units. Dog can go swimming.

KEY WEST

HAMPTON INN

2801 North Roosevelt Blvd, Key West 33040 305-294-2917
Located in a tropical paradise, offers 157 spacious, comfortable, and affordable guest rooms overlooking Gulf of Mexico or tropical gardens, pool and jacuzzi, shops, parking, bar. Serves complimentary continental breakfast. Explore Hemingway's haunts, beautiful historic homes, and fabulous gourmet restaurant. Shopping, fishing, diving.
RATE: Inquire DOG: small dog allowed at nominal fee

LAKE WALES

CHALET SUZANNE COUNTRY INN

3800 Chalet Suzanne Drive, Lake Wales 33853

941-676-6011, 800-433-6011 Hosts: Hinshaw family

This interesting Swiss-style country inn is located near the state's center. There are 30 individualized rooms on a 70 acre estate, an excellent restaurant, a pool, private lake, and grassy air strip. Gardens nearby. RATE: min $125 includes breakfast for two, packages available DOG: allowed at $20 charge per pet per night. Some space to run.

LONGBOAT KEY

HOLIDAY INN

4949 Gulf of Mexico Drive, Long Boat Key 34228

914-383-3771, 800-813-HOLIDAY

Offers 146 rooms, restaurant, lounge, swimming pool, beach, tennis, boating rentals. RATE: min $79 DOG: allowed with $50 refundable pet charge if no damage.

RIVIERA BEACH RESORT

5451 Gulf of Mexico Drive, Longboat Key 34228

941-383-2552 Hosts: Bernie and Linda Weiss

This resort is located on one of the most secluded tropical beach settings on Longboat Key. Spacious apartments overlook gardens and calm blue waters of the Gulf of Mexico...a lovely beach setting. There is a private white sand beach for swimming, sunning, and fishing. Sailboat rental, tennis, golf courses nearby. The ambiance is relaxed and friendly. Near shops, gourmet restaurants. RATE: Min offseason May-Dec $470-$650 per week for 2 persons per bedroom. DOG: allowed if 15 lbs and under only. Need prior agreement and an additional security deposit.

MARATHON

FARO BLANCO Marine Resort

1996 Overseas Highway, Marathon 33050

305-743-9018, 800-759-3276

This friendly and luxurious marine resort in the Florida Keys offers 4 restaurants, 2 lounges, a full service marina, an olympic size freshwater swimming pool, picnic areas, boat charters and rentals, snorkeling and diving on live barrier reef. Accommodations include cottages, houseboat staterooms, apartments, condos. Get there by car or plane. RATE: min cottage about $65 per night dbl. sport fishing packages available. DOG: $18 not allowed in condos.

MIAMI BEACH

NEWPORT BEACHSIDE CROWNE PLAZA RESORT (Holiday Inn)

16701 Collins Ave, Miami Beach 33160-4299
305-949-1300, 800-327-5476

Offers 350 South Florida rooms and 28 suites with sun drenched beaches washed in blue Caribbean waters. This hotel has 450' of beach, its own fishing pier and artificial reef, olympic size pool, kiddie pool, whirlpool, games and evening entertainment. There are world famous restaurants, cocktail bars, a cappuccino bar, fitness center, beauty salon, shops. In area, deep sea fishing, golf, waterskiing, cruises, and much more. RATE: high-moderate, inquire. DOG: maximum size 25 lbs.

OCEAN FRONT HOTEL

1230 Ocean Drive, Miami Beach 33139 305-672-2579

Located on the oceanfront in the heart of Miami Beach's art deco district. Offers 27 nice rooms and penthouse suites, TV, bar, safe, views, phone, and the Les Deux Fontaines French Restaurant. RATE: min $125 DOG: welcome at $15 per day.

NAPLES

WORLD TENNIS CENTER RESORT AND CLUB

4800 Airport Road, Naples 33942 800-292-6663

Located about 2 miles from the powdery beaches of the Gulf of Mexico, this resort is not just for tennis. It features 82 tropically landscaped acres, and 148 2-bedroom condos for daily or longer rental. Mediterranean style architecture and lush gardens.

There is a 2500 seat stadium, whirlpool spas, aerobic classes, jacuzzis, stocked fishing lakes, ball courts, miles of roadways to jog, hike, bike, or walk, a heated swimming pool, sun deck and pool-side restaurant. 16 tennis courts and instruction available. Golf packages are available. There are 200 restaurants to explore. RATE: $125 min. DOG: welcome in a few condos. No extra charge.

- ## ORLANDO
DELTA ORLANDO RESORT

5715 Major Blvd, Orlando 32819 407-351-3340

Offers 800 guest rooms on 25 landscaped acres, 3 heated outdoor pools, saunas, tennis courts, 9 hole mini-golf, games courts, Health Club use, 3 restaurants. Located 15 minutes to Walt Disney World Resort, Universal Studios near hotel, Sea World 3 miles. RATES: min sgl about $75. Special packages. No charge for children under 18. DOG: allowed at fee of $25 per stay.

- ## PALM BEACH GARDENS
EMBASSY SUITES HOTEL

4350 PGA Blvd, Palm Beach Gardens 33410
407-622-1000, 800-EMBASSY

This hotel offers 160 suites, TV, phone, kitchenette, located at Interstate 95 near Palm Beach. Restaurant features steak and seafood. Complimentary breakfast. Has outdoor pool, fitness center, jogging trail, tennis, golf course nearby. Locally, Palm Beach and Worth Ave have shopping, theater, deep sea fishing, golf, miles of white sand beaches, water sports. RATE: min. winter $129 DOG: allowed with $100 non-refundable fee.

- ## PALM BEACH
FOUR SEASONS RESORT PALM BEACH

2800 South Ocean Blvd. Palm Beach 33480
407-582-2800, 800-332-3442

Offers 210 elegant luxury beachfront accommodations with private terraces, rerstaurant, sparkling Atlantic with silken sand beach, pool, tennis, spa and health club. Excellent golf nearby. Also cruises, polo, theater. RATE: summer min sgl $140. special pack.

DOG: welcome but must observe rules. Can never be left unattended in room. Cannot go on Pool Deck, Beach or restaurant. When outside dog must be on leash (6 ft max); must pick-up dog mess; cannot disturb other guests.
"Pet sitters" available for small fee through hotel.

HEART OF PALM BEACH HOTEL

160 Royal Palm Way, Palm Beach 33480 407-655-5600
This is a charming European style hotel located in the heart of the island. Swim in the Atlantic or relax around pool. Shop on Worth Ave, visit restaurants and clubs. Near golf, tennis, polo, fishing, water sports, theater. Rooms are large with refrigerator, color TV, most with terraces. Restaurant on property. RATE: min $129 in winter, special packages. Summer & Fall $69
DOG: allowed, but cannot be walked on hotel property (take off). Must be leashed at all times. Owner responsible for damages.

PALM COAST
SHERATON PALM COAST RESORT

300 Clubhouse Drive, Palm Coast 32137 904-445-3000, 800-654-6538
This very attractive resort offers 154 rooms and suites, and 2-bedroom villas, restaurant, lounge, entertainment. Activities include 4 golf courses, 18 tennis courts, 2 pools, beach, fitness room, marina, fishing, boating, jogging trails, games, playground. Located 27 miles from Daytona Beach Intl Airport and 22 miles from St Augustine. RATE: Inquire DOG: allowed, no charge

PANAMA CITY
MARRIOTT'S BAY POINT RESORT

4200 Marriott Dr, Panama City Beach 32408 800-874-7105
Offers 1,100-acre full service resort with a private beach, located 15 minutes from airport. 355 guest rooms, 5 restaurants, 2 18-hole golf courses, 12 clay tennis courts, 4 swimming pools, 2 health clubs, sauna, boating, children's program. RATE: Inquire DOG: small dog allowed. $50 non-refundable fee.

PONTE VEDRA BEACH
MARRIOTT SAWGRASS RESORT

1000 TPC Boulevard, Ponte Vedra Beach 32082 904-285-7777
This premier sports resort is an enchanted place where land and sea sea come together. There are 538 guest rooms or beach and golf villas, and a host of dining and entertaining options.
There are 3 pools, lounge with live music, health and fitness center. Service is superior. Recreational activities include world-class golf on 5 surrounding championship courses. Tennis courts are on 5 different surfaces, including grass. Guests swim in two lagoon-like pools with tropical foliage, and can fish, sail, explore beach and marshlands on foot, bike, boat, or horseback ride.
Many sightsee in St Augustine nearby. Special children's programs for age 5-12. RATE: about $100. Special packages. Inquire.
DOG: allowed in several buildings on ground floor.
$25 non-refundable pet fee.

SUGAR LOAF KEY
SUGAR LOAF LODGE

Sugar Loaf Key 33044 305-745-3211
Located 13 miles from Key West, overlooking Gulf of Mexico on beautiful Sugar Laof Key. Complete vacation resort provides tropical surroundings, good fun, good food, and good drinks, in friendly family atmosphere. Resort offers all waterfront rooms, color TV, restaurant, cocktail lounge, entertainment, porpoise shows, tennis courts, shuffleboard, miniature golf, fresh water pool, salt water beach, marina, bait and tackle, fishing, diving, a 3,000' air strip.
RATE: Min sgl $65, dbl $75. No charge children under 12.
DOG: charge $10 per pet. Allowed in designated areas only on resort property.

SAFETY HARBOR, TAMPA BAY
SAFETY HARBOR RESORT & SPA

105 N. Bayshore Dr., PO Box 248, Safety Harbor 34695
813-726-1161, 888-237-8772
Offers ultimate range of spa packages from nightly to full range. Fall sampler $109 to 7 night $2,039 package of services and beauty routines. All sorts of aerobics, pool, tennis, healthy gourmet meals

and much more. You decide what to attend. Also, lots of activities for men while he waits for you, including sports-specific learning in golf, tennis, deep sea fishing, boxing and more. RATE: variety of packages, inquire. DOG: small dog allowed up to 20 lbs.

SARASOTA
COQUINA ON THE BEACH

1008 Ben Franklin Drive, Sarasota 34236 941-388-2141
Host: Thomas Quigley, manager
This resort is directly on Lido Beach on the Gulf of Mexico. Take a dip in the heated pool or walk to the beach at your doorstep. You can water ski, picnic, and swim. The location is convenient to other cultural attractions. Offered are 1-2 room efficiency apartments, with cable TV and laundry facilities. RATE: Minimum Feb & March $139; Jan, Apr-Dec $89-109. Children 18 yrs and under free. DOG: $25 non-refundable fee. Owner must clean-up after pet. Dog must be leashed at all times. Dog not allowed in pool or on beach.

STUART
INDIAN RIVER PLANTATION BEACH RESORT

555 NE Ocean Blvd., Stuart 34996 800-444-3389, 407-225-3700
This lovely resort offers 200 tropical acres on Treasure Coast, north of Palm Beach. Features 300 rooms, suites, and oceanside villas, restaurants, plus a broad selection of recreation...including 3 golf courses, beaches, 13 tennis courts, 77 slip marina, 4 swimming pools, in a beautiful natural setting. Fishing, snorkeling, sailing, hiking, and more. RATE: min $135 DOG: $75 non-refundable fee for entire stay.

TREASURE ISLAND
SEA HORSE COTTAGES

10356 Gulf Blvd., Treasure Island 33706 813-367-2291, 800-741-2291 Host: Tom & Roseanne Petit
Located in a serene island setting of palms, rolling waves, white sands and cool trade winds off the Gulf of Mexico. Housekeeping cottages and apartments have microwave, refrigerator, TV, phone, outdoor grill. No maid service. Nearby Busch Gardens, Zoo, and

performing arts center. Orlando is 2 hours drive with Disney World and MGM, and Universal studios. RATE: min sgl about $60
DOG: small dog under 20" and under 20 lbs allowed @ $10 charge. There is a park across street to walk pet. Must keep on leash and pick up after dog. May not take on beach.

WINTER PARK
LANGFORD RESORT HOTEL

300 E. New England, PO Box 970, Winter Park 32790
407-644-3400
This is a 220 room and suites holiday paradise in North Orlando. Offers olympic size pool in tropical setting, children's pool, health spa, excellent restaurant, evening dance band. Located a comfortable drive from Orlando attractions. RATE: min sgl $65
DOG: allowed at $25 charge.

GEORGIA

Charming Georgia offers many historic sites of the Civil Road. Atlanta is a hallmark of southern hospitality, as well as a center of industry. Savannah, several hours from Atlanta, retains its own charm. Blues, jazz, and some raggae and hard rock are all represented in the nightlife of these cities. Popular vacation spots include the Chattahoochee National Forest, and a chain of islands along the coast...Jekyll Island, Sea Island, and St Simons Island, which can be reached by car.

ATLANTA
HAWTHORN SUITES HOTEL

1500 Parkwood Circle, Atlanta 30339
770-952-9595, 800-338-7812
Large 1-2 bedroom suites, complimentary breakfast, swimming pool, tennis courts. RATE: min $69 DOG: allowed

DOUBLETREE HOTEL

7 Concourse Parkway, Atlanta 30328 770-395-3900, 800-222-TREE
Offers 370 Elegant rooms overlooking a lake. RATE: $135, complimentary breakfast DOG: allowed

BLAIRSVILLE
7 CREEKS - HOUSEKEEPING CABINS

5109 Horseshoe Cove Road, Blairsville 30512 706-745-4753
Hosts: Marvin and Bobbie Hernden
Offers 6 cottages in one of the South's most phorographed areas, located in the midst of rugged mountainous country, with the Appalachian Trail, 3 large TVA lakes, beautiful waterfalls, and numerous recreational areas, all within a short driving distance. Fishing, swimming, hiking, and jogging opportunities abound. Walks in the woods on this 70 acre property are popular. Picnic shelters badminton, horseshoes, and tetherball also offered. Within one hour's drive guests find several golf courses, gold and gem panning, canoeing, river rafting, craft shops, flea market and state park. Children enjoy watching and patting the resident pony, goats and other farm animals. RATE: cabin size varies, 2-night minimum. $60 per day 1-2 persons; $325 per week. Bring own linens or rent. otherwise cabins fully furnished. DOG: Dogs allowed. They must be housebroken, clean, free of fleas, and quiet. Owner must control dog at all times, on leash or under voice control. Owner must clean-up hair and cover furniture if dog jumps on it. There are areas to walk the dog and a lake for dog and people swimming with lots of space for fun.

BLUE RIDGE
BLUE RIDGE MOUNTAIN CABINS

P.O. Box 1182, Blue Ridge 30513 706-632-8999
Hosts: Theresa Meehan and Peter Feldbrugle
These rental vacation cabins are open year 'round, located in the beautiful North Georgia Mountains. They are nicely furnished and fully equipped. May be rented by night, weekend, or week. Most are located only 1-4 miles from Lake Blue Ridge, easily reached by car.

Guests can go tubing or whitewater rafting on the Toccoa and Ocoee Rivers, swim and boat on Lake Blue Ridge, fish for trout in rivers and streams or go for a hike and picnic in the Chattahoochee National Forest. Also, shop, play golf and tennis, go bowling, visit auto races or dine in fine restaurants. RATE: min. daily $70; weekly $435. DOG: Dogs are permitted in a few cabins. Dog must be friendly, housebroken, and deflead. $10 per dog per stay fee. If there is a flea problem following rental, there is a $35 additional charge. Therefore rentals must be guaranteed with VISA, Mastercard, or Discover. Arrangements must be made in advance for dog. Owner is responsible for damages.

PINE MOUNTAIN
CALLAWAY GARDENS RESORT

PO Box 2000, Pine Mountain 31822 800-282-8181, 404-663-2281

This is a place "prettier than anything since the Garden of Eden" and much more. More than 750,000 people from all over the U.S. visit this resort annually. Set on 14,000 acres, the Gardens include horticultural displays, plus world-class golof, tennis, fishing, hunting, fine dining, and lodging. Accommodations range from 350 single rooms to 155 secluded cottages and 49 delux lodgings in villas. Dining is delicious at 7 unique restaurants. RATE: Inquire DOG: If guests are staying overnight at the resort, their dog must be boarded outside. They suggest the Canine Country Club for boarding animals with prior arrangements. During the day you can pick-up your dog and have him visit the resort with owners. Dog must be on leash and be well-behaved. They can visit throughout the Gardens, go on numerous walking trails in woodland areas and lakes, but not inside buildings.

CLARKESVILLE
HABERSHAM HOLLOW CABINS

Route 6, Box 6208, Clarkesville 30523 706-754-5147

Hosts: C.J. and Maryann Gibbons

This is a peaceful oasis of solitude and serenity situated on seven wooded acres, nestled in Northeast Georgia Mountains. Stroll through woods on the property or drive five minutes to a state park or 15 minutes to Tallulah Falls. The resort is close to shopping, fishing, swimming, boating, whitewater rafting, canoeing, golf, horseback riding, and hiking areas. Cabins have full kitchens, fireplaces, air conditioning, color TV, decks, picnic tables. RATE: Inquire. DOG: Well mannered dogs are allowed in cabins. Must be leashed outside.

CLEVELAND
VILLAGIO DI MONTAGNA

Highway 129 North, Cleveland 30528 800-367-3922
Luxury villas in the northeast mountains to relax and enjoy. In-room jacuzzis and riverfront palazzo rooms, health Club, swimming pool. RATE: minimum $80 DOG: allowed

DILLARD
DILLARD HOUSE

P.O. Box 10, Dillard 30537 706-746-5348
This is a year 'round mountain resort, 100-year-old working farm, restaurant, tennis, swimming, horseback riding, golf, waterfall rides...a perfect home base when hiking in the mountains. Lots of Southern hospitality. RATE: moderate, inquire
DOG: allowed at $5 per night.

JEKYLL ISLAND
VILLAS BY THE SEA

1175 N. Beachview Drive, Jekyll Island 31527
800-841-6262 (outside GA), 800-342-6872 (in GA)
This resort is a hotel condominium on a 17 acre property with villas of various sizes on or near Jekyll Island beachfront. Pool and bike rentals. This enchanting island offers golf, tennis, beach, bosting, fishing, historic attractions, plus breathtaking natural beauty in a year 'round semi-tropical climate. Once an escape for the Morgans, Goulds, and Rockefellers, the island is now a state park. RATE: Vary according to season and accommodation. Min 1-bedroom in vacation season $109. Weekly rates available. DOG: non-refundable $41 for 1-bedroom unit, $44 for 2-bedrm unit, $47 for 3-bedrm unit. There is a state leash law in effect. Many guests bring their dogs with them to enjoy the property and the island, with its numerous paved bike paths.

SAINT SIMON ISLAND
THE ISLAND INN

301 Main Street, Plantation Village, St Simon Island 31522
800-673-6323

Southern hospitality in a serenely beautiful setting.
RATE: minimum $45 DOG: allowed in specific rooms at $9 per day

SAVANNAH
BALLASTONE INN & TOWNHOUSE

14 E. Oglethorpe Ave, Savannah 31401 800-822-4553, 912-236-1484

Offers 23 lovely rooms, antiques, courtyard, fireplaces, located near river. Breakfast complimentary. RATE: min. $100
DOG: allowed in 4 rooms @ $10 per night charge

OLDE HARBOR INN BED & BREAKFAST

508 East Factors Walk, Savannah 31401 800-553-6533, 912-234-4100

Experience cobblestone streets, quaint shops, and ships passing just outside your window. Offers charming luxury suites with elegant furniture. Evening cordials. RATE: minimum $95 DOG: allowed

RIVER STREET INN

115 E. River Street Savannah 31401 912-234-6400

This is a 44 room historic Inn overlooking River Street and the Savannah River. Breakfast included in rate. RATE: Inquire
DOG: allowed

MARRIOTT-SAVANNAH RIVERFRONT

100 General McIntosh Blvd, Savannah 31401 912-233-7722

Marriott hotel on the riverfront, adjacent to shops and dining.
RATE: moderate DOG: allowed

VILLA RICA
AHAVA PLANTATION BED & BREAKFAST

2236 S. Van Wert Road, Villa Rica 30180
770-459-2863, 404-459-4978
Hosts: Larry & Dianne Camp
True hospitality in this antebellum home, about 30 minutes from Atlanta. Offer 5 bedrooms and 2 suites, airconditioned. Southern-style breakfast before fireplace. Enjoy farm animals.
RATE: minimum $65. No smoking in rooms; ok outside.
DOG: Shady, fenced out-door kennels available for dog @$10 per night, per pet. There is a wooded section behind house with streams and hiking area.

HAWAII

At the present time Hawaii has a quarantine law in effect of 120 days. No dog can enter without going through quarantine which is not practical for those wishing to vacation. Hawaii residents with a dog do have some vacation options within the State at major resorts. However, we will not list these here.

IDAHO

This is a lovely state for vacation. There are 8 national forests and 17 state parks, including the Sawtooth National Forest with recreation area. Sun Valley is popular, North Idaho has many lakes for fishing and recreation. Coeur d'Alene and Priest Lake are scenic areas.

CASCADE
NORTH SHORE LODGE

175 North Shoreline Drive, Cascade 83611
800-933-3193, 208-632-2000
Cabins at Warm Lake open all year. Lodge includes a lounge, store, restaurant, gas and oil, boat and canoe rental, docks for mooring, swimming area, hiking trails, water skiing, fishing, horseshoe pits, volleyball, wildlife viewing, horseback riding with local outfitter, a Saturday night Bar-B-Que (at reasonable charge) RATE: Cabin maximum occupancy from 2-10 persons. Minimum rate $50 per ngt (4 persons) $90 per ngt (10 persons) . DOG: Welcome. Must be leashed at all time; messes cleaned up. Lots of space for fun.

COEUR d'ALENE
COEUR d'ALENE INN

414 West Appleway, Coeur d'Alene 83814
208-765-3200, 800-251-stay
This is an affordable new resort, very modern in design. Offers 123 well appointed rooms, manicured grounds, restaurant, grille, bar, climate controlled indoor/outdoor pool, fitness center. There are shops, area restaurants, a resort golf course, and private beach. Nearby skiing. RATE: about $45. Packages available.
DOG: allowed. no charge

ISLAND PARK
ELK CREEK RANCH

Box 2. Island Park 83429 208-558-7404
Elk Creek Ranch is in the heart of Idaho's trout country in a beautiful lake setting. They offer their private lake. Other waters nearby are renowned and draw anglers from coast to coast. There is a varied bird population. In addition, nearby there is horseback riding, boating, hiking, picnicking, and other out-door activities for guests and family members. This accommodation offers large living quarters and wholesome home cooked meals served family style. Eight cabins of various sizes are available, and a rustic main lodge. RATE: $75 per day DOG: Welcome. Owner is required to clean up after dog if they use groomed lawn. There are plenty of forest areas surrounding.

KETCHUM
HEIDELBERG INN

PO Box 5704, 1908 Warm Springs Road, Ketchum 83340
208-726-5361, 800-284-4863
This lodge in a park-like setting offers spacious rooms with microwave and refrigerator, TV, some kitchenettes, indoor spa, heated swimming pool in summer, fireplaces. There is a golf course and tennis complex across the street. Sawtooth National Recreational area is 7 miles north. RATE: Inquire DOG: allowed in "smoking" rooms @ $5 per night. Ketchum/Sun Valley area has a very extensive pet-friendly hiking, biking, skiing, trail system.

NORDMAN
ELKIN'S ON PRIEST LAKE

HCO-1, Box 40, Nordman 83848 208-443-2432
This fine log cabin resort is open all year and offers full service, fine dining, cocktail lounge, long sandy beaches, spacious cabins, and a marina. There are hiking and jogging trails, ski trails, a golf course nearby, game rooms, mountain bike trails.
RATE: cabin min. daily rate about $100, variable, seasonal.
DOG: must be on leash at all times on property. Charge of $5 per night or $30 per week.

PRIEST LAKE
HILL'S RESORT

HCR 5, Box 162A, Priest Lake 83856 208-443-2551
Hosts: the Hill family Open year around
This 50 unit resort is located along the sandy shores of Luby Bay at Priest Lake, within view of the Selkirk mountain range and woods. Hill's has been named an outstanding family resort by two natioanl magazines, Better Homes and Gardens and Family Circle. Activities include water sports, boating, hiking, jogging along trails, fishing, hunting, tennis, pickleball, bike riding, golf, cross country skiing, and snowmobiling. Rentals available for bikes, canoes, boats, skiis and snowmobiles. Enjoy the casual elegance of an award wining restaurant or enjoy a cocktail by the stone fireplace.
RATE: Vary considerably. Minimum cabin offseason about $125.
DOG: On leash only on property. Leash law in effect June 15 through Sept 30. Fee $10 per night or $60 per week.

SAGLE
BOTTLE BAY RESORT & MARINA
on Lake Pend Oreille

1360 Bottle Bay Road, Sagle 83860 208-263-5916
Host: Dorette and John High
Located on a quiet well-protected bay, the resort offers a variety of water sports or just lazy sun-filled days. There is a sandy beach , sailing, fishing, water skiing, and Bottle Bay burgers and sunset dinners. The resort offers modern log cabins with kitchens. There is a restaurant and cocktail lounge. Also, an RV park.

Points of interest in area include golf courses, restaurants, shops, Glacier National Park, trails for hiking, skiing, mountain bike rentals, boat rentals. RATE: housekeeping cabins summer $85 per 2 people. $7.50 each addit. Lakefront 2-bedroom cabin $115 per night.

SANDPOINT
LAKESIDE INN

106 Bridge Street, Sandpoint 83864 800-543-8126, 208-263-3717
A very nice family resort inn located on Lake Pend Orielle. Private park, waterfront and boat moorage, restaurant. Amenities include complimentary breakfast, waterfront rooms, suites, and kitchens, jacuzzi. Lake cruises available, as well as golf and parasail packages. Boat rentals. RATE: moderate. Inquire. DOG: welcome at $5 per pet, per night.

STANLEY
MOUNTAIN VILLAGE RESORT

P.O. Box 150, Stanley 83278 208-774-3661, 800-843-5475
Host: Cindy Dalzell, manager
Cozy all season resort located in the heart of the Sawtooth Mountain near Salmon River. Meadows with wild flowers, steelhead fishing, rafting, hiking, biking on trails. Sandy beaches for swimmers and boaters. Trail rides into back country, photo opportunities, ski trails. Offers 60 unit lodge with coffee, TV, telephone, and use of natural hot spring. Restaurant. RATE: Inquire DOG: allowed in smoking rooms @ $5 plus tax. Resort is in mountains with hundreds of miles of trails and lakes for doggie fun with owner.

SUN VALLEY
RIVER STREET INN BED & BREAKFAST

100 Rivers Street West, Ketchum 83340
PO Box 182, Sun Valley 83353
208-726-3611
This is a lovely little Inn with views of Bald Mountain, within walking distance of shops, restaurants. All accommodations are spacious parlor suites with Japanese soaking tub, shower, phone, TV, Easy access to incredible recreation areas. RATE: $130 min. (dbl) DOG: 1 or 2 dogs @ $10 per night with manager prior approval.

Illinois has Chicago, a city of some charm and interest from its central business district, The Loop, to Magnificent Mile shops and artistic and cultural offerings. There is the Shawnee National Forest in the southern part of the State, as well as State parks. Galena, in the Northwest part is former home of Ulysses S. Grant, and also a recreation area.

BLOOMINGTON

JUMER'S CHATEAU

1601 Jumer Drive, Bloomington 61704 800-285-8637, 309-662-2020
This chateau brings Europe to the Midwest. There is old world charm, rich colors, and objects d'art to give guests a truly unique experience. Accommodations are delux and service impeccable. Dining features authentic German and American "house specialties" and a fully stocked wine cellar. Limousines provide luxurious transport to airport or shopping centers. There is a swimming pool, game room, sauna, and whirlpool, cocktail bar, and attractive grounds. Rooms and suites are luxurious.
RATE: minimum about $89 DOG: $25 deposit upon check-in. Refundable on check-out upon inspection.

CHICAGO see CITIES section of this book.

JONESBORO

BLACK DIAMOND RANCH

off Rt 127 bet Alto Pass & Jonesboro, Jonesboro 62952
618-833-7629
" Old West" atmosphere offering year 'round lodging, cabins, hiking, horseback riding, and more, in Southern Illinois. RATE: Inquire
DOG: will allow well-behaved dog at owner discretion

TRAIL OF TEARS LODGE & SPORTS RESORT

1575 Fair City Road, Jonesboro 62952 618-833-8697
Located in Southern Illinois. Offers lodging, meals, cabins, horse trail rides, fishing, archerv. miniature golf, and more.
RATE: inquire DOG: can be allowed at manager discretion.

LINCOLNSHIRE
MARRIOTT LINCOLNSHIRE RESORT

Ten Marriott Drive, Lincolnshire 60069 847-634-0100
This resort offers the atmosphere of a country club...the excitment of a night on the town. For non-stop fun try golf, tennis, racquet-ball, aerobics, sailing, canoeing, swimming in indoor and outdoor pools, cross-country skiing in season, health club, theater. For non-stop leisure, sit poolside, get a massage, relax in a whirlpool, or picnic at the lake. There are 2 restaurants and lounges. Nearby, guests find shopping, a theme park, and Lake Michigan sport fishing. RATE: min $150. Many packages, inquire. DOG: allowed in 1st floor rooms. Must be in carrier in room. Guest responsible for any damages.

ROBINSON
QUAIL CREEK COUNTRY CLUB & RESORT

1010 E. Highland, PO Box 243, Robinson 62454
800-544-8674, 618-544-8674
Offers rooms and suites, restaurant, golf, swimming pool, tennis. RATE: min $40 DOG: allowed if kept in kennel in room, take out during the day. No charge.

WHITTINGTON
REND LAKE RESORT

R.R. #1, Box 73B, Whittington 618-629-2211
Located on Rend Lake. Offers first class lakeside rooms within Wayne Fitzgerrell State Park. Balconies, decks, fireplaces, restaurant. You can swim, fish, or boat. Tennis courts, horseback riding and golf are nearby. RATE: Inquire. DOG: Resort has own kennel on property. Must keep dog in kennel and take him out during the day to play and walk. No charge.

INDIANA

A major city is Indianapolis with interesting museums, and buildings. Eagle Creek Park is within the city. There are shops, good dining, opera and symphony. Southern Indiana has forests, hills, and small towns. Northern Indiana includes shores of Lake Michigan the Amish Country, and popular Indiana Dunes National Shoreline.

BATESVILLE
INDIAN LAKES RESORT

7234 S. SR 46 Batesville 812-934-4767

This is a membership resort. Non-members can come for vacation one time to see how you like it, at regular rate.

Offers 54 fully furnished rustic cabins, sleeps 4, patio, swimming pools, golf, tennis, beach. RATE: $75. Special golf and tennis packages. DOG: allowed at $5 per night.

BLOOMINGTON
LAKE MONROE VILLAGE RESORT

8107 S. Fairfax Road, Bloomington 812-824-2267

Offers 7 fully furnished and heated/air conditioned A-frame log cabins in a wooded setting. Available year 'round. Outdoor pool. Short drive to golf, tennis, beach. No restaurant. RATE: moderate, about $25.00 DOG: allowed. No charge.

DERBY
OHIO RIVER CABIN RENTALS

Star Route Box 149C, Derby 812-836-2289

Offers 3 modern view cabins with kitchens on river. Boating, fishing, swimming, hiking. RATE: moderate DOG: allowed

FRENCH LICK
FRENCH LICK SPRINGS RESORT

8670 W. SR 56, French Lick 47432 800-457-4042, 812-936-9300

Known as a complete golf destination, this year 'round resort offers 485 renovated rooms, swimming pool, health spa, 10 tennis courts, beach nearby, 2 18-hole golf courses, horseback riding, skiing. Complete range of recreational activities for young and old alike. Lots of special packages for recreation, spa, and holidays.

RATE: Inquire DOG: allowed @ $10 per night.

PATOKA LAKE VILLAGE

Lake Village Drive, RR #2, Box 255 E, French Lick 47432

812-936-9854 open all year

The Pines at Patoka Lake Village is a nature retreat for both the sports minded and those who want a peaceful get-away. Located in the heart of the Patoka Lake recreational area, these luxury log cabins near the lake are surrounded by pine woods. There are 3 hiking trails on this property. Also, miles of hiking and biking trails at the State Recreational area adjacent, plus a 9,000 acre lake, beach, and picnic sites. Popular activities include boating, fishing, skiing, cave exploration, canoe trips, theme parks, horseback riding, and golf. RATES: cabins dbl May 1-Oct 31 @ $75 per day, $450 per week. Damage deposit is $75, refundable after cabin inspection. Cabins have central heat, color TV, kitchen, barbeque grill and picnic table. DOG: allowed. Refundable deposit covers dog as well as guests. Dog required to be on leash outside and owners must clean up after them. There is lots of space for dog and owner activity.

• INDIANAPOLIS

MARRIOTT HOTEL

7202 E 21 Street, Indianapolis 317-352-1231
Offers 252 rooms, TV, restaurant, bar, two swimming pools. It is a short drive to golf and tennis. Located 10 minutes to downtown area. RATE: high moderate DOG: allowed

RADISSON HOTEL

8787 Keystone Crossing, Indianapolis 317-846-2700
Offers 400 rooms and suites, TV, restaurant, pool, health facilities. Short drive to golf and tennis. Free parking. RATE: high moderate DOG: allowed

NEW ENGLAND SUITES HOTEL

3871 W. 92 Street, Indianapolis 317-879-1700
Offers 40 suites, TV, microwave, and refrigerator. RATE: moderate DOG: allowed

• LA PORTE

PINE LAKE HOTEL

444 Pine Lake Avenue, La Porte 219-362-4585
Offers 146 luxury rooms, swimming pool, fundome, min-putt course, shops, and baeutiful lakes. Walk to beach and golf.
RATE: $79.95 DOG: under 20 lbs allowed

PORTAGE
RAMADA INN

6200 Nilton Road, Portage 46368
219-762-5546, 800-437-5145

Formerly Indiana Dunes Hotel. Offers 158 rooms, swimming pool, near golf and tennis. Inn is near Indiana Dunes National Lakeshore with 14,227 acres of sandy beaches, swimming, hiking, picnic shelters, and more. RATE: about $50 DOG: $10 pet charge

IOWA

Des Moines, Grand Rapids, Iowa City, and Dubuque are major cities. The seven Amana Colonies lie in Eastern sector, founded in the 19th century as a utopean religious community. Much of way of life and original buildings are preserved. The major recreation area is in the northwest corner of the State, which has 6 lakes, including West Okobiji.

DES MOINES
DES MOINES MARRIOTT

700 Grand St, Des Moines 50322 515-245-5500

Offers confortable hotel rooms and reasonable rates. restaurant
RATE: moderate DOG: small and medium allowed.

ARNOLDS PARK
FILLENWARTH BEACH RESORT
on West Lake Okoboji

P.O. Box 536, Arnolds Park 51331 712-332-5646

West Lake Okaboji is heralded as one of the three most beautiful blue waters in the world. It is very clean, spring-fed lake that covers 17 square miles. There is a rocky shore so dock is used for sunning and fishing. This is a large and well-maintained resort. Accommodations available include cottages, duplexes, rooms and apartments. Each has air conditioning, heat, carpeting, bath, equipped kitchen, patio, color TV, and phone. Linens are provided. Daily maid service in season. Baby sitters available. Complimentary rowboats, canoes, and paddleboats. There are many summer sttractions nearby including an amusement park, malls, restaurants, shops, and the Gospel Tabernacle. There are jet ski, rollar blade, and bicycle rentals, plus scuba shops. There are 6 golf courses nearby, theat ers, antiques, state parks and a 10-mile fitness trail. RATE: variable according to accommodation. Example: a small apartment is $520 per week. DOG: Welcome. They can swim in the lake, go hiking in the wooded areas on trails, and meet and play with other dogs.

OKOBOJI
VILLAGE EAST RESORT

P.O. Box 499, Okoboji 51355 712-332-2161, 800-727-4561
Great year around vacation accommodations in stunning surroundings with exciting activities all year...18 holes of golf on Brooks championship course, indoor and outdoor tennis, racquetball courts, jogging track, pool, and athletic club. Beach nearby. Wonderful restaurant. Offers 97 confortable rooms. RATES: Inquire, moderate DOG: allowed, with lots of space for fun.

KANSAS

Topeka is a major city. Agriculture the State mainstay. There is fishing in reservoirs and the state parks have marked nature trails. In the Santa Fe Trail area you can hike a National Recreation Trail system at Dillon Nature Cernter, Hutchinson.

COUNCIL GROVE
COTTAGE HOUSE HOTEL AND MOTEL

25 N. Neosho, Council Grove 800-727-7903
Offers 36 rooms and breakfast. Located near two lakes and a golf course. RATES: moderate DOG: allowed

KANSAS CITY
BEST WESTERN INN

501 Southwest Blvd, Kansas City 66103 800-368-1741
Offers 113 rooms, swimming pool and spa, game room, shopping nearby. Continental breakfast. RATE: moderate, inquire DOG: allowed.

OVERLAND PARK

MARRIOTT, OVERLAND PARK

10800 Metcalf Ave, Overland Park 66210
913-451-8000; 800-228-9290
Offers over 400 guest rooms and suites, cable TV, restaurants and lounge, indoor/outdoor swimming pools, whirlpool, exercise room, nearby golf and tennis, Country Club Plaza, Woodlands greyhound and thoroughbred racing. RATES: min. weekend rate about $90. DOG: allowed. Guest responsible for damage.

VASSAR

LAMONT HILL RESORT

Rt. 1, Hwy 368, Pamona Lake, Vassar 66543 913-828-3131
Offers 10 rooms within walking distance to Pamona Lake, restaurant, 9-hole golf, breakfast served. RATE: min. $22 DOG: allowed, no charge. Cannot leave alone in room.

KENTUCKY

Recreational opportunities abound for fishing, golf, hiking, and some riding and hunting. Visitors often visit the Daniel Boone National Forest. In addition, there are 34 state parks. Louisville is a major city. One well known event is the Kentucky Derby in May. Lexington area is known for racehorse breeding farms and tobacco.

BENTON

COZY COVE on Kentucky Lake

Rt 5, Box 534, 1917 Reed Road, Benton 42025 800-467-8168, 502-354-8168 Hosts: Bob and Marge Norman
This is a waterfront resort, private and family owned and operated with 12 cottages of various sizes on 12 acres with 1,500 ft of shoreline and a safe and sandy beach. At the resort, there are many activities and games. Boat rentals and guide services available. Hunting and fishing fall packages. Area attractions include golf, tennis, horseback riding, and restaurants. RATE: cabin about $90. seasonal variable. DOG:No dogs allowed during summer. Dogs allowed in the spring and fall with manager approval and a $50 fee for cleaning.

BURNSIDE
VILLAGER RESORT

P.O. Box 267, Burnside 42519 606-561-4707 open Mar-Oct
Host: Dave Baugh
Located on Lake Cumberland, this resort offers 20 individual air-conditioned 2,3,4 bedroom cottages with kitchens, porches, color TV. Recreational facilities include tennis, basketball, volleyball, and lake swimming. A swimming pool and golf course located within minutes on Burnside Island. Other places of interest include various State parks and recreational areas, and Daniel Boone National Forest.
RATE: min 2-bedrm (4-6 people) daily $90; weekly $400.
DOG: one dog per unit allowed. $25 charge. Dog will enjoy forest, lawn, lake swimming, and shoreline walks.

BOWLING GREEN
ALPINE LODGE BED & BREAKFAST

5310 Morgantown Road, Bowling Green 502-843-4846
Offers a Swiss Chalet on 10 acres. 5 rooms, 2 suites, full country breakfast, swimming pool, nature trail. RATE: inquire
DOG: allowed.

CADIZ
COUNTRY INN

154 Hospitality Lane, Cadiz 42211 502-522-7007
Host: Steve Bearden
This Inn is a cozy place to stay in a location convenient to a golf course, Berkley Lake, an outlet mall, TVA's Land Between the Lakes Recreation Area, restaurants and more. There is a swimming pool. Service is prompt and friendly. RATE: min. sgl $46.80. Children 18 years and under stay free. DOG: allowed with deposit.

GILBERTSVILLE
THE MOORS RESORT & MARINA on Kentucky Lake

570 Moors Road, Gilbertsville 42044 800-626-5472
This lake resort and marina has a log-cabin style lodge with conference facilities, 27 cottages from 1-4 bedrooms, Jamestowner houseboats, swimming pool, restaurant with home style cooking, gift shop.

The resort offers professional fishing and hunting guide service, Sportsman's Quest and recreational facilities. Guests are urged to bring their fishing gear and water toys. Boats of various kinds can be rented or bring your own to their slips. Recreational activities for children and adults include softball, volleyball, basketball, beach games, and more. RATE: min. 1 bedrm cottage $65 per day. DOG: Dog welcome in cottages, and also on campgrounds. A $50 refundable fee is charged, if no damage upon departure. Dog required to be on leash in resort. Lots of wide open space and shoreline to exercise and swim.

HARNED
MOUNTAIN LAUREL LAKE

Rt 1, Box 46, Harned, 40144 502-756-2737

Hosts: Larry and Patti Mattingly

Offers secluded cabins and lake, designed for romantics and nature lovers, nestled in a wilderness setting. Located 50 miles from Louisville in Breckenridge County. Relaxing vacation cabins on lakefront or woodlands with modern kitchens, heating / air conditioning, your own fishing boat, spas. Lake is 25 acres. Hiking trails. RATE: min weekday $139. (3 night minimum)

DOG: allowed.

LEXINGTON
GRIFFIN GATE MARRIOTT RESORT

1800 Newtown Pike, Lexington 40511 800-228-9290, 606-231-5100

Want to go to Bluegrass country? This resort is a magnificent 19th century southern mansion on 250 acres of rolling Bluegrass, offering 358 rooms and 25 suites. For recreation try golf, tennis, swimming in indoor and outdoor pools, volleyball, badminton, or croquet, and the health club. This resort is one of the top 75 resort golf courses in the country. Several dining facilities. For entertainment, spend a day at the fabulous Kentucky Horse Park, visit historic homes, or shop in Lexington. RATE: special packages available. Example: per couple $195 includes room for 1 night, breakfast, dinner, and use of resort facilities. DOG: allowed with a 1x $20.00 fee.

LOUISVILLE
THE SEELBACH

500 Fourth Ave, Louisville 40202 502-585-3200, 800-333-3399
This grand hotel offers 321 delux guest rooms in the heart of Louisville. Comfort, charm, and grace provided. Restaurant.
RATE: min $170 DOG: $50 pet deposit required; partly refundable.

OWENSBORO
RAMADA RESORT

1 Executive Blvd, Ownesboro 800-626-1936, 502-926-8000
Offers 650 rooms and 38 suites near the Ohio River. Restaurant, exercise area, sauna, tennis, swimming pools, shopping galleria.
RATE: moderate DOG: allowed with $50 deposit against damages

LOUISIANA

Baton Rouge is the capital. The Kisatchee National Forest has trails for hiking. There are various state parks and a State Arboretum in Ville Platte. New Orleans is the largest city, and the birthplace of jazz. Tour the French Quarter, and the Garden District uptown to see large estates. There are parks within the city, as well as museums and shopping. Cajun country lies west of the city. Throughout Louisiana, try the delicious variety of seafoods.

BATON ROUGE
NEWCOURT INN

1-10 exit 151, Port Allen 70767 504-381-9134, 800-826-3375
Offers 70 rooms, enclosed courtyard, 24-hour security, free breakfast, swimming pool. Located 3 miles from downtown Baton Rouge. RATE: moderate DOG: allowed with $5 charge. Owner is responsible for damages.

RED ROOF INN at Baton Rouge

11314 Boardwalk Drive, Baton Rouge 504-275-6600, 800-THE ROOF
Baton Rouge is a historic destination worth seeing. Lush, stately plantations along the shady reaches of Great River Road. Is also home to interesting Cajun cabins in Bayou Grosse Tete.
RATE: moderate DOG: allowed, no charge. Dog must be housebroken and not have fleas. Owner liable for damages.

CHENEYVILLE
LOYD HALL PLANTATION, BED & BREAKFAST

292 Loyd Bridge Road, Cheneyville 71325 318-776-5641
Innkeepers: Dr & Mrs Frank Fitzgerald
Offers 4 rooms, carriage house, country cabin and cottage on 600 acres of a working cotton plantation. Kitchens, porches, and pool. Jogging, hiking, bicycling, and bird watching. RATE: $95 min. DOG: Should be contained in kennel in cabin or cottage. Can run on property. Owners have two large dogs and a fenced kennel area.

FLORIEN
TORO HILLS RESORT

Highway 171 South, Florien 71429 800-533-5031
Offers rooms and suites, restaurant, 18-hole championship golf course, 2 swimming pools, 2 tennis courts. RATE: inquire DOG: is allowed, must be contained when in room.

LAFAYETTE
BOIS DES CHENES, BED & BREAKFAST

338 N. Sterling, Lafayette 70501 318-233-7816
Innkeepers: Majorie & Coerte Voorhies
Rated a top bed and breakfast in country. Located in interesting area. Offers 5 rooms and baths, private entrances, TV, tours of Atchafalaya. children permitted. French spoken. Cajun tradition. RATE: min. $85 DOG: no charge. Can be exercised in back yard. Owners have dogs. No smoking.

LAKE CHARLES
ISLE OF CAPRI HOTEL

3033 Hilton Drive, Bossier City 71111 800-221-4095
On Lake Charles, tropical island getaway with comfortable rooms, lounge, swimming pool, and more. RATE: inquire
DOG: allowed at 1x charge of $25.

NEW ORLEANS
DAUPHINE ORLEANS

415 Rue Dauphine, New Orleans 70112 504-586-1800

This 109 room French Quarter hotel embodies the essence of old New Orleans. It is located near the nightspots of Bourbon Street near antique stores, art galleries, riverfront, and aquarium. The hotel is a serene oasis with a fine staff. There is a palm-filled courtyard, swimming pool, valet parking, a fitness and exercise room, cable TV, and library. RATE: min $129. children under 12 free. DOG: allowed. No charge.

NEW ORLEANS HILTON RIVERSIDE

Poydras at Mississippi River, New Orleans 70140
800- HILTONS, 504-584-3980
Located in the heart of New Orleans, within walking distance of the Aquarium, as well as the enchanting French Quarter and fine antique shops, this hotel offers various types of accommodations, plus a riverboat casino, the Queen of New Orleans. World-renowned cuisine, hot jazz, indoor and outdoor tennis, golf studio, fitness classes, sauna, racquetball, a jogging track, and more. For dog owners, self-guided walking tours can be made. RATE: min. $125, packages available. DOG: small dog welcome with owner responsibility form signed.

RUE ROYAL INN, BED & BREAKFAST

1006 Rue Royal, New Orleans 70116 800-776-3901, 504-524-3900
An 1830's Creole townhouse in the heart of the French Quarter. Rooms and suites with refrig., jacuzzi. RATE: min. $90 DOG: allowed. no restrictions

THE RATHBONE INN, BED & BREAKFAST

1227 Esplanade Ave, New Orleans 70116 800-947-2101
Indulge yourself in a 1850's Greek Revival Mansion, jacuzzi, and tropical patio area. 9 rooms with kitchenettes and private baths. Enjoy the French Quater. RATE: min $90 DOG: allowed, no restrictions.

• RUSTON

HOLIDAY INN RUSTON

P.O. Box 1189, Ruston 71273 318-255-5901

Offers 231 guest rooms located on 22 acres of beautiful grounds. Two swimming pools, restaurant. RATE: about $50 DOG: allowed no charge

ST FRANCISVILLE

BUTLER GREENWOOD, BED & BREAKFAST

8345 US Hwy 61, St Francisville 70775 504-635-6312
Innkeeper: Anne Butler

Offers 5 cottages on extensive 2200 acre grounds. Lots of historic charm. Nature hikes, swimming pool. No smoking in house. RATE: about $90 DOG: allowed. Must be well-behaved.

ST FRANCESVILLE HOTEL ON THE LAKE

P.O. Box 440, (Hwy 61 & LA 10) St Francisville 70775
504—635-3821

Offers 101 guest rooms nestled in wooded area overlooking lake. Has restaurant, olympic pool, live entertainment. RATE: inquire DOG: small dog allowed. no charge.

MAINE

In Maine, tour anywhere along the wonderful coastline, see inland villages, Acadia National Park with mountains and shoreline, and State parks throughout the State. Special picturesque towns are Bar Harbor, Camden, Boothbay Harbor, and Bethel. Dining in Maine ? Enjoy the lobster !

BAR HARBOR

BAR HARBOR INN

Box 7, Newport Drive, Bar Harbor 04609 800-248-3351,
207-288-3351

Located on a grassy knoll overlooking beautiful Frenchman's Bay, the Inn is surrounded by 8 acres of lawns and gardens. Offers elegant guest rooms, fine restaurant and terrace, heated outdoor pool and spa. A superior inn with superior service.
RATE: Inquire. Packages available DOG: $10 charge

WONDER VIEW INN

Box 25, Bar Harbor 04609 207-288-3358, 800-341-1553

This Inn overlooks Frenchman Bay on Mount Desert Island, minutes from Acadia National Park and Bar Harbor. Explore mountains, coast, play golf, deep-sea fish, rent a canoe, bicycle, sail, or just relax by a large heated pool. Delightful Spring, Summer, and Fall. RATE: min. summer $80. DOG: welcome. Charge $10 for stay 1-5 days, additional $10 if longer. Do not leave unattended. Walk in wooded area of property. Restrain in public areas. Not allowed in swimming pool. Owner responsible for damages.

BETHEL
THE BETHEL INN AND COUNTRY CLUB

P.O. Box 49, Bethel 04217 207-824-2175

Accommodations in village offer relaxed resort environment on 200 acres. Perfect family vacation. There is an 18-hole Cornish designed golf course, golf school, health club, heated outdoor swimming pool, and sauna. In winter, there is cross-country skiing. Close proximity to Sunday River. Accommodations include choice between traditional New England Inn or contemporary townhouses. Fine dining with Maine lobster and famous prime rib. RATE: Example: 1-bedrm townhouse $110 dbl 2-ngt weekend. Varies. Inquire. DOG: Quiet dog welcome at no charge.

BOOTHBAY
THE LAWNMEER INN

P.O. Box 505, W. Boothbay Harbor 04575
207-633-2544, 800-633-7645

A lovely Inn at water's edge on island of Southport...5 minute drive across a swing bridge to bustling Boothbay Harbor. Facilities include rooms and a guest cottage, excellent restaurant, lawns, decks near water. Boat dock. Visit villages, lighthouses; see seals. RATE: min. summer room $68, cottage $128. DOG: One small dog per room. Cannot be unattended unless caged. Use grassy pet relief area and clean-up after pet. Dog must be leashed and quiet.

CAMDEN
THE HIGH TIDE INN

U.S. Rte 1, Camden 04843 207-236-3724

Offers an inn, cottages, and motor inn on the ocean. Private beach overlooks Penobscot Bay. Green lawns. 7 beautiful acres at base of Mt Megunticook. RATE: Inquire DOG: allowed in cottages , no charge.

CENTER LOVELL
HEWNOAKS LAKE KEZAR

P.O. Box 65, Center Lovell 04016 207-925-6051
Host: Jessie Volk
Offers 6 cottages of various sizes, available on what was previously a beautiful country estate in uncrowded forested areas. Guests do what they want to do when they want to do it. Entirely self-catered. Tour, fish, swim, boat, hike the trails, climb the mountains, explore glacial caverns of Lost River or spectacular Flume gorge and waterfalls, watch birds, play golf, explore nearby communities, hunt for minerals at world famous Ruggies Mine, and more. White Mountains national parkland nearby, as well as Lake Kezar, which is one of the ten most beautiful lakes, has sparkling waters, a loon population, Pine Tree Belt, marina, and 2 beaches. RATE: vary according to property rented.
Min. spring $698, summer $798, and up
DOG: welcome, except on beach. Deposit may be required. no charge.

FREEPORT
THE FREEPORT INN

335 US Rt 1 So. Freeport 04032 800-99-VALUE, 207-865-3106
This Inn is just minutes from 3 state parks with gorgeous views of Casco Bay and its wildlife. Five museums and many attractions. close by. Above all, Freeport is a mecca for the value conscious shopper, with over 110 factory outlets available in the village, among them LL BEAN, BROOKS BROS., and ANNE KLEIN. This 25 acre Inn property is high on a hill. All rooms have bath, color cable TV, heat, phones, and movies. Guests stroll across the lawn, take canoe trips on the river, or relax by the pool.
RATE: Jan-Mar $49.95, July-Oct $99.95, Mar-June & Oct-Dec $59.95 DOG: allowed in specific rooms. Guests must notify Inn in advance if dog will be with them. No other restrictions.

KENNEBUNKPORT
THE COLONY

Ocean Avenue & King's Highway, PO Box 511, Kennebunkport 04046
207-967-3331, 800-552-2363

Discover the spectacular Maine coast at this hotel, built in the grand oceanfront resort hotel tradition. It is splendidly situated in a glorious garden setting above the Atlantic. Activities include golf, tennis, sailing, and fitness packages. There is a heated salt water swimming pool, private sandy beach and safe swimming, beautiful gardens and verandas, with unexcelled ocean views.
RATE: min summer $199 dbl, with meals DOG: Welcome at fee of $22 per day. Dogs can use beach here. Owner must clean-up after dog. He is not allowed where food is being served.

• MONHEGAN ISLAND
THE ISLAND INN

Box 128, Monhegan Island 04852 207-596-0371, 800-722-1269
Hosts: Philip Truelove & Howard Weilbacker
This Inn is located on Monhegan Island, a small beautiful island in Penobscot Bay, 10 miles offshore. Seventeen miles of footpaths run along cliffs and through pines. The Inn offers 36 varied accommodations, facing meadows or ocean. There is a dining room. You get there by boat from Boothbay. RATE: min. $88
DOG: There are no cars on the island so it is an exceptionally safe haven. All dogs welcome. No restrictions.

• OAKLAND
ALDEN CAMPS
on East Lake, Belgrave Lakes Region

RFD 2, Box 1140, Oakland 04963 207-465-7703
This easily accessible camp has 18 cottages with 1-3 bedrooms, located in a prine grove on the shore of East Lake. Each unit has electricity and plumbing. Linens/towels provided. There is a bath, screened porch, and wood stove. Refrigerators may be rented. Meals served in dining room. The many activities available include: fishing, if you catch fish they can be served in dining room. golf. There are 2 courses nearby. swim. There is a sand beach dock and float for sunbathers. waterski. Instruction available. boats. Various rentals available. tennis. 1 clay court. Games. Badminton, volleyball, children's swing sets. Hike. camp has 40 acres on lakeside and 100 acres across road. basketball 1/2 court.

RATE: Summer season example:
2-3 persons $75 per person daily. $450 per person weekly for a cottage, 3 served meals and maid service. Inquire about offseason rates A general deposit is required.
DOG: Camp prefers that dog remain home. However, they state that "If you cannot enjoy a vacation without your pet there's a daily charge of $25. Your dog will be accepted on condition that it does not disturb other guests or damage camp property".

RANGELEY
TOWN & LAKE MOTEL & LAKESIDE COTTAGES
on the shore of Rangeley Lake

P.O. Box 47, Main Street, Rangeley 04970 207-864-3755
Set in the lush green wilderness of Maine's North Woods is picturesque Rangeley Lake. This area has hundreds of miles of Lakes and wooded shorelines, mountains, and streams. These cottages are at the edge of the village...shopping, restaurants, and churches. Guests play lawn games, swim, go canoeing, hike, mountain climb and more. Nearby is an 18-hole golf course and public tennis court, also snowmobiling and skiing at the Saddleback Mountain. This is a really good area to exercise your dog hiking.
RATE: Motel room sgl $45, dbl $55. 2-bedrm lakefront cottage with fireplace $120 night. color TV.

ROCKPORT
OAKLAND SEASHORE COTTAGES & MOTEL

714 Commercial Street, Rockport 04856 207-594-8104
Located between Rockland and Camden, 1,2,3 room units, some with kitchenettes. Private beach. Rustic area, Trees, wildlife and birds. On 80 acres. RATE: about $50 in cottages in summer
DOG: allowed. no charge. Can run and play on the 80 acres and swim on the beach.

ROCKWOOD
THE BIRCHES RESORT & WILDERNESS RAFTING

P.O. Box 81 MI, Rockwood 04478 800-825-9453

Offers an 11,000-acre Wilderness Resort on Moosehead Lake, remote cabins, lakeside dining, marina, fly fishing pond, 2 lakes. Hike, fish, boat, mountain bike, canoe, sea and whitewater kayaking, ski, wildlife watching. RATE: cabin $75 min. off-season DOG: allowed at $8 per dog, per day in summer.

WELD
KAWANHEE INN
Lakeside Lodge and Cabins

Summer address: RR #1, Box 119 Webb Lake, Weld, Maine 04285
Winter address: 7 Broadway, Farmington 04938
Summer phone: 207-585-2000, winter: 207-778-3809
Host: Martha Strunk, Sturges Butler Open May 15-Oct 15
This Inn is a mountain lakeside resort and housekeeping cabins in the pines of the Maine woods. Far from the surging crowds, the Inn offers vacation comfort in a simple, natural atmosphere. Offers 11 housekeeping cabins of various sizes. Restaurant provides delicious home cooked food. The sloping white sand beach is ideal swimming, especially for children and non-swimmers. Canoes are available. There are many mountain trails that will provide great exercise for guests with a dog. Resort can provide picnic lunch. Gold panning is popular. There are 2 waterfalls, fun for swimming. Bring your own mountain bikes, tennis equipment, golf clubs, for use at nearby facilities. RATE: min. cabin rental by week $600. Discount 10% pre and post season. DOG: Welcome in several cabins. No dog on beach please. No other restrictions. Dog welcome in all cabins in Fall and Spring.

WINDHAM
SEBAGO LAKE LODGE & COTTAGES

White's Bridge Road, P.O. Box 110, No. Windham 04062
207-892-2698 Host: Debra & Chip Lougee
Sebago Lake is a Maine vacation region. The crystal clear waters are ideal for fishing, hiking, boating, sunbathing, water skiing, and swimming. The Lodge is at a quiet lakefront location with 700' of lake frontage, including swimming and boat docking areas. Free use of canoes and rowboats, picnic tables, grills. Fishing licenses and water skiis available.

In autumn the foliage is unsurpassed, and antique shopping, country fairs, and harness racing are popular. Accommodations include a variety of rooms and cottages. RATE: 1-2 bedroom cottage $600 per week. Available weekly only in season. Nightly off-season. DOG: Dog by prior arrangement, only no "barkers". Fee is $8 per day. Dog must be controlled and leashed at all times on property and not left unattended inside or outside. "Pooper scooper" is available to clean.

MARYLAND

Visitors enjoy the shoreline around Chesapeake Bay and the Eastern Shore, the Cumberland Narrows area, Baltimore, Annapolis, Ocean City, the Assateague Isld National Seashore with Sandy Point State Park . a good place for swimming and fishing. Baltimore is the major city with museums, a national aquarium, an IMAX movie theater, and inner harbor shopping malls.

ANNAPOLIS

HOWARD JOHNSON'S

69 Old Mill Bottom Road 21401 410-757-1600, 800-213-7432
Offers 70 rooms and an outdoor pool. RATE: moderate
DOG: allowed

LOEW'S ANNAPOLIS

126 West Street 21401 410-263-7777, 800-526-2593
Offers 216 rooms, restaurant, exercise room. RATE: inquire
DOG: allowed

BALTIMORE

HOLIDAY INN - INNER HARBOR

301 West Lombard St, Baltimore 21222 410-685-3500
Located in the heart of downtown a few blocks from Inner Harbor. Offers 375 guest rooms, a 50 foot pool, sauna, and fitness facilities. RATE: Inquire DOG: allowed. no charge

CAMBRIDGE

SARKE PLANTATION

6033 Todd Point Road, Cambridge 21613 410-228-7020, 800-814-7020

This waterfront property is located in the heart of Chesapeake Bay County on the shore. Offers 27 acres with 5 bedrooms, bath, fireplace, suite, continental breakfast. RATE: $50 DOG: allowed. Dog can run. Lots of space.

EASTON

GROSS' COATE PLANTATION

11300 Gross Coate Road, Easton 21601 800-580-0802, 410-819-0802

Lovely secluded luxury mansion on Wye River with superb service, privacy, and relaxation. Cottages and suites with fireplaces, pool, dock, canoes, spa. Sixty acres in country, green lawns and some immense trees. RATE: $295 dbl per night; $495 dbl per night for cottage. Includes breakfast, snacks, and open bar.
DOG: Welcome. Dog has lots of beautiful space to run on the grounds, and can swim in the river. Not restricted to a leash.

THE TIDEWATER INN

101 E. Dover Street, Easton 21601 800-237-8775, 410-822-1300

This Inn is a luxury getaway, restored to its original perfection. RATE: inquire DOG: can stay in kennel facility in hotel, and come out during the day.

FALLSTON

MOUNTAIN LAKE RENTALS

2605 Greene Lane, Fallston 21047 800-846-7386

Offers 60 lakefront Deep Creek Lake chalets, cabins, or townhouses Close to Wisp. Exercise room, outdoor pool. RATE: vary, inquire DOG: allowed

GREENBELT

MARRIOTT GREENBELT

6400 Ivy Lane, Greenbelt 20770 301-441-3700, 800-228-9290

Offers 283 rooms, restaurant, exercise room, 2 swimming pools, tennis courts. RATE: moderate DOG: allowed

OAKLAND

HARLEY FARM BED & BREAKFAST

16766 Garrett Highway, Oakland 21550 301-387-9050
A beautiful, relaxing 65-acre farm. Hot tubs, fireplaces, horses, duck pond, views. RATE: Inquire DOG: allowed when not full. Owner has a collie, cats, and other pets. Dog must be well-behaved and get along with others. Lots of space to run on 65 acres.

OCEAN CITY

FENWICK INN

13801 Coastal Highway, Ocean City 21842 800-492-1873
Offers 201 spacious, attractive rooms with refrigerators, an indoor pool, hot tub, game room, and rooftop restaurant. RATE: weekends $39. There are golf packages. DOG: allowed if 30 lbs and under @ $10 per night.

GEORGIA BELLE SUITES & LODGE

12000 Coastal Highway, Ocean City 21842 410-250-4000
100 oceanview rooms and suites, TV, outdoor pool.
RATE: $169 dbl DOG: allowed, except not in July & August if too full. Call to check. No charge for dog.

SHERATON FONTAINEBLEAU HOTEL

10100 Ocean Highway, Ocean City 21842 800-638-2100, 410-524-3535
A major hotel in the year 'round resort area of Ocean City with newly remodeled guest rooms. Bath, private balconies, refrigerator, color TV with free cable and HBO, inroom coffee maker, complimentary USA TODAY. Hotel on a clean, wide beach. Two oceanfront restaurants, piano bar, night club. Health spa, jacuzzi, sauna, and exercise equipment. Heated swimming pool, game room. Nearby, golf, deep sea fishing, shops. RATE: min $65 weekdays, weekend $75. Special packages available. DOG: Allowed @ $15 per day. There is exercise area for dog. Beach restricted during summer months, off-season no restriction on beach.

SOLOMONS
HOLIDAY INN at Solomons Island

P.O. Box 1099, 155 Holiday Drive, Solomons 20688
800-356-2009, 410-326-6311

This is a seven acre waterfront retreat located in historic Calvert County two miles from Chesapeake Bay and 55 miles from Washington D.C. The hotel and marina offer southern charm and fine customer service in 326 guest rooms. Leisure activities include power and sail boats, health club, aerobics, a large pool, tennis, volleyball, sport fishing on Chesapeake Bay, golf at Chesapeaske Hills Golf Club, sunset cruises, walks at nature parks and River Walk, and shop. RATE: min about $80 dbl. Special packages available. DOG: permitted. no charge. no restrictions.

TILGHMAN ISLAND
THE TILGHMAN ISLAND INN

21384 Coopertown Road, Tilghman Island 21671 800-866-2141, 410-886-2141

In the heart of some of the most beautiful unspoiled country left in the East is this contemporary, luxurious, and intimate resort. It offers private tennis courts, swimming pool, croquet court, fishing, biking, docking facilities, and bar. The formal and informal dining rooms feature innovative American cuisine. The Inn is located on the water at Knapps Narrows and the Chesapeake Bay. Working bay craft are seen daily. This area has over 500 miles of creeks, rivers, and bayshore to explore. RATE: min $110 DOG: $10 per ngt

MASSACHUSETTS

This state has many attractions for dog owners. Travel along the coast. See Boston and New England seacoast towns along the Cape Cod National Seashore between Eastham and Provincetown which offers good recreation. The two resort islands of Martha's Vineyard and Nantucket are popular and can be reached by ferry and plane. Hyannis and Hyannis Port are popular, while Provincetown has excellent beach and trails for walking and horseback riding. In the Berkshires area are hills, New England villages, ski areas, festivals, and a music festival at Tanglewood in the summer.

BOSTON see CITIES section of this book.

CHATHAM on Cape Cod
QUEEN ANN INN

70 Queen Anne Road, Chatham 02633 PO Box 747
800-545-4667, 508-945-0394

This large romantic timeless inn offers spacious privacy and excellent cuisine. There is Old Cape Cod atmosphere, spacious rooms, gardens, fireplaces, whirlpools, tennis courts, heated pool. Nearby beaches, trails, roses, fish piers, lighthouses. Guests sail, swim, deep sea fish. This is a wonderful base to explore Cape Cod.

RATE: min Jan-May $127, summer $157.

DOG: well-behaved dog allowed @ $21 fee.

HYANNIS PORT
HARBOR VILLAGE

P.O. Box 635, Hyannis Port 02647 508-775-7581
Hosts: Tim Fuller and Sandra Roas

Twenty 1-3 bedroom cottages located on a delightful privately owned 17-acre pennisula, with pine trees and paths to ocean beach. Fireplaces, kitchens, linens furnished. One mile from Hyannis. Golf, tennis, fishing, boating available locally. Get there by boat or fly . RATE: 3-night minimum stay; rate depends on cottage size and time of year. Off-season 5/1-6/30 and 9/4-10/31,

1 bedroom 2 people $90 night

3 bedroom 6 people $125 night

Summer: 7/1-9/3 min $1000 week 1 bedroom.

DOG: allowed with prior consent of manager @ $100 week charge.

MARTHA'S VINEYARD
HIDDEN HILL

P.O. Box 1644, Vineyard Haven, Martha's Vineyard 02568
508-693-2809 Host: Dorothy Mayhew Open May-October

This accommodation on this beautiful island consists of apartments and 2 cottages on four acres of land, available for weekly rental. They are set in a natural meadow of wildflowers, fruit, evergreens, and windblown oaks. Well-behaved dogs are welcome in cottages.

No howling or barking. Dog can run on this beautiful four acres, and also enjoy many sightseeing and seaside activities with owners. RATE: cottages (2 people) about $600–700 per week. Inquire about ferry reservations. DOG: charge $25 per week.

NANTUCKET

JARED COFFIN HOUSE

PO Box 1580, Nantucket 02554 508-228-2405, 800-248-2405
This popular Inn has 60 rooms in four buildings. Interiors are elegant, food is scrumptous, service is friendly. Nantucket offers interesting shopping, great biking and walking, spectacular beaches. There are cobblestone streets and restored mansions and cottages in this charming place. RATE: offseason min about $55, summer min about $80. DOG: Dog is permitted with owner in certain rooms with manager approval. Please advise if bringing a dog. $10 charge. No restrictions.

THE NANTUCKET INN

27 Macy's Lane, Nantucket 02554 508-228-6900, 800-321-8484
A short trip from Cape Cod brings you to Nantucket Island with its picturesque harbor, historic homes, quaint shops, and miles of beaches. An enchanting and architecturally unique spot in America. This Inn offers 100 guest rooms and suites, refrigerator, bath, color TV. There are indoor and outdoor swimming pools, whirlpool spas, a health and fitness center, tennis courts, restaurant and lounge. Reach by ferry or air. This island is a great place to take a dog, especially with miles of deserted beaches where a dog can run and swim, while the owner relaxes in the sun. Sailing or fishing arrangements can also be made outside the Inn.
RATE: min standard, winter $50, summer $175
minimum cottage, winter $80, summer $190. Ask about packages.
DOG: allowed, 1 x nonrefundable fee of $25. Dog owner must let housekeeping know when dog is out of room for cleaning.

PITTSFIELD

BERKSHIRE HILTON INN

Berkshire Common, Pittsfield 01201 413-499-2000, 413-445-8090

This Inn offers 175 rooms located in the heart of the colorful Berkshire's, minutes from Tanglewood and other sttractions. It provides comfortable, spacious rooms and restaurant. Skiing close by, indoor pool. RATE: Inquire DOG: This Inn has a "no pets" policy but dogs are often allowed as an "exception" according to reservations. Speak to this hotel directly when making reservations.

PROVINCETOWN
HARGOOD HOUSE AT BAYSHORE

493 Commercial Street, Provincetown 02657 508-487-9133
Hosts: Ann Maguire, Harriet Gordon, Louise Davy
This charming Cape Cod style apartment complex is on a private beach within walking distance of town. Kitchens, decks, views, private entrances, lawn chairs. Offers 20 apartments, studio to 2-bedrm. RATE: min offseason (studio) $81 daily
min inseason studio 6/22-9/7 $697 week.
DOG: allowed with advance permission. Has rules of pet etiquette, inquire. No charge for dog.

SANDWICH
PINE GROVE COTTAGES

P.O. Box 74 358 Rte 6A, East Sandwich 02537 508-888-8179
Open May-October
For a Cape Cod vacation in your own private pine scented atmosphere, try a Pine Grove Cottage. You are free to come and go as you like, and are minutes away from wonderful beaches, golfing, boating, fishing, superb restaurants, and shops typically Cape Cod. There are historic sites, summer theater, and the world famous National Seashore Park. On-site swimming pool and play area. RATE: Variable daily, weekly, inseason, offseason. Inquire. Linen provided. DOG: Dog Welcome. No restrictions.

STOCKBRIDGE
WILLIAMSVILLE INN

Rt 41, West Stockbridge 01266 413-274-6118
Fifteen rooms offered in this Inn on 10 acres, swimming pool, tennis, skiing, restaurant, fireplaces. RATE: Inquire
DOG: allowed at manager discretion

WILLIAMSTOWN
THE WILLIAMS INN on-the-Green

Williamstown 01267 413-458-9371

This Inn is in a beautiful village in the Berkshires on the Mohawk Trail. It is modern and colonial style, offering 100 guest rooms and 2 suites, with bath, color TV, heat, and AC. Facilities include elevators, indoor swimming pool, saunas, spa, dining room and tavern lounge. The accent is on friendly and gracious way of life. This geographic area is rich in culture, such as art, theater, performing arts and dance. For sports enthusiasts there are two 18-hole golf courses, tennis, hiking, fishing, and several ski areas. RATE: min sgl $85 DOG: welcome in first floor rooms at $5 per ngt

MICHIGAN

Visitors usually stop to see Detroit, the major city, which has shopping, museums, the Belle Isle park in the Detroit River with recreation facilities. The Lake Michigan shoreline has ideal beaches and placid waters; resort area. Northern towns attract and campers and has many trails.

BAY CITY
BAY VALLEY RESORT HOTEL

2470 Old Bridge Road, Bay City 48706 800-292-5028

If golf is your game, there is a Jack Nicklaus & Desmond Muirhead designed course waiting for you, features water on 13 holes. Hotel resort amenities and accommodations on-site. RATE: Inquire DOG: allowed. no charge

CADILLAC
CABERFAE PEAKS SKI AND GOLF RESORT

Caberfae Road, Cadillac 49601 616-862-3300

This resort is located right in the heart of beautiful Manistee National Forest on 140 acres. Main offerings are golf, lots of nature, and skiing. Attractive lodge has two floors of room accommodations. RATE: inquire DOG: well-behaved dog welcome.

CADILLAC SANDS RESORT

6319 E M-115, Cadillac 49601 616-775-2407
This is a 55 unit resort located on a lake, open all year. It has a restaurant, swimming pool, boating, fishing, golf. RATE: Inquire
DOG: allowed, $40 charge

MCGUIRE'S RESORT

7880 Mackinaw Trail, Cadillac 49601 616-775-9947, 800-632-7302
Offers 123 comfortable rooms and suites, superb dining, pool, golf, tennis, boating, skiing, jogging, bicycling, and hiking, all on 320 acres. RATE: minimum $59 DOG: allowed in smoking rooms @ $10 per night charge.

DETROIT

WESTIN HOTEL

Renaissance Center, Detroit 48243 313-568-8200, 800-228-3000
Lovely hotel located on a river. Offers 1392 attractive rooms, swimming pool, whirlpool, restaurant, parking.
RATE: $155; packages available DOG: smaller dogs allowed.
Call hotel directly to check on medium or larger sizes.

DRUMMOND ISLAND

WOODMOOR on Drummond Island

26 Maxton Road, Drummond Island 49716
800-999-6343, 906-493-1000
Locally owned Woodmoor encompasses 2000 beautiful acres of woods and water. Includes a 60 room log lodge, an outstanding golf course, The Rock, restaurant on the waterfront, pool, tennis, fishing, fitness, skiing, hunting, botanical trips.
Cabins and homes for rent. Small boats available. Get there by 10-minute ferry trip from Detroit, fly, or go by boat. Variety of accommodations. RATE: Example: 2 bedrm, 2 bath log cottage, kitchen, fireplace, sleeps 8. $300 per night; $1,500 7 nights.
DOG: allowed in cabins. 1 x charge of $30.

FOUNTAIN
CHRISTIE'S LOG CABINS

6503 E. Sugar Grove, Fountain 49410 616-462-3218
Offers six cabins on Round Lake, available all year. Fishing, boating.
RATE: $45 minimum DOG: allowed

FRANKFORT
CHIMNEY CORNERS RESORT on Crystal Lake

1602 Crystal Drive, Frankfort 49635 616-352-7522
This resort is in a northwest Michigan area geared to vacation fun. In addition to the resort itself, there is shopping, drama, and night life in the closest big towns. Resort activities include: enjoy 1000 ft of private Crystal Lake beach; swim in clear, sparkling water; sail on 9 miles of lake, surrounded by wooded hills; walk and hike in 300 acres of forest, fields, and old orchard. Also, the resort adjoins Sleeping Bear National Lakeshore with its miles of forests, dunes and lakeshore...almost a wilderness. The resort has tennis, shuffleboard, basketball, volleyball. Golf courses nearby. Row boat available or bring your own. There are playground areas. Jet skiis are banned. Cottages and apartments are housekeeping. No phone or TV. RATE: seasonal rates vary. Minimum cottage on beach off-season, daily $90, week $540. DOG: No dogs in Lodge or apartments. Dog welcome in cottages. $30 fee for necessary special cleaning. No dog on the beach, and please leash dog when walking on resort property.

GAYLORD
MICHAYWE RESORT

1535 Opal Lake Road, Gaylord 49735 517-939-8914, 800-322-6636
Offers 42 vacation home rentals and other units in a resort community. Has lake, beach, sunning, 3 golf courses, tennis, skiing, boating, swimming pool. Horseback riding in area. RATE: Inquire DOG: some homes available for dog owners and pet.

HONOR
FOUR SEASONS

8841 Deadstream, Honor 49640 616-325-6992, 800-347-9728
Offers 6 cabins and one house rental on lake. Ski, fish, boat.
RATE: cabin $480 per week, house $1200 per week DOG: allowed

MT. PLEASANT
HOLIDAY INN

5665 E. Pickard, Mt Pleasant 48858 800-292-8891, 517-772-2905
Offers 184 rooms, restaurant, 2 swimming pools, fishing, golf, tennis, boating, fitness, skiing. RATE: min. summer weekend $89
DOG: allowed in hotel, not condos.

WAKEFIELD
INDIANHEAD MOUNTAIN RESORT

500 Indianhead Road, Wakefield 49968 800-3 INDIAN, 906-229-5181
Located in the Lake Superior area this is Big Snow Country's most complete resort village, nestled on top of a mountain. Family oriented ski programs for all ages and skill levsls. Lodging has a variety of options, chalets, condos, lodge. Available health and fitness club, racquet club, indoor pool and spa, sauna, restaurant and bar. RATE: minimum lodge room $72, chalet $130 per night.
DOG: allowed in most units. Inquire.

WALLOON LAKE
SPRINGBROOK HILLS

P.O. Box 219, Walloon Lake 49796 616-535-2227
This is a resort community of individual vacation home rentals, available to accommodate 1 to 200 people. Management can arrange catering, rental of saddle horses with guide, canoes, boats, golf, hunting or fishing guides, snowmobile trips and tours. Fine fishing is available within 20 miles in great lakes, inland lakes, rivers and streams. The Jordan River State Forest is nearby with hiking trails surrounding...and a large pond for dogs to enjoy.
RATE: depends on availability and number of people. $80-$150 for a 2-bedroom home, 2 people typical. Special golf packages. Special Spring & Fall Mushroom outings. Temporary guest membership optional for use of clubhouse and swimming pool. DOG: welcome

WHITEHALL
THE WATER'S EDGE on White Lake at Lake Michigan

6195 N. Murray Road, Whitehall 49461 616-894-4331
Cottages available on two sandy beaches. Boats available for guest free use...canoe, rowboat, paddleboat, and sailboat. Fishing charter

boats available. Nearby are located dune rides, amusement parks, golf courses, horseback riding, and restaurants. Blue Lake Camp provides concerts, plays, and personalities during the summer. RATE: Example: 5-person cottage with kitchen and 2 baths $595. One room with bath for 3 people $325. Weekly rates available. Inquire DOG: Stays with owner. No restrictions or charge.

MINNESOTA

Minneapolis and St Paul are the major cities. Both have parks, shopping, and sports. The State has many lakes and beaches. Wilderness areas of the Northwoods and Lake Superior are popular.

BEMIDJI
RUTTGER'S BIRCHMONT LODGE

530 Birchmont Beach Rd, NE, Bemidji 56601

218-751-1630, 1-888-RUTTger HOST: Randy Ruttger

With sparkling water, whispering pine forests, and a sandy shore, this Lodge is a quiet getaway or an activity-filled vacation, as you wish. It is situated on 1700 ft of sandy beachfront on Lake Bemidji. Guests enjoy swimming, sunning, fishing, and boating. Other activities include tennis, golf, hiking, biking. A new indoor recreation center houses a heated swimming pool, sauna, whirlpool, exercise rooms. There is an extensive supervised children's play program. Meals are delicious. Accommodations include lodge rooms, deluxe cottages, or new town houses. The Lodge has a commitment to quality and seeks to combine old fashioned hospitality with modern comfort, for an unforgetable trip. RATE: Mininum 1-bedroom standard beachfront cottage 1-2 persons $120 weeknight. $640 weekly. Inquire about offseason discounts. DOG: Small dogs are permitted in cabins only. They must be on leash when on the resort. There is an $8 charge per night. Dogs can run free on a nature trail with owners.

ELY
LODGE OF WHISPERING PINES

Big Lake, BOX 327R, Ely 55731 218-365-2129

Wilderness resort for the family. Sandy beach, fishing, picnics, hiking trails, cross-country skiing, dog sled trips. Housekeeping cabins. RATE: min $395 per week. DOG: $50 per week. Must be on leash in resort.

GRAND MARAIS

NOR'WESTER LODGE

Gunflint Trail, Box 550, Grand Marais 55604
800-992-4386, 218-388-2252

This Lodge is a resort and canoe outfitter located on historic Gunflint Trail, surrounded by Boundary Waters Canoe Area Wilderness with its abundent wildlife. Rustic warmth and old-fashioned hospitality combine with comfortable surroundings and modern conveniences. Dining in restaurant features good food and home-made baked goods. The resort offers a sand beach, play area, shops, canoes, boats, fishing guide, hiking trails, mountain biking, wildlife photography, hunting, skiing, and snowmobiling.
Nor'Wester Outfitters offer professional canoe adventures in the Boundary Waters Canoe Area Wildreness. Minimum rate for 3 days is $180. Dogs, leashed or under control, are allowed in BWCA.
RATE: Minimum housekeeping cabins (2 people) $129 daily; $774 weekly. Seasonal specials. DOG: The Lodge prefers that pets be left at home. If not possible, the charge is $40 per week, or $6 per day. Dog must not be left alone in cabin, and is not allowed on furniture. Noisy dog not allowed. An obediant dog can run free on side roads and on hiking trails. Restricted in winter. Dog allowed in housekeeping cabins only.

MINNEAPOLIS /ST PAUL

BEST WESTERN KELLY INN

161 St Anthony, St Paul 55105 612-227-8711
Offers 127 rooms and suites, swimming pool, restaurant. Located minutes from area attractions. RATE: $71 min sgl, $110 suite
DOG: allowed

REGAL MINNEAPOLIS HOTEL

1313 Nicollet Mall, Minnesota 55403 612-332-6000, 800-522-8856
Offers 320 rooms and 5 suites. Blocks from theatres, shopping.
Has restaurant, swimming pool, sauna, jacuzzi RATE: Inquire
DOG: allowed, no charge

SHERATON PARK PLACE

1500 Park Place Blvd. Minneapolis 55416
612-542±8600, 800-542-5566
Located on the edge of downtown Minneapolis. Offers 298 rooms, 32 suites. Swimming pool, exercise room, health club. Near the downtown area. RATE: Inquire DOG: allowed

NEVIS
FREMONT'S POINT
Big Mantrap Lake

Rt 1, Box 119 M, Nevis 56467 218-652-3299,800-221-0713
Offers housekeeping cottages and lodge with fireplaces on wilderness lake peninsula. Horseback riding nearby. Near Paul Bunyan State Forest and Heartland Trail RATES $625 per week. Overnights available DOG: $10 per day charge. Lots of space to run on this 15 acre property.

NISSWA
ALLURING PINES RESORT ESTATE on Lake Hubert

PO Box 202C, Nisswa 56468 218-9633-2694
Open all year. A beautifully landscaped estate with 2-3 bedroom cabins and condos. Safe sandy beach, tennis courts, canoes, hiking, biking, good fishing. Five minutes to golf, ski. RATE: minimum is $295 per week. Special off season rates. DOG: allowed offseason Only...not June - Sept. Inquire.

RAY
ARROWHEAD LODGE & RESORT

10473 Waltz Road, Ray 56669 218-875-2141
Near Lake Kabetogama on Minnesota-Canadian border, central entrance to Voyageurs' National Park. Offers 11 cabins, TV, sandy beach, boats, hiking trails, nearby golf and tennis. RATE $51 DOG: allowed

TOFTE
BLUEFIN BAY ON LAKE SUPERIOR

PO Box 2125, Tofte 55615 218-663-7296, 800-258-3346

This year 'round elegant resort offers a beautiful Lake Superior setting from shoreline condos and motel units, some fireplaces. Swimming pool, exercise room, tennis courts. fishing, hiking, skiing. RATE: minimum $69 DOG: allowed in some units, No charge.

WALKER

ANDERSON'S GRAND VU LODGE on Leech Lake

HCR-84, Box 1235, Walker 56484 218-547-2326, 800-842-0783
Spacious, private lake-side homes and lodge. Activities include beach, waterskiing, fishing, pony rides, bonfires. Eleven acres of grounds with paved roads. RATE: $140 sgl , $450 week DOG: allowed at $75 per week charge.

FORESTVIEW LODGE

HCR 84, Box 594, Walker 56484 218-836-2441, 800-223-6922
Full service resort with 21 cabins, fireplaces, restaurant, protected harbor, water sports, hiking, golf, tennis, horses nearby. RATE: minimum $365 weekly. DOG: allowed

MISSISSIPPI

Try the 312 mile drive along the Natchez Trace Parkway for a variety of homes, beaches, and huge old oak trees. The Gulf Islands National Seashore has beeches and wilderness. Ocean Springs is popular. Jackson is the capitol.

BILOXI

THE BREAKERS INN

2506 Beach Blvd, Biloxi 39531 800-624-5031, 601-388-6320
A quality accommodation on the Mississippi Gulf Coast, this Inn is located next to a 26 mile beach. Offers 28 delux 1-2 bedroom suites with breathtaking views, full kitchens, color cable TV, HBO, and a washer-dryer. In addition to the extensive beach, activities include Breakers swimming pool, tennis courts, and playground. There are championship golf courses in the area, and charter boats set out daily for fishing. 12 casinos within 5 miles. Area national and state parks await nature lovers, plus amusement attractions.

RATE: minimum summer $99; winter $55
DOG: $20 non-refundable charge for 1 day - 1 week. Over 1 week $35 not refundable.

GULF BEACH RESORT

2428 Beach Road, Biloxi 39531 800-323-9164, 601-385-5555
Offers 226 rooms on beach, 3 swimming pools, restaurant, golf packages. RATE: Inquire DOG: allowed with $25 non-refundable deposit.

• GULFPORT
BEST WESTERN SEAWAY INN

9475 Hwy 49, Gulfport 39503 601-864-0050, 800-822-4141
Offers 180 rooms, restaurant, jacuzzi, swimming pool, golf packages. RATE: Inquire DOG: allows dogs up to 25 lbs @ $3.00 per ngt.

• LONG BEACH
PARADISE BEACH RESORT

220 West Beach Blvd, Long Beach 39560 800-538-7752, 601-864-8811
Offers 100 rooms on the beach, swimming pool, entertainment, tennis courts, golf packages. RATE: Inquire DOG: $50 non-refundable deposit

• LOUISVILLE
LAKE TIAK-O'KHATA RESORT

Smyth Lake Road, P.O. Box 160, Louisville 39339 601-773-7853
Offers cabins on a lake. RATE: Inquire DOG: small dog allowed in cabins.

• OCEAN SPRINGS
SEVEN OAKS GULF HILLS RESORT

13701 Paso Road, Ocean Springs 39564
800-638-4902, 601-875-4211
Resort offers on premises, 65 rooms in quiet neighborhood, large swimming pool, 18-hole golf course, 7 tennis courts, restaurant and lounge. Five minutes to beaches and casinos. Friendly courteous staff. RATES: Inquire DOG: allowed with $100 deposit, $75 of which is refundable.

Among the attractions are St Louis and Kansas City. Hannibal, outside St Louis is Mark Twain's home. Recreation and beauty are offered at Mark Twain National Forest, Lake of the Ozarks, and Table Rock Lake in the Ozark hill region of southern Missouri. Branson attracts many visitors to theatres.

• CAPE GIRARDEAU
HOLIDAY INN

1-55 & William Street, RtK, Cape Girardeau 63702 573-334-4491
Offers guest rooms, restaurant, swimming pool, game area, tennis, jogging. RATE: moderate DOG: allowed

• KANSAS CITY
WESTERN CROWN CENTER

1 Pershing Rd, Kansas City 64108 800-228-3000, 816-474-4400
Offers 725 rooms and 49 suites, several restaurants, swimming pool, putting green, tennis, exercise club. RATE: min sgl $185, DOG: small dog allowed @ $5 per night

• KIMBERLING CITY

KIMBERLING OAKS RESORT
on Table Rock Lake

#4 Vista Haven, Lake Road 13-50, Kimberling City 65686
407-739-4461 Host: Donna Thornhill
This resort is located on a lovely cove. There are 10 cottages and a tanning salon. Nearby are jet ski's, water slides, horseback riding, plus tennis and basketball courts. The resort has a beautiful, large filtered pool, patio, picnic area, wooden play area, and game room. The park-like lawn with over 100 tall oak trees slopes gently to the lake edge and boat dock. The Kimberling City shopping center is nearby; thirteen miles from shows at Branson.
RATE; 1-2 person unit $45 with kitchen, bath, TV
1-4 person cottage $63 with kitchen, bath, TV.
DOG: small dog accepted. Clean-up after dog, inside and outside.

• LAKE OF THE OZARKS
HOLIDAY INN RESORT

Bus Rte 54, Box 1930, Lake Ozark 65049
573-365-2334, 800-532-3575

Offers 213 rooms and suites in a recreational area, restaurant, lounge, 3 pools, marina, miniature golf, exercise area, playground. No direct lake access. RATE: moderate DOG: $5 per day charge

LONE OAK POINT RESORT

HCR 69, BOX 482, Sunrise Beach, Lake of Ozarks 65079
573-374-7992

Small family - oriented resort. Housekeeping units, condos, cabins, located lakeside on a wooded peninsula, pools, spas, tennis, fishing, game room, jogging, hiking. Open mid-March-Nov. Golf packages
RATE: Inquire
DOG: allowed if 15 inches high or less, in the off-season only.

• OSAGE LAKE

CEDAR OAKS LODGE & GOLF COURSE

Rt 4, Box 160 B, Stockton 65785 417-276-3193

Offers Lodge, golf, swimming pool, marina, games, fishing, boat rental. RATE: min $42 DOG: allowed if well behaved and friendly No charge.

• ST LOUIS

AIRPORT MARRIOTT

1-70 at Lambert Airport, St Louis 63134 800-228-9270,
314-423-9700

Located 20 minutes from downtown. Offers 607 rooms, restaurant, tavern, and extensive sports facilities...2 pools, tennis, exercise room, putting green. Golf nearby. RATE: min about $50
DOG: allowed 1 x non-refundable fee per visit of $25

REGAL RIVERFRONT

200 S. Fourth St, St Louis 63134 800-242-8333, 314-241-9500

Offers 850 rooms and suites, 3 restaurants, swimming pool, health club. RATE: about $100 DOG: allowed. nominal charge

• SHELL KNOB

BASS HAVEN RESORT

HCR 1, Box 4480, Shell Knob 65747 417-858-6401
Host: John & Judy Engelthaler

This is an 8-unit resort with "The Most Beautiful View on Table Rock Lake" There is a lighted dock with a fishing platform, a swimming pool, recreation room, volleyball and badminton, oak decks overlooking the lake, guest laundry, anc charcoal grills. The resort has 12 acres of park-like setting providing ample room for walking, jogging, picnics, and just relaxing. They are off the beaten track, quiet and peaceful. Each unit has color TV, air conditioning, heat, bath, kitchen. Nearby guests can find restaurants, groceries, gas, tennis courts, 2 golf courses, and 2 public marinas.
RATE: min. offseason $35 one person; $5 each addtl.
Inseason $40 one person; $6 each addtl.

WHEATLAND
ANGLER'S RESORT

on Lake Pomme de Terre in the Osage Lakes Region of Missouri Ozarks

Route 2, Box 2832, Wheatland 65779 417-282-5507
Laura Darrell & Darla Guinn

At this resort there is 7,800 acres of excellent fishing for Muskie, Bass, White Bass, Blue Gill, Catfish, and more. The resort has 10 cabins with carpeting, heat, TV, pans, dishes, linens, crib, picnic table, barbeque grill. There is a convenience grocery, live bait, tackle, ice. There is lake fishing and a playground. Fishing boat included in cabin rental. Located in a 11,200 acre wooded area where hunting is permitted, hiking on public lands at the front door, and there are miles of shoreline to explore, wade, swim. The resort is also a canoe outfitter for river float trips in fairly easy waters. Dog can go on float trip also. Nearby, restaurants, tennis courts, beaches, golf, music shows, hiking trails, shopping. crafts, water skiing. RATE: Min $30 per day DOG: Well-behaved dog welcome. Must be attended at all times by owner. One time charge of $5 per stay.

MONTANA

This State has many national parks and recreation areas, 8 wildlife refuges, 10 national forests, and 15 wilderness areas. Flathead Lake and Glacier Nat. Park are popular

BIG SKY
BUCK'S T-4 LODGE (Best Western)

P.O. Box 160336, Big Sky 59716 800-822-4484, 406-995-4111
Offers 75 delux accommodations. Fishing, horseback riding, skiing, white water rafting. Nearby golf and tennis. RATE: high moderate DOG: allowed.

CONDON
HOLLAND LAKE LODGE

S.R. Box 2083, Condon 59826 406-754-2282, 800-648-8859
This year 'round lodge is a gateway to the Bob Marshall Wilderness located on the shores of Holland Lake. Accomodations include 9 sleeping rooms in the lodge and 5 comfortable lakeside cabins, sleeping 4-8 people each. Activities include horseback riding, as a major activity. Experienced outfitter and his wranglers will guide guests on a one-hour, half-day cookout or overnight ride. Customized guided summer trips in Bob Marshall Wilderness are a specialty of the Lodge. Fall Big Game hunting is available beginning in September. For fishing and water-sports enthusiasts, canoes can be rented, as well as other boats. While hikers will enjoy miles of trails in forests nearby. Other summer activities include swimming, volleyball, hiking. Other winter activities include skiing, snowmobiling, ice skating, ice fishing, sledding, and dog sled rides. RATE: minimum cabin with kitchen (max 4) $70 DOG: Dog owners welcome in 5 cabins available on lake. There are great hiking trails and fields to run dogs, which are safe for them.

DARBY
WEST FORK MEADOWS RANCH

Coal Creek Road, Darby 59829 406-349-2468, 800-800-1437
Hosts: Guido and Hanny Oberdorfer
Charming guest ranch located on the edge of the Bitterroot Wilderness. Airport pickup, superb dining and service, European hospitality. Activities include horseback riding, pack trips, fishing, boating, mt biking, hiking, jeep excursions. RATE: Inquire. DOG: allowed in the off-season.

GALLATIN GATEWAY
320 GUEST RANCH

205 Buffalo Horn Creek, Gallatin Gateway 59730 800-243-0320, 406-995-4283

Open all year, Western resort with 1-3 bedroom luxury log accommodations. Near Big Sky and Yellowstone Park. Restaurant. Activities include horseback riding, trout fishing, barbeques, hay-rides, hiking. Winter sleigh rides, hiking, skiing, jacuzzi.

RATE: Inquire DOG: allowed on leash at ranch @ $10 per night.

PRAY
CHICO HOT SPRINGS LODGE

Post Office Drawer D, Pray 59065 406-333-4933

Located in Montana's Paradise Valley, 30 miles north of Yellowstone, lodge offers lots of activity in a comfortable mountain setting. Swim, ride, bike, hike, ski, float trips, and guided dog sled treks. Soak your cares away in relaxing natural mineral hot spring pools. Accommodations include rooms, cabins, cottages, chalet, houses.

RATE: Example: min room with bath, summer $75

Log cabin $80. 5-bedrm house $300. Rates for weekly and off-season inquire.

DOG: $5 fee per animal. Dog must be housebroken. Problem barkers asked to go outside. Dogs especially enjoy trails and river swimming.

SEELEY LAKE
LODGES AT SEELEY LAKE

Boy Scout Road, Box 568, Seeley Lake 59868 406-677-2376, 800-900-9016

Offers log cabins with kitchens nestled in larch trees. Large beach, and 2 docks on Mt. Lake. Lodge for indoor activity. Fishing, boating, swimming, hiking, biking, golf, skiing. A year 'round vacation headquarters. RATE: Inquire. DOG: allowed at $5 per night charge.

TAMARACKS RESORT

PO Box 812, Seeley Lake 59868 800-477-7216, 406-677-2433

Owners: Jeff and Sue Heagy

This resort consists of 16 acres and over 1500 ft of lake frontage and mountain views, located in the beautiful Lolo National Forest. There are 13 cabins of various sizes and styles , all with heat kitchens, and bathrooms. There is a log recreation building, a boat launch, beach and games area. The resort offers mountains, lakes, and snow in winter. Summer activities are endless. From easy hiking on many scenic trails to more challenging trails in the Bob Marshall Wilderness or the Mission Mountain Range. There is mountain biking, canoeing, horseback riding, fishing, swimming, and golf nearby. In winter, there are 300 miles of grommed snow-mobile trails, cross-country skiing, ice fishing, and ice skating, photography and more. There are also many shops, activities, and restaurants in the nearby town of Seeley Lake. RATE: Min 1-bedrm $45 off-season. DOG: rate $5 per pet. No restrictions.

NEBRASKA

Nebraska boasts the Nebraska National Forest and 7 state parks. Northwest area is rugged, beautiful land, with ridges, pines. Lake McConaughy is a state recreation area with beaches.

ASHLAND
CABINS IN A NEBRASKA STATE PARK

For information and reservations for state parks contact 800-826-PARK
(Example) EUGENE T. MAHONEY STATE PARK
28500 W. Park Hwy, Ashland 68003 402-944-2523
This park overlooks the picturesque valley of the Platte River. This premier 574 acre park is open all year. Secluded on wooded ridge tops are 41 modern, housekeeping cabins. They have air conditioning/hear, foreplace, TV, refrigerator, range, and outdoor deck. 40 guest rooms in Lodge. There is a pool, marina, tennis courts, horseback riding, golf driving range, miniature golf course, fishing in 2 lakes, nature and hiking trails, and many park activities. RATE: cabin 2-bedrm $80 per night (sleeps 4)
DOG: accepted in cabins. Not permitted in Lodge, marina, pool, or public buildings. They must be leashed at all times when on park grounds.

BELLEVUE
AMERICAN FAMILY INN motel

Hwy 73-75 & Lloyd St, 1110 Ft Crook Road, So Bellevue 68005
800-253-2865, 402-291-0804
Hosts: John & Phyllis Hobbs
This motel features budget prices in a good recreational location. It has 107 luxurious rooms. Featured are complementary coffee, waterbeds, featherbeds, honeymoon suite, outside entry doors, 32 channel cable TV, VCR, movie rentals, restaurant next door, library, kitchenettes, heated outdoor pool, volleyball and basketball courts, laundry facilities. There is a picnic area near outdoor pool that would be convenient for guests with a dog. Nearby, numerous parks and recreational areas, among them Fontenelle Forest, a 1220 acre virgin forest with scenic trails, animal sanctuary, and Hayworth Park. RATE: minimum $32.95
DOG: There are designated pet rooms for guests with a dog. Dog must be declared when checking in or will be asked to leave. Pet rooms are cleaned with a pet vacume and sprayed with insect spray not harmful to pets. Dog must be removed or confined to carrier at time of cleaning. Aggressive dogs not allowed. There is a minimal daily charge for the dog.

CRAWFORD
BUTTE RANCH

803 W. Ashcreek Road, Crawford 69339 308-665-2364
This ranch bed and breakfast is open May to Dec. It offers 4 rooms and kitchenettes. Good hiking and hunting area. RATE: moderate
DOG: allowed

ELWOOD
SUNSET SHORE RESORT
at Johnson Lake

20 Bullhead Expressway Dr 28, Elwood 68937 308-785-2298
308-785-2298 Open April-Sept Host: Greg Medo, Owner
"Fun for the entire family" is the theme of this playground spot. that can't be beat for recreation such as swimming, boating, water skiing, fishing, golfing, or just plain relaxing. Johnson Lake has

a surface area of 3000 acres and 21 miles of shoreline. Resort offers 10 large modern cabins with 2/dbl beds and kitchenettes rental boats, a general store, and restaurant-lounge. The beach is of fine sand. Golf can be enjoyed on one of the midwest's finest grass greens...Lakeside Country Club. RATE: cabin 2 persons $58 DOG: allowed on 6' leash.

NORTH PLATTE
STOCKMAN INN

1402 S. Jeffers, PO Box 1303, North Platte 69101
308-534-3630, 800-624-4643
This 150 room Inn is located only minutes from Buffalo Bill's Ranch State Historical Park. It features a lounge, outdoor swimming pool, fireplace restaurant, and cable TV. Nearby are shopping and outlet malls, 3 public golf courses, and Lake Maloney. Travelers in this area with a dog are welcome.
RATE; min. $46.95 DOG: welcome. no restrictions or fee.

ORCHARD
DIAMOND E TROUT RESORT

P.O. Box B, Orchard 68764 800-658-3244, 402-893-3002
Hosts: John & Aletha Eley, owners
Open April 1-mid-October
This resort is located on the wooded and crystal clear Big Springs Creek, surrounded by rolling hills. The resort offers good fishing, paddle boating, hiking, and a relaxed pace. Local attractions include the ashfall fossil beds. a zoo, golf course, school house, antique shops, restaurants, municipal pool. There are 4 modern cottages, each sleeping about 7 persons. This 30 acre resort offers plenty of space for guests and their dogs to just roam around. RATE: Mon-Thurs (2 adults) $260, Fri-Sun $210 DOG: Fee Mon-Thurs $30, weekend $20.

SPRINGVIEW
BIG CANYON INN

HC 82, Box 107 402-497-3170, 800-437-6023

Offers 4 rooms in a ranch style home. Good hiking and horseback riding in area. Breakfast served. RATE: $36 dbl DOG: allowed in house if well behaved. No charge.

NEVADA

Los Vegas is the gambling mecca; Reno is less crowded. Lake Tahoe is the Nevada playground with crystal blue water and fine boating, fishing, and mountain sports. Golf, fishing in summer, and hike 100 miles of hiking trails.

LAKE TAHOE
LAKE TAHOE RESERVATIONS

Crystal Management Group Vacation Rentals
774 Mays Blvd, Suite 7, Incline Village 89451 702-831-8988
Offers condos and homes for rent on North and South shore. Rentals require a security deposit of $200-$300 and non-refundable cleaning fee. Linens and kitchen utinsels provided. Call for detailed listing. Some accommodations allow a dog.

Lake Tahoe Accommodations
255 Kingsbury Grade, PO Box 3824, Stateline 89449 800-228-6921
This real estate firm has properties that allow a dog in the Lake Tahoe area.

RENO
TRUCKEE RIVER LODGE

501 W. First Street, Reno 89503 800-635-8950, 702-786-8888
Non-smoking hotel. Offers 227 rooms, suites, kitchenettes, health club, TV, coffee. Activities in area: biking, canoeing, backpacking, fishing, golfing, skiing, tennis, and more. RATE: Min. $34
DOG: $10 day, $50 week. There are 9 miles of biking and jogging paths along the Truckee River.

LAS VEGAS
ALEXIS PARK RESORT

375 E Harmon Ave, Las Vegas 89109 800-582-2228

This resort is a green oasis in Las Vegas with 20 acres of greenery, streams, and waterfalls. Amenities include restaurants, swimming pools, putting green, tennis, health club, entertainment, lounge. There are 500 1-2 bedroom suites, jacuzzis, fireplaces. RATE: inquire DOG: allowed with $200 deposit, $50 non-refundable.

NEW HAMPSHIRE

Lots of outdoor recreation and quaint towns. White Mountain national forest occupies 770,000 acres in the north, as well as Monadnock State Park. Hamption Beach is popular. The central part of the state has lovely little villages and clear lakes. Fall foliage in the forests is lovely. Antique shops are situated throughout the state.

BARTLETT

THE COUNTRY INN AT BARTLETT

Rt 302, Box 327, Bartlett 03812 800-292-2353, 603-374-2353
Host: Mark Dindorf

This Inn is surrounded by the White Mountain National Forest. It is a great base for hiking, mountain biking, sightseeing, or just relaxing. Offers a hearty breakfast and expert trail advice, a hammock and a hot tub. There are Inn rooms and cottages of various sizes, with fireplaces. Inn is also near Crawford Notch State Park with trails and waterfalls, Mt. Willard, and Mt Washington. RATE: example: cottage with kitchenette (2-bedrm) bath, about $55. Inquire. DOG: Dog welcome in cottages. Inn residents include a cat and a dog. Your dog must not be left unattended.

FRANCESTOWN

THE INN AT CROTCHED MOUNTAIN

534 Mountain Road, Francestown 03043 603-588-6840
Host: John & Rose Perry

This is a quiet, secluded, and charming 170 year old ivy-covered Colonial Inn, 1300 Ft above sea level on Crotched Mountain. It has an unspoiled setting and panoramic views, yet only 75 miles from Boston. Various activities are available. There are 2 clay tennis courts, a large pool, wading pool , hiking and mountain climbing, 3 golf courses nearby, fishing in mountain streams, ponds, and lakes and browsing in picturesque New England towns. Ski area nearby. RATE: Modified Am Plan (lodging, dinner, bkfst) About $70 per person, dbl occupancy; $115 single. Deposit required. DOG: Dog welcome. Fee $5 per night.

• FRANCONIA NOTCH
LOVETT'S INN

Route 18, Franconia Notch 03580 800-356-3802, 603-823-7761
Hosts: Sharon & Anthony Ayrutine
This charming historic Inn in the White Mountain Region offers 6 guest rooms with bath, living room, porch, bar, and 3 dining rooms with New England dishes. Surrounding the Inn are 11 cottages with fireplaces. There is an outdoor grill and spa. Children welcome. Activities available in area include golf, tennis, biking, hiking, museums, shopping, theater, skiing. RATE: moderate DOG: Dog welcome. They will enjoy grounds, meadow, pond and brook, and hiking trails with you. Inn has about 10 acres.

• GORHAM
ROYALTY INN

130 Main Street, Gorham 03581 800-43-relax, 603-466-3312
Host: the King family
This Inn is located in Gorham, a few minutes from the White Mountains. On the premises guests find a restaurant, heated indoor and outdoor pools, jacuzzi, health club, racquetball, and game room. There are refrigerators and kitchenettes. Nearby, a golf course, tennis courts, and a playground on the town common. The White Mountain National Forest has plenty of challenging terrain for hikers, climbers, and skiers. RATE: about $50 (2 persons, 2 beds)
DOG: Allowed @ $5 per night or $10 per stay

• JACKSON
DANA PLACE INN

P.O Box L, Pinkham North, Rt 16, Jackson 03846
800-537-9276, 603-383-6822

This Inn is on 300 acres in Pinkham Notch, at the base of Mount Washington, and surrounded by 750,000 acre White Mountain National Forest. The Inn is a special place. It is an updated colonial farmhouse with a variety of 35 rooms. The dining experience in this romantic country Inn setting is enjoyable. Activities :

In summer, swim in indoor pool or swimming hole, tennis, hiking, excursions, shop local stores and galleries.

In fall, hike, drive, bike ride through White Mountains amidst brilliant fall color, use indoor pool , tennis, fish on Ellis River.

In winter, ski, winter hike, use indoor pool and just relax before the roaring fire.

In spring, ski in Tuckerman's Ravine, hike, walk the trails, swim, and play tennis. RATE: Special packages. Inquire directly.

DOG: Guests with dog can stay in an exterior room. Dog cannot be left unattended while you are away from the Inn. Also, dog not allowed in Main Inn. Lots of space for running in the woods.

JACKSON VILLAGE
THE WENTWORTH RESORT HOTEL

Box M, Jackson Village 03846 800-637-0013, 603-383-9700

This accommodation is in the charming village of Jackson, located at the foot of Mt Washington, bordered on the east by the beautiful Jackson Falls of the Wildcat River, and on the west by an 18-hole golf course...surrounded by White Mountain National Forest. It offers comfortable accommodations, memorable dining, and outstanding recreation. There is golf, swimming, tennis, and hiking on hundreds of well-marked trails in surrounding forest. Rivers and streams are known for fishing, canoeing, and white water rafting. In winter, guests find four major mountains for downhill skiing offering 28 lifts and 100 trails. Also ice skating, and sleigh riding on snowy golf course. RATE: room about $100 dbl. Condo, 2 bedroom about $200. Modified American Plan available.

NORTH CONWAY · KEARSARGE VILLAGE
ISAAC E. MERRILL HOUSE INN

P.O. Box 8, Kearsarge Village, North Conway 03847
800-328-9041, 603-356-9041

This Inn offers traditional country hospitality at the base of Mt. Cranmore in North Conway's historic Kearsarge Village. Amenities include views of cathedral Ledge, river swimming, fireplace dining room, breakfast and tea and pastries served daily. Located 1 1/2 miles to shopping district and 1 mile to Mt. Cranmore. The historic Kearsarge Village is a charming group of cozy homes and country estates, fine walks and lovely drives. Beautiful Kearsarge Brook winds through the village and adds to the enjoyment of woodsy walks. To the east lies Rattlesnake Range, to the north is Mt Kearsarge and Mt Bartlett with remarkable views. Opportunities abound for mountain climbing, hiking, camping, fishing, hunting, swimming, golf, tennis, and horseback riding.
RATE: minimum $55 DOG: Dog accepted. No restrictions, no charge. There is open land for dog to run, and a river.

LYME
LOCH LYME LODGE

70 Orford Road, Lyme 03768 603-795-2141, 800-423-2141
Host: Paul & Jody Barker, Open Menorial Day-September.
This Lodge has been taking guests since 1918. From May-Sept 25 cabins and rooms in the Main Lodge are available. Dogs are permitted in cabins only. The Lodge overlooks a spring-fed lake surrounded by hills. There are 125 acres of woodlands, fields, and lakeshore for hiking, fishing, and relaxing. Tennis courts, Boats, canoes, and kayakis available. This is a rustic vacation spot ...no luxury, phones, TV or bar. But lots of space, fresh air, and clean water. Meals provided. There is a private lake waterfront, cabins with fireplaces, peace and quiet. Lots of casual family activities. RATE: Cabins $430 min. per week (2 people)
B & B rates or modified American Plan available. See brochure.
DOG: Well behaved dogs allowed in cabins only. Prohibited from beach area. Up-to-date vaccinations please.

NORTH CONWAY
STONEHURST MANOR

P.O. Box 1937 (Rt 16), North Conway 03860
603-356-3271, 800-525-9100

Set on a secluded hillside among tall pines, this elegant manor was originally part of the 500-acre summer estate of carpet-baron Erastus Bigelow. Today the manor operates as a unique luxury Inn with 33 acres. Located near North Conway Village, in Mt Washington Valley. It offers an outdoor pool, hot tub, tennis court, walking trails, skiing in winter. Manor rooma and condos are set on manor grounds with kitchens and fireplaces. There is an extensive dining menu. RATE: min $75 per room per night. DOG: One room is reserved for a guests with a dog. Charge $10 extra per pet. 33 private acres of walking trails.

PITTSBURG
LOPSTICK LODGE & CABINS

First Connecticut Lake, Pittsburg 03592 800-538-6659, 603-538-6659

This accommodation offers 9 comfortable housekeeping cabins of various sizes, with a spectacular view of First Connecticut Lake. Each has a kitchen, hot shower, dishes, refrigerator, etc.
The mountain location offers panoramic views and friendly hospitality. Animals abound...deer, rabbit, fox. This is a fishing and hunting area. Activities include hiking to the top of Mt Magalloway or to Fourth Connecticut Lake. Fish for trout , salmon, in pond and streams. In winter, snowmobile on groomed trails to neighboring Maine, Vermont, Canada, and cross-country ski.. RATE: min $30 per person per night, DOG: $7 per night in cabins.

RINDGE
WOODBOUND INN

62 Woodbound Road, Ringe, 03461 800-688-7770, 603-532-8341
Host: the Kohlmorgen's

This is a 200 acre, self-contained full-service, country resort located on the shores of the 2 1/2 mile Lake Contoocook, 65 miles from Boston. Offers restaurant, woodland, sandy beaches, and meadows featuring an abundance of leisurely and recreational on-site activities, including swimming, boating, fishing, hiking and climbing, skiing, ice skating, tobogganing, picnicking, golf, putting, tennis, volleyball, biking. Horseback riding nearby. In this area, guests are interested in Mt Monadnock, with its easy and well-marked trails and views. The Cathedral in the Pines, an outdoor shrine. Friendly Farm, a "petting zoo" in Doublin. Historic homes, bridges, villages, auctions, and antiques. There are more than 200 lakes and ponds, forests and trails...all away from public roads. RATE: Example: 1 bedroom cottage, sgl $125, includes room and hearty country breakfast. Modified American Plan available. Also, special extended stay rates. DOG: Welcome at lake front cabins. Must be with owner outside cabin. Not allowed in Main Inn.

SUNAPEE
DEXTER'S INN and Tennis Club

P.O. Box 703, Sunapee 03782 800-232-5571, 603-763-5571

Host: Michael and Holly Durfor, Open May-October

The Inn embodies the essence of a true New England Country Inn, with estate-like grounds and gardens. The Inn boasts breathtaking views, spacious library, lounge, porch, meeting facilities, 3 tennis courts, tennis instruction with a pro on staff, swimming pool, horseshoe pits, more. There are 3 excellent golf courses within a Paul Bunyan golf drive, and excellent antiques and gift shopping throughout the area. Breakfast and dinner served daily. Meals are bountiful and distinctive. Guests will enjoy the New Hampshire countryside with Lake Sunapee to the east, and Mt Sunapee to the south. Lawns, gardens, meadows and woods surround the Inn in which guests can hike, bike, and canoe. RATE: Minimum sgl $95 with meals, Minimum Holly Cottage (4 people) $375 with meals. Inquire about packages. Children welcome. DOG: Permitted in annex rooms or Holly Cottage at $10 per day, plus any damages.

SUGAR HILL
THE HILLTOP INN BED & BREAKFAST

Sugar Hill 03585 603-823-5695

Host: Mike & Meri Hern

This is a charming Victorian Country inn, built circa 1895, 6 hrs from New York and 2 1/2 hrs from Boston. It has antique furnishings. There are 6 guest rooms with bath; non-smoking. Also, a 2-bedrm cottage. Fine dining during foliage season. All room rates include a large country breakfast.

Activities in area include skiing, swimming, canoeing, fishing, biking, hiking, waterfront trails, horseback riding, wind surfing, glider and plane rides, summer stock theater, No. Conway outlet shopping, exploring the White Mountains. RATE: minimum room $70, cottage $200 (2-4 people)
DOG: welcome. Charge is $10 per night. Dog stays with you in guestroom. They will enjoy running in fields. There is a closed-in deck to sit outside. Dog walking service available. Snacks given. Lots of hiking trails and swimming areas.

TROY
THE INN AT EAST HILL FARM

Troy 03465 603-242-6495, 800-242-6495
Host: Dave and Sally Adams
The Inn is a casual and carefree family vacation resort at the foot of picturesque Mount Monadnock. It combines farm activities and resort fun. There are 2 outdoor pools, 1 indoor pool, whirlpool, wading pool, sauna, lake beach, tennis, shuffleboard, recreation rooms, boats, fishing, waterskiing, square dancing, and mountain climbing. Also, winter cross-country skiing, skating, sleigh rides and a children's program. Nearby, guests can find golf, summer theater, auctions, movies, bowling, churches, and the Cathedral in the Pines. Children's activities abound. They enjoy petting the barnyard animals, hunting for eggs, feeding pigs and calves, hay rides, swimming, organized activities, games, fishing While children are busy, parents enjoy freedom.
RATE: A deposit of $125 per family is applied to the last day of the reservation. Rate includes rooms, 3 meals daily, use of boats, tennis courts, pony rides and more. Adult weekly $460, daily minimum $65. DOG: Dogs are allowed in some units at $10 per day. They must be on leash at all times. They can hike and can also swim in pond on property.

WHITEFIELD
THE SPALDING INN

Mountain View Road, Whitefield 03598 800-368-VIEW, 603-837-2572 Host: Diane E. Cockrell, owner
Open: May 15 - October 31

This charming, warm, and hospitable Inn is located in the heart of the White Mountains, set amidst 200 acres of lawns, orchards, and perennial gardens... a perfect escape from the stress of city life. There is an established tradition of superb food, complete but unobtrusive service, grand mountain views. Children welcome. Offers 4 clay tennis courts, 9 hole golf course, heated swimming pool, biking, carriage roads for walking, 200 acres for hiking. The summer stock theater is nearby. The Appalachian Trail system is near the Inn.

RATE: Dogs accepted in cottage suites, 1-4 bedrooms, living room, kitchen, fireplace. $150 minimum rate includes breakfast-2 people. Weekly from $650 in cottage. Full meal plan available from $200 per day, per couple. Golf packages and theater packages. Baby sitting and dog sitting can be arranged. 2 night minimum stay.

DOG: The Spalding Inn loves dogs. There are 3 resident English Springer Spaniels. This property has 220 acres for them to walk, and miles of country roads to explore.

NEW JERSEY

The State of New Jersey has a large park system with 36 parks, 11 forests, recreation areas, marinas, and recreational facilities. The Jersey Shore is public beach front that stretches from Sandy Hook to Ocean City, a family oriented resort area, to Wildwood and Cape May with its Victorian bed and breakfasts.

LONG BEACH ISLAND, BEACH HAVEN
ENGLESIDE INN

30 Engleside Ave, Beach Haven 08008   609-492-1251

Accommodation located on oceanfront on Long Beach Island. Restaurant, swimming pool, wide sandy beach on ocean.

RATE: $72 minimum DOG: allowed offseason only (not summer) @ $10 per night charge

CAPE MAY
MARQUIS DE LAFAYETTE HOTEL

501 Beach Dr, Cape May 08204 609-884-3431

Offers comfortable rooms. Dog allowed in certain rooms.

RATE $236 per ngt in dog room. DOG: $20 per night charge

• OCEAN GROVE
PARKVIEW INN

23 Seaview Ave, Ocean Grove 07756 908-775-1645
Located very near beach. Continental breakfast given.
RATE: $50 DOG: allowed with refundable deposit. Owner has large dog in residence in summer. Need owner approval to bring your dog in. Offseason no dog is there. Your dog allowed with no problem.

• SOMERS POINT
RESIDENCE INN BY MARRIOTT

900 Mays Landing Road, Somers Point 08244 609-927-6400
This is a residence accommodation for the Greate Bay Resort and Country Club located across the road. The Country Club offers golf, fine dining, and nightlife. Minutes from Atlantic City.
RATE: moderate DOG: allowed with $50 non-refundable fee.

• WARREN
SOMERSET HILLS

200 Liberty Corner Road, Warren 908-647-6700, 800-688-0700
An elegant hotel in beautiful Watchung Mountains. Offers 111 rooms, gracious dining, entertainment, outdoor pool, fitness center.
RATE: Inquire DOG: Hotel has a kennel for dogs on property. Pet must be kept in kennel at night.

• WILDWOOD
JADE EAST MOTEL

510 E. Fourth Ave, North Wildwood 08260 609-522-1867
Offers ocean view rooms and efficiencies, heated pool, near beach.
RATE: minimum $40 dbl DOG: allows quiet, friendly dog. No barking, @ $10 per night. Dogs not allowed on beach. Also be advised it is hot in summer. Spring and Fall preferable for a dog. There are limitations on what a dog can do in this area.

LONG BEACH LODGE

539 E 9th Ave, North Wildwood 08260 609-522-1520
Comfortable rooms offered in recreation area. RATE: minimum $45
DOG: allowed off-season only, Fall and Spring. No charge.

WOODCLIFF LAKE
WOODCLIFF LAKE HILTON

Tice Blvd & Chestnut Ridge Road, Woodcliff Lake 07675
800-445-8667, 201-391-3600
This luxury hotel in northern New Jersey is located on 21 acres of gently rolling hills and delightful fruit orchards. It features delicious cuisine at three distinctive restaurants and attentive service. There are a variety of sports amenities including tennis, indoor and outdoor pools, putting green, and ball courts. Walkers and runners will love the scenic trails through fruit orchards.
RATE: minimum about $100 DOG: Dog owner required to sign a waiver taking full responsibility for any damage or cleaning needed.

NEW MEXICO

Picturesque New Mexico has various areas of interest, from Santa Fe Taos, and Albuqurque, to the Carlsbad Caverns. There are about 45 state parks and various recreation areas such as Angel Fire, and Ruidoso.

ALBUQUERQUE
HOWARD JOHNSON LODGE

7630 Pan Americam Freeway, Albuquerque 87109
800-446-4656, 505-828-1600
This is a new hotel 45 minutes from Santa Fe. Offers pool, playground, exercise room, continental breakfast, TV.
RATE: moderate DOG: allowed

ALTO
HIGH COUNTRY LODGE

P.O. Box 134, Alto 88312 800-845-7265, 505-336-4321

Offers 32 cabins in tall pines next to Alto Lake, with kitchen, TV, phone, fireplace, porch, enclosed heated pool, spa, tennis court, fishing. RATE: Inquire DOG: allows 2 dogs maximum @ $10 per pet.

ANGEL FIRE
ELK HORN LODGE

Angel Fire 87710 505-377-2811
A fine new 15-room hotel with restaurant in Angel Fire resort area on 10,000 acre private ranch. Road runner tours.
RATE: inquire DOG: $10 charge per night

CHAMA
THE LODGE AT CHAMA

P.O. Box 127, Chama 87520 505-756-2133
This is a world renowned luxury resort and foremost outdoor sporting retreat, now owned by the Jecarilla Apache Tribe, is dedicated to continuing excellence and high standards. Offers 32,000 acres of magnificent managed environment landscapes, to be explored on horseback or on foot. Wonderful animal photography in breathtaking surroundings, fishing in lakes and streams, riding, skiing, and hunting in season. Also, a working cattle ranch. Professional guides available. Only 22 guests admitted at one time. Nearby towns of Santa Fe and Taos offer shopping and restuarants.
RATE: lodging only $200, includes meals, Lodging and activities $375. Inquire about specifics.
DOG: You can bring your pet by making special arrangements directly with the Reservations Manager.

SPRUCE LODGE

P.O. Box 365, Chama 87520 505-756-2593
This Lodge consists of 12 cabins on the bank of the Chama River. There are cool, relaxing surroundings for those who want to get away from it all or fish. The cabins are clean and remodeled, with or without kitchenettes and porch. 1-6 person units.
RATE: minimum 1-person cabin w/kitchen $45 DOG: welcome. No restrictions.

• LAS CRUCES
HILTON INN

705 South Telshor Blvd, Las Cruces 88011 505-522-4300
Overlooks Las Cruces and the beautiful Mesilla Valley. Offers luxurious accommodations, swimming pool, jacuzzi, exercise room, golf packages, restaurant with Southwestern cuisine.
RATE: Inquire DOG: allowed

• RUIDOSO
DEE DEE CABINS

Box 844, 310 Main Street, Ruidoso 88345
800-345-4848 505-257-2165
A premier 5-acre cottage resort in the beautiful upper canyon in a forest setting. Minutes from all recreation sites.
RATE: moderate, inquire DOG: allowed. Must never be left alone in cabin.

INN AT PINE SPRINGS

Hwy 70E, Ruidoso Downs 800-237-3607
Secluded, friendly, all-season Inn. Watch horse racing, hike, fish, shop, play golf, ski, bike. The Ruidoso area is surrounded by a national forest. RATE: moderate, inquire DOG: allowed on leash.

• SANTA FE
THE INN OF THE ANASAZI

113 Washington Ave, Santa Fe 87501
800-688-8100 505-988-3090
This is a beautiful and unusual Inn. Huge cactus, massive hand carved doors, and textiles, paintings, carvings and baskets represent New Mexico's three cultures...Native American, Hispanic, and Anglo. There are 51 guest rooms and 8 suites with fireplaces, reflecting the region's diverse heritage. The restaurant serves an exciting and colorful cuisine of southwest foods. There are tours and fireside chats with artists, historians, and archaeologists, spanning past and present for guests. RATE: minimum $195
No charge for children. DOG: dog allowed @ $30 charge.

CASA DE LA CUMA, BED & BREAKFAST

105 Paseo de la Cuma, Santa Fe 87501 505-983-1717
Offers 7 rooms and casitas with kitchens; flowers, patios.
RATE: minimum $60 DOG: $10 charge

ELDORADO HOTEL

309 W. San Francisco St, Santa Fe 87501 800-286-6693
Gracious hotel with first class amenities. RATE: inquire
DOG: allowed. No charge. Owner liable for any damage.

MARRIOTT RESIDENCE INN

1698 Galisteo St, Santa Fe 87501 800-331-3131, 505-988-7300
An all-suite hotel, kitchens, fireplaces, swimming pool.
RATE: moderate, inquire DOG: allowed at $8 per day and $50 cleaning fee.

• SAPELLO

SURPRISE VALLEY RANCH

HC 68, Box 28, Sapello 87742 505-425-8028
Host: Hal Hoover, General Manager
This is a working ranch with cabins, located in the heart of the beautiful Santa Fe National Forest, bordering the Pecos Wilderness. Nestled in a valley forested with aspen, pine, and spruce, near the Sapello River abounding with trout. Stocked ponds also available. Fishing license required. Activities include riding, hiking, and fishing. Cabins with bath have fireplaces and kitchens, they can accommodate up to 6 people each. No TV. Hunting and pack trips available. RATE: minimum $60 DOG: allowed at $15 1 x fee.

• SILVER CITY

BEAR MOUNTAIN GUEST RANCH ,Bed & Bkfast

2251 Bear Mountain Road, PO Box 1163N, Silver City 88962
800-880-2538, 505-538-2538
Host: Myra B. McCormick, owner and manager
This bed and breakfast will help you enjoy tranquil, uncrowded Southwest New Mexico with mild temperatures year 'round.

There are 13 rooms, 2 cottages, and a 5 bedroom house available. Guests can visit national forests, wilderness areas, state parks, mesas, mountains, deserts, Indian ruins, watch and photograph birds, animals and wild plants. RATE: 1 person $54; 2 people $95 with meals. Special rates available. DOG: Dog can stay in the same room as owner. When outdoors, dog must be on leash at all times. Dogs can run free along open roads, since ranch is out from town. No charge for dog.

TAOS
INN ON LA LOMA PLAZA, Bed & Bkfast

315 Ranchitos Road, Box 4159, Taos 87571
800-530-3040, 505-758-1717

This is a luxury walled estate that takes reservations for guests with dogs on adjacent lovely property. Some fireplaces and TV. Inquire for these lovely accommodations at the above number.

NEW YORK

New York is most notable for New York City, an ideal place for a big city vacation...and literally "the center of everything"...finance, shopping, museums, theater, Central Park, United Nations, wonderful ethnic restaurants. Outside the immediate city, visit Long Island mansions, museums, nature areas and villages along the coast. The elegant resorts in the Hamptons attract celebrities and tourists. Other points of interest are the Hudson Valley, Catskills, Niagra Falls, and the Adirondacks.

CANANDAIGUA
CANANDAIGUA INN ON THE LAKE

770 South Main Street, Canandaigua 14424 800-228-2801
716-394-7800

This elegant full-service resort is located in the Finger Lakes Region on Canandaigua Lake, about 1 hour from Rochester by road. Offers 134 very comfortable rooms and suites and fine service. There is a lakeside swimming pool, fitness center, cable TV, games,

Nearby, skiing, golf, snorkeling, windsurfing, boats, fishing, Sonnenberg Gardens, racing, shopping, concerts. RATE: min sgl about $45, dbl $79 with breakfast. special packages available. DOG: allowed, no charge.

DE BRUCE
DE BRUCE COUNTRY INN
on the Willowemoc within Catskill Forest Park

R.D. 1, Box 286A, De Bruce 12758 914-439-3900

Charming Inn on own private preserve. Adjacent wooded trails, wildlife and game, fishing, country walks, swimming pool, fitness, delightful dining on terrace, view of trout pond, with valley and mountains beyond. RATE: includes bkfst and dinner, Min. $85 DOG: Friendly, well-behaved dogs, taken good care of by owner, are allowed at the Inn at manager descretion. Inquire about your dog.

DOVER PLAINS
OLD DROVER INN

Old Route 22, Dover Plains 12522 914-832-9311

Host: Alice Pitcher and Kemper Peacock

This is a lovely dog-friendly Inn located in Dutchess County. In continuous operation since 1750, this historic Inn at the foot of the Berkshires features elegant gourmet country dining and overnight accommodations. Day trips can easily be taken to Hudson Valley, and the Berkshires. Riding, golf, skiing, hiking, historic mansions, are available in the area. RATE: minimum midweek $150 dbl. includes breakfast. DOG: This Inn has 3 Yorkshire Terriers in residence. Guest dogs must get along with these and other dogs. Charge $20 per night, per dog.

DUNKIRK
FOUR POINTS HOTEL HARBORFRONT

30 Lake Shore East, Dunkirk 14048 800-525-8350, 716-366-8350

This superior ITT Sheraton hotel has 132 rooms and is located in Chautauqua County, the State's grape-growing region. It is on Lake Erie, near Chadwick Bay Marina with 400 slips. Includes restaurant, lounge, night club, fitness room, swimming pools. Sport fishing and boating are popular on Lake Erie. Ski, Hike, explore lighthouses. RATE: minimum sgl $75 DOG: charge $10

GILBOA
GOLDEN ACRES FARM AND RANCH

Gilboa, 12076 800-252-7787, 800-847-2151, 607-588-7329
This is a 600 acre family "KOSHER" Farm and Ranch high in the Catskill Mountains, with modern resort comforts. There is an outdoor and indoor pool, spa hot tub and sauna, a special children's program, and evening programs.
Activities include hayrides, horseback riding, pony rides, marshmellow roasts. Guests can pet and view farm animals, such as cows, horses, goats, sheep, ducks, chickens, cats, dogs and more. There are various games, fishing, boating, tennis, swimming, archery, spa hot tub, indoor recreation areas with mini golf and workout room. Nearby is an 18-hole golf course, bowling, auctions.
All meals prepared in accordance with Jewish Dietary Laws. All you want to eat and a large variety of everything.
RATE: Daily adult minimum about $110 (any 2 nights)
DOG: Accepted at fee of $5 daily or $25 weekly. Pet must be leashed in central areas. No hyper or large dogs.

HAMPTON'S
BASSET HOUSE INN

128 Montauk Highway, East Hampton 11937 516-324-6127
This Inn is 1 1/2 miles from "the most beautiful village in the United States"...East Hampton, Long Island. The Inn has 12 bright and airy rooms with bath, two with fireplaces. The hosts will make you feel at home. There is easy access to the village beaches, country walks, restaurants, and more. A beautiful year 'round area.
RATE: about $125 min. sgl with bath, includes breakfast
DOG: allowed. Inquire.

BOWEN'S BY THE BAYS

177 West Montauk Highway, Hampton Bays 11946
516-728-1158, 800-533-3139 Host: Kevin & Eileen Bowen

Located in the heart of the Hamptons, a 2-hour drive from New York City, this affordable resort offers seven 1-3 bedroom cottages and nine motel rooms. Amenities include swimming pool, tennis court, playground, on 3 1/2 landscaped acres. Close to ocean and bay beaches, and resort area attractions.
RATE: Inquire. Depends on season of year. DOG: Allowed. Guests with dog allowed in cottages only.

• INLET
ROCKY POINT LAKESIDE LODGES

P.O. Box 570, (Route 28) Inlet 13360 800-442-2251, 315-357-3751
Townhouse rentals available in the heart of the Adirondacks in Fulton Chain of Lakes. Most owners do allow dogs in rentals. Be sure to mention dog for proper rental placement.
Units have fireplace, TV, 3 bedrooms, bath, spa. Also spa, pool, 2300' of beautiful shore, beach, tennis, 25 boat docks, golf courses nearby, horseback riding, hiking, 5 restaurants.
RATE: minimum $150 autumn/spring for 2 nights, $210 summer for 2 nights; weekly $150 per night.
DOG: no charge noted. General deposit required.

• LAKE PLACID
BEST WESTERN GOLDEN ARROW HOTEL

150 Main Street, Lake Placid 12946 518-523-3353
Vacation in the beauty of the Adirondacks. Rooms, suites, condo apartments available in this resort-type hotel with restaurant, lounge, and night club. Guests swim in heated indoor pool or relax on private white sand beach fronting mirror Lake. Free canoes and boats. Fish, take dog sled rides, hike. There is a putting green. Golf courses in vicinity. RATE: minimum offseason $60 dbl.
DOG: Welcome. must follow house rules:
leash on property and in Lake Placid; putting green off-limits to dog; bring a "pooper scooper" and bags; and do not leave dog unattended in room. Charge: $10 small dog, $25 large dog.

HOLIDAY INN, LAKE PLACID RESORT

One Olympic Drive, Lake Placid 12946 518-523-2556

This 40 acre resort offers superb accommodations, dining, and recreation at the center of the village overlooking beautiful Lake Placid. Chalets, guest rooms with fireplaces, mini-suites and condos are available. There are 6 unique dining rooms, a private trout stream and 50 acre trout preserve, 5 tennis courts, and an extensive health club. There is also Camp Majano, a secluded island 17 acre retreat located on one of the major islands on Lake Placid lake. It can be used by groups.

RATE: minimum about $85. DOG: Any size dog allowed. Must not be left unattended. $50 deposit against damages required.

LAKE PLACID HILTON RESORT

One Mirror Lake Drive, Lake Placid 12946 800-755-5598, 518-523-4411

Offers superior service, exceptional accommodations, delightful cuisine, and activities, on the shores of Mirror Lake, overlooking the Adirondack's High Peaks. Amenities include all rooms facing the lake and mountains, live entertainment in the Lounge, indoor and outdoor heated pools, whirlpools, exercise room.

In Spring, enjoy woods and fishing. In Summer, there is tennis, golf, carriage rides, hiking, swimming, and boating. Fall is a "flaming leaves" spectacle. Winter is the time for skiing, ice skating, bobsled, dogsled rides, and more. Area has Olympic Winter Games and major shows. There is lots of space surrounding.

RATE: about $135 per day per room. DOG: Welcome, but cannot be left alone at any time. Deposit required. Owner responsible for any damage.

NEW YORK CITY see Cities section of this book

NIAGARA FALLS

NIAGARA FALLS RADISSON

Third & Old Falls Streets, Box 845, Niagara Falls 14303
800-333-3333, 716-285-3361

This 400 guest room hotel is located in the heart of Niagara Falls, 1600 ft from the Falls. Amenities include an indoor skylit swimming

pool, jacuzzi, spa, saunas, a fully equipped fitness center, and delightful dining. This international tourist destination has a vast selection of attractions, shopping, including New York State's largest state park. Walking trails and beautiful scenery are plentiful. This hotel hosts several dog shows throughout the year.
RATE: variable. Off-season low $46
DOG: welcome with a $50 deposit.

PURLING
TUMBLIN FALLS HOUSE, Bed & Bkfst

P.O. Box 281, Purling 12473 518-622-3981
Host: Hugh & Linda Curry
This house sits high atop a cliff, hidden in trees, and near enough to Shinglekill Falls for the steady gentle sound to be relaxing. Country breakfast served. Activities include swimming, fishing, hiking, birding, skiing. There are antiques at Saugerties, 20 minutes away. A bit further is Woodstock. RATE: minimum $55 for 1-2 persons per room. DOG: Owners have 2 dogs on premises. Guest dogs allowed most of the time. Call and discuss specific dates... holidays may be busy. Dogs and owners utilize numerous trails, several swimming holes, and forested areas. Cannot leave dog in room unattended. Property also has outside dog run and fenced area for short periods. Charge $6 per day, per pet, as well as fees for special services of dogsitting or feeding.

RICHFIELD SPRINGS
FIELDSTONE FARM

R.D. #3, Rose's Hill Road, RB-168, Richfield Springs 13439
315-858-0295, 800-336-4629
This is a very nice family vacation resort with various size cottage and apartment rentals, kitchens. Offers resort-type activities at family rates. No maid service. No livestock but lots of recreational opportunities. 190 acres with lovely woods and streams provide hiking, fishing, boating. Outdoor pool, tennis court, games, rec hall.
RATE: example: small cottage 1-2 people $60 day, $280 per week
DOG: allowed. Cannot run loose and owner must clean-up after them. Constant barking not acceptable. Charge $40 per week or $6 per day.

• SACKETS HARBOR
ONTARIO PLACE HOTEL

103 General Smith Drive, Sackets Harbor 13685 518-646-8000
This is a nice 32 room hotel on the harbor in beautiful historic Sackets Harbor, near Watertown. This area is a vacation center. RATE: $69 dbl DOG: one room is available for guests with a dog. Has 3 single beds. Inquire for further information.

• SARANAC LAKE
THE POINT

HCR #1, Box 65, Saranac Lake 12983
800-255-3530, 518-891-5674. Host: Claudia & Bill McNamee, mgrs
Open year 'round, The Point is a lovely "fantastic hideaway" ten acre private estate, widely recognized for upscale excellence. Between ancient forests and swimming lakes, this resort was an Adirondack retreat for the very wealthy and their friends...the home of the Rockefellers. Join new friends for a house party in the woods. There are 11 large, distinctive guest quarters spread among 4 buildings. The Great Hall's interior has massive logs and enormous stone fireplaces with antique furnishings, superb food and drink, and an environment of exquisite beauty.
There is no menu. The finest cuisine is served "en famille" and will delight the most sophisticated palates. Breakfast served in rooms. Activities include hiking in balsam-scented woods, fishing, sailing, water skiing, swimming, and sunning. Bicycle, go horseback riding, golf is nearby, and guides are available for wilderness hiking. Ski and ice fish in winter. RATE: minimum all inclusive, 2 people $775, min stay 2-night weekend. DOG: allowed.

THE HOTEL SARANAC of Paul Smith's College

101 Main Street, Saranac Lake 12983 800-937-0211, 518-891-2200
In the tradition of Adirondack hospitality, this college owned full-service hotel can help you enjoy spectacular scenery and fresh mountain air and participate in non-stop recreation. Golf, tennis, swimming, canoeing, skiing, snowmobiling, shopping, all are within minutes of the hotel. There are Olympic sites, international

competitions, and guided hiking or fishing trips.
The hotel offers 92 guest rooms, 5 mini·suites, a restaurant, gift shop and bakery. At your doorstep is the Village of Saranac Lake.
RATE: about $49.95 bed & breakfast special. DOG: allowed.

TANNERSVILLE
DEER MOUNTAIN INN

Rte 25, Tannersville 12485 518-589-6268
Offers 8 rooms in a 1900's mansion on 15 wooded acres. There is European ambiance throughout. RATE: inquire DOG: will accept a dog. Space to run and play.

TICONDEROGA
THE RANCHOUSE AT BALDWIN on Northern Lake George

R.R. #1, 79 Baldwin Road, Ticonderoga 12883 518-585-3528
Open May-October
This is a lakefront accommodation situated directly on the north shore of beautiful Lake George in a private residential setting. Activities offered are swimming, boating, fishing, and games for the whole family, as well as walking or bicycling in beautiful Adirondack lake country. In the area are forts and museums, arts and entertainment, tennis, an 18-hole golf course, fishing tournaments, windsurfing, autumn foliage, Oktoberfest, and more.
RATE: $425-$600 per week DOG: dogs accepted.

TUPPER LAKE
THE WAWBEEK RESORT, on Upper Saranac Lake

553 Panther Mountain Road, Tupper Lake 12986 518-359-2656
Open all year, except November and April
This resort is ideally located in the heart of the Adirondack Mountains on the shores of Upper Saranac Lake. On-site facilities include swimming beach, boats, tennis, trails, gameroom, more than 30 miles of cross-country skiing. Activities in the immediate area include downhill skiing, cross-country sking, golf at 2 18-hole courses, horseback riding, canoeing, and hiking along marked trails.

Accommodations range from rustic to super confortable. Available are cabins, cottages, and a mountain lodge. The restaurant is acclaimed for fine dining and lounge, overlooking Upper Saranac Lake. RATE: Various accommodations from about $125 per room (dbl) includes continental breakfast. Weekly rates. Most units have cooking facilities. DOG: Dog allowed at $20 per dog. They may swim at beachfront but not at beach. There is a lot of other waterfront for them to play in. On property, dog must be on leash and owner responsible for pooper scooper detail.

WINDHAM
POINT LOOKOUT MOUNTAIN INN

Route 23, East Windham 12439 518-734-3381
Host: Mariana Di Toro, Rosemary Jensen, Lucio Di Toro
This is a charming cliffside Inn on the historic Mohican Trail in the beautiful Northern Catskills. Comfortable rooms, color TV, and beautiful panoramic views. Close by hiking, historic landmarks, state parks, skiing. Cafe, outdoor decks and tap room are popular with exciting menues and views of 5 states. Inn located 2 hours north of New York City. RATE: minimum weekend $80 dbl slightly higher minimum during foliage season.
DOG: allowed at charge of $15 per day, plus a $100 security deposit, refundable. Dog must be quiet and well-behaved. Must have leash, collar, ID tags and written vaccinations. Inquire about further dog policies and restrictions on grounds. Longer walks can be taken with your dog. Inn can advise.

NORTH CAROLINA

Take the scenic drive on the Blue Ridge Parkway. It extends 250 miles from the Virginia State line to Great Smoky Mountains National Park. The Triangle area of Raleigh, Durham, and Chapel Hill, and the Triad area of Greensboro, Winston-Salem, and High Point are the largest towns. Vacationers seek the barrier islands, the outer banks, which stretch along the coast with lots of vacation spots, charming towns, and sea life at beaches...along an extensive oceanfront.

ATLANTIC BEACH
ATLANTIS LODGE

P.O. Box 310, Atlantic Beach 28512 800-682-7057, 919-726-5168
Host A.C. and Dorothy Hall
This is a lodge in a beautifully wooded, ocean-front site on coast. Most units are suites with kitchens, patios, and decks. For recreation shell, fish, swim, windsurf, play games. There is an outdoor pool and library. Nearby, find 8 golf courses, a country, restaurant.
RATE: summer $83 per day, dbl DOG: allowed in most units. Make advance arrangements for dog. Charge $2 per night. House rules include: There is a maximum of 2 dogs. Must be kept on leash outside room. Owner must clean-up after pet in all public areas. Dog must be kept quiet and not left unattended. Any damage charged to guest.

BEECH MOUNTAIN
BEECH MOUNTAIN SLOPESIDE CHALET RENTALS

503 Beech Mountain Pkwy, Beech Mt 28604
800-692-2061, 704-387-4251
This agency has 47 chalets and townhouses for rent. Some available with kennels. Inquire.

CASHIERS
HIGH HAMPTON INN & COUNTRY CLUB

P.O. Box 338, Cashiers 28717 800-334-2551, 704-743-2411
This Inn has a proud history which goes back more than a century. Many persons whose names adorn Southern history have visited this 1400 acre estate...a place where time stands still and very little changes except the seasons. The architecture is rustic and blends with the lush green beauty of the area. Rock Mt and Chimney Top Mt stand guard over the Inn in this southern Blue Ridge Range.
The Inn has 130 rooms and guest cottages, and also a number or privately owned vacation homes near the golf course for rent. The cuisine is American. There is a social hour and evening entertainment. Resort activities include 18-hole golf course, tennis, swimming at Hampton Lake, boating, sailing, canoeing, rowing,

fishing. No license required. Nature walks and fitness trails with exercise stations, various sports and games, and bird watching.
RATE: Inquire DOG: Dogs not allowed in rooms but stay in kennel on Inn property at night. Guests water and feed their own dogs. There are several hiking trails on which dogs can be taken without a leash.

CORNELIUS
HOLIDAY INN at Lake Norman

P.O. Box 1278, Cornelius 28031 704-892-9120
Inn located 20 minutes from Charlotte and close to Lake Norman recreation. Offers 120 guest rooms and suites, restaurant and lounge, an outdoor swimming pool. Golf and sailing available nearby.
RATE: $56 minimum, incl bkfst. DOG: $10 per pet for entire stay

HOT SPRINGS
DEER PARK CABINS

P.O. Box 617, Hot Springs 28743 704-622-3516
Two cabins available for rent, kitchen, TV, picnic area, fireplace, dog kennel. Jog the nature trail. Open all year. RATE: Inquire
DOG: allowed. kennel available.

KILL DEVIL HILLS
RAMADA INN at Nags Head Beach

P.O. Box 2716, 1701 So Virginia Dare Trail, Kill Devil Hills, 27948 800-635-1824, 919-441-2151 open all year
This 172 room Inn is located on a wide, sandy beach in the Outer Banks...a perfect place to relax and unwind. There are many historic sites and sporting activities available. See nearby quaint fishing villages, beautiful gardens, light houses, and the Wright Bros. Memorial. Activities include deep sea fishing, shell collecting, and hand gliding. There is an indoor heated pool and spa. The oceanside restaurant, Peppercorns, offers delicious meals.
RATE: First floor rooms, offseason rate $54, summer $119
DOG: Dog welcome in first floor rooms. One $10 charge. Dog cannot be left along in room. "Potty deposits" must be removed from hotel grounds. Scooper can be borrowed. Dogs can go on beach except May 15-Sept 15. Nags Head, 1 mi. so. allows dogs year around.

NAGS HEAD, KITTY HAWK AREA
REAL ESTATE FIRMS OFFERING VACATION RENTALS

. Duck's Real Estate , Nags Head area, 919-261-2224

has 120 cottages, 22 townhouses, and condos, some of which have a kennel on property and will allow dogs.

. Southern Shores Realty, Kitty Hawk area, 800-334-1000

has 400 cottages, 16 townhouses and condos. Some allow dogs. This area has golf, fishing, beach, tennis, horseback riding, boats, jogging, nature trails for walking your dog and yourself.

NEW BERN
SHERATON GRAND NEW BERN HOTEL, INN, AND MARINA

P. O. Box 130, New Bern 28563 919-638-3585

Offers 172 rooms, restaurant, swimming pool, golf privileges, tennis waterfront, bicycles,, canoes, boats, jogging, nature trails.

RATE: Inquire DOG: small dog allowed in 2 pet rooms.

RALEIGH
PLANTATION INN RESORT

6401 Capital Blvd, Raleigh 800-992-9662

Offers 95 rooms and suites, restaurant, swimming pool, golf privileges, waterfront, fishing pier, playground, jogging, nature trail.

RATE: Inquire DOG: $25 non-refundable fee, plus $5 each additional night.

VELVET CLOAK INN

1505 Hillsborough St, Raleigh 27605 800-334-4372, 919-828-0333

Offers 171 rooms, restaurant, swimming pool, jacuzzi, and an exercise area. RATE: Inquire DOG: allowed at $15 1 x charge

RODANTHE
HATTERAS ISLAND RESORT

P.O. Box 9, Rodanthe 27968 919-987-2345

Resort offers 35 cottages, and 28 rooms and 14 efficiencies. There is a restaurant, swimming pool, picnic area, waterfront, fishing pier, laundry, play ground, and dog kennel.

RATE: Inquire DOG: dog welcome, allowed in cottages at fee of $75.

A favorite scenic drive is the Pembina Gorge area, a beautiful forested valley and river. Theodore Roosevelt National Park is popular, as are the state parks. Lake Sakakaula and Devil's Lake areas offer recreational opportunities.

GOLDEN VALLEY
KNIFE RIVER RANCH

R.R. #1, Box 21A, Golden Valley 58541 701-983-4290
Hosts: Ron and Lois Wanner
This rustic ranch offers vacations in cabin accommodations with trail riding, hunting, swimming, canoeing, fishing, tubing, hiking, photography, camp fires, streak fries.
RATE: cabin 2-people $55 per night, $5 each addtl person. There is an extra charge for horseback riding, guide canoe rental, and horse boarding. DOG: allowed in cabins if in a kennel.

MINOT

This city is a hub for the lakes and gardens section of the State. Recreation areas include Devil's Lake and Lake Sakawea.

BEST WESTERN SAFARI INN

1510 26 Ave SW, Minot 800-528-1234, 701-852-4300
Offers 100 rooms, hot tub, TV, swimming pool, games room.
RATE: moderate DOG: small dog allowed

OHIO

Cincinnati and Cleveland are the major cities. Resort areas include hiking the trails in Wayne National Forest, and the Lake Erie islands resort area; Catawba Point, and Put-in-Bay a port village of South Bass Island.

CINCINNATI
HOLIDAY INN NORTH

2235 Sharon Road, Cincinnati 45241 513-771-0700, 800-308-DOME
This is a full service hotel and Holidome recreation area, with an olympic pool, indoor volleyball, golf, fitness, restaurant.
RATE: $99 dbl DOG: allowed in room but not in Holidome .

SHERATON SPRINGDALE HOTEL

11911 Sheraton Lane, Cincinnati 45246 513-671-6600, 800-325-3535
Beautiful surburban hotel with swimming pool, erercise room, and restaurant. RATE: $95 dbl DOG: allowed

CLEVELAND
THE RITZ-CARLTON

1515 W. Third Street, Cleveland 44113
216-623-1300, 800-241-3333
A gracious 4-star hotel offering 208 elegant rooms, 21 suites, fine restaurants, fitness center, swimming pool. High level of service. RATE: $159 dbl DOG: allowed if 20 lbs and under.

HURON
CLARION INN - TWINE HOUSE

132 N. Main Street, Huron 44839 419-433-8000, 800-947-3400
Located in the Sandusky area. 61 room Lake Erie hotel, restaurant, and entertainment, boating. Near recreational area.
RATE: $54 dbl DOG: allowed

LOUDONVILLE
LITTLE BROWN INN MOTEL

940 S Market Street, Loudonville 44842 419-994-5525
Offers 20 rooms near Mohican State Park and Amish Country. Skiing, hunting, boat rentals, golf, in a rural setting.
RATE: $40 dbl DOG: allowed

MARIETTA
BEST WESTERN MARIETTA

279 Muskingum Dr., Marietta 45750 800-528-1234, 614-374-7211
Offers 47 rooms on the Muskingum River. Free dockage. Golf and tennis nearby. RATE: $48 dbl DOG: allowed

NEWARK
CHERRY VALLEY LODGE

2299 Cherry Valley Road, Newark 43055
614-788-1200, 800-788-8008

This is a picturesque lodge on 13 country acres. Offers 120 rooms, restaurant, swimmming pool, fitness center. RATE: minimum dbl $124 DOG: allowed, with a refundable deposit. There is a wooded area for running and play with owner.

PORT CLINTON
L K INN

1811 Harbor Road, Port Clinton 43452
419-732-2111, 800-282-5711
Offers 66 rooms on a lake. Swimming and boating, walking.
RATE: minimum $35 DOG: allowed, any size, no charge

PAINESVILLE
RIDER'S INN , Bed & Breakfast

792 Menton Avenue, Painesville 44077 216-354-8200
Offers 11 rooms and bed and breakfast. Activities in the area include golf, tennis, boating. RATE: $75 dbl DOG: allowed

PORTSMOUTH
HOLIDAY INN

US Route 23N, Portsmouth 43662 614-354-2851, 800-HOLIDAY
Offers 100 rooms close to park, 2 golf courses, excellent fishing and boating on the Ohio River, seven stocked state park lakes and ponds. RATE: $50 dbl DOG: allowed

SANDUSKY
RADISSON HARBOUR INN

2001 Cleveland Road, Sandusky 44870 419-627-2500,
800-333-3333
Offers 237 rooms in a waterfront hotel with a resort atmosphere. Swimming, boating, fitness, walking. RATE: $149 dbl.
DOG: allowed with refundable $50 pet deposit against damages.

WARREN
AVALON INN & RESORT

9519 E. Market St, Warren 44484 330-856-1900, 800-528-2566
Resort offers 144 attractive rooms, 2 18-hole golf courses, pool, 3 tennis courts, saunas, exercise facilities, restaurant. RATE: $80 dbl DOG: allowed with permission of reservations manager

Oklahoma City is a major city. Drives to Wichita Mountains Wildlife Refuge and Ouachita National Forest in Southeast are popular. Visitors to the Southwest will find many natural attractions, magnificent parks and lakes, and local museums.

STATE PARK RESORTS

This State has some fine resorts , many with cabins or cottages as well as a lodge. Guests with a dog are allowed in cottages. They are not allowed in Lodge. They must be on leash while in the park. Kennels, where available, are complimentary. Resort cottages feature full maid service.

RATE: for central reservation service for all park resort cabins, call 800-654-8240 nationwide. Minimum rate about $58

Information about resorts follows:

BEAVER BEND 47 cabins, golf course, hiking trails, fishing, boating, swimming, tennis, riding.

QUARTZ MOUNTAIN 16 cabins, golf course, hiking trails, fishing, boating, swimming, waters skiing, archery, games.

LAKE MURRAY 88 cabins, air strip, golf course, hiking trails, fishing, boating, swimming, water skiing, archery, tennis, riding.

LAKE TEXOMA 67 cabins, air strip, golf course, hiking trails, fishing, boating, swimming, riding, games, tennis

ROMAN NOSE 16 cabins, golf course, hiking trails, fishing, boating, swimming, archery, riding, tennis, games.

WESTERN HILLS GUEST RANCH 54 cabins, air strip, golf course, fishing, boating, swimming, water skiing, riding, tennis, volleyball.

AFTON

MONKEY ISLAND EAST BAY RESORT

Off SH-125S, Afton 800-728-0968

Has five cabins for rent, available to dog owners. RATE: moderate

DOG: allowed

KINGSTON

SOLDIER CREEK RESORT & MARINA on Lake Texoma

Box 341, Kingston 73439 405-564-3670

Lake Texoma cabins and homes rentals, TV, swimming pool,

restaurant, marina, boats. "Best fishing on the lake".
RATE: inquire, moderate DOG: small dog allowed

OKLAHOMA CITY
CLARION HOTEL

4345 N Lincoln, Oklahoma City 73112 405-528-2741, 800-252-7466
Offers comfortable rooms, restaurant. RATE: inquire DOG: dog is allowed with extra fee.

HILTON INN

2945 Northwest Expressway, Oklahoma City 73112 800-848-4811, 405-848-4811
Offers 212 rooms near a lake. Cabanas, suites, cafe, swimming pool. RATE: inquire DOG: allowed up to 15 lbs

OREGON

This is a wonderful state to visit with a lots of space, beaches on an entire 300 mile coast are clean, white sand, and available to all. Crater Lake National Park is popular. There are 225 State parks, including a unique "forest park wilderness" within the city of Portland which has trails and animal species. Mount Hood draws visitors. The entire State invites you to hike, bike, fish, golf.

BEND
THE RIVERHOUSE

3075 N. Highway 97, Bend 97701 800-547-3928
This resort is located on the banks of the beautiful Deschusets River. There are 220 rooms. Recreation available includes indoor and outdoor heated pools, spas, saunas, golf courses, Nautilus exercise room, jogging trails, entertainment, dancing, shopping nearby. Three restaurants. Mt. Bachelor Nordic and Alpine skiing nearby. RATE: minimum approx. $55 DOG: allowed. Do not leave alone in room.

CAMP SHERMAN

COLD SPRINGS RESORT and RV Park

Cold Springs Resort Lane, HCR 1270, Camp Sherman 97730
503-595-6271 Host: Jim McLean

Located on the Metolius River, this small resort has cabins and RV park that welcome dogs. Acres of beautiful lawn roll gently down to the river. There is a footbridge, picnic tables and bar-b-ques. Within the resort guests hike, bike, fish, walk, watch wildlife and relax. Nearby is the Central Oregon Cascade Range in the heart of the Metolius River Wildlife Preserve and Recreation Area. Guests can enjoy golf, horseback riding, raft trips, canoeing, water skiing, and windsurfing. Hikers entering the Mt Jefferson Wilderness Area can experience scenic lakes, meadows, and wildflowers. Also, several small western towns are nearby. RATES: Minimum cabin dbl summer $91. Children under 6 free. RV rate dbl daily $16. DOG: Dog fee in cabins is $5 per night. There is a dog walking area and an entire forest to hike and bike with your dog.

CANNON BEACH

HALLMARK RESORT at Cannon Beach

1400 S. Hemlock, P.O. Box 547, Cannon Beach 97110
503-436-1566, 800-345-5676

This Pacific oceanfront resort overlooks famous Haystack Rock. The resort features oceanfront accommodations, fireplaces, kichen units, spa suites, exercise room, indoor pool, sauna, and 2 swirl pools. RATE: Minimum oceanfront bedroom (dbl) $139. Non-view (1-3 persons) $49. Minimum higher May 27-Sept 30. Inquire. DOG: Allowed with $10 per day non-refundable fee. Dogs allowed only in selected rooms. Please notify us of your pet arrival. Dogs are not to be left alone in room. Leash law in effect in area.

HAYSTACK RESORT

3339 So Hemlock, P.O. Box 219, Cannon Beach 97110
800-499-2220

This is a quality beach resort motel located in Cannon Beach at Tolovana Park, one block from beach overlooking beautiful Pacific.

Everything is new at the facility, except the view. Comfortable, clean, new accommodations are featured, with ocean views, fireplaces, kitchens, color TV and HBO, complimentary coffee, and a daily newspaper. There is a handicapped unit. Guests can swim in indoor heated pool and spa, walk the beach, hike the surrounding areas, and explore the communities. RATE: minimum, sleeping room (dbl) $89. Minumum suite 1-4 people, $139.
DOG: Welcome. Fee $5 per day.

SURFSAND RESORT

P.O. Box 219, Cannon Beach 97110 800-547-6100, 503-436-2274
Resort on the Pacific Ocean with a magnificent view of Haystack Rock. Heated swimming pool. Activities in immediate area include bike trails, fishing and crabbing, marked trails for day hikes, horseback riding along beach, visits to parks with picnics, whale and bird watching, tennis courts, art feativals, and more.
RATE: in low season rate about $129. Also houses for rent at about $169.
DOG: This is a "dog friendly" resort. Dogs welcome in most rooms at fee of $5 per day. Cannot leave dog unattended at any time. "Bowser bags" available at front desk for $12.

COOS BAY
RED LION INN

1313 N. Bayshore Dr., Coos Bay 541-267-4141
Offers 143 units in this resort area. Swimming, fishing, restaurant.
RATE: minimum $69 DOG: allowed

EUGENE
VALLEY RIVER INN

1000 Valley River Way, Eugene 800-543-8266, 541-687-0123
Offers 257 units, located on the banks of the beautiful Willamette River. Hiking, biking, swimming pool, shopping. RATE: min. $79
DOG: allowed.

GLENEDEN BEACH
SALISHAN LODGE

Highway 101, Gleneden Beach 97388
541-764-2371, 800-452-2300
This Lodge is a secluded, 400 acre forested nature preserve perched on the headlands overlooking Siletz Bay where the towering evergreens of Oregon's Coast Range meet the rolling dunes of the Pacific. A 2-hour drive from Portland, the Lodge offers first class service. 3 restaurants, 14 meeting rooms, library, wine cellar, gift shop, and 205 guest rooms with wood-burning fireplaces, balcony, carport. Activities include a par-72 golf course, indoor tennis center, fitness center with pool, sauna, nature trail system, fishing, shopping.
RATE: Minimum $110 DOG: Charge of $10 per night. Dog may not be left alone in guestroom.

GOLD BEACH
IRELAND'S RUSTIC LODGES

1120 E. Ellensburg Ave, Gold Beach 97444 541-247-7718
Offers seven 1-2 bedroom cabins in a wonderful landscape. Fireplace and deck overlook the sea. Motel rooms also available.
RATE: moderate. inquire DOG: allowed

JOT'S RESORT on the Oregon Coast

P.O. Box J, Gold Beach 97444 800-367-5687 541-247-6676
Here is where the Pacific Ocean and Rogue River meet to create unique recreational opportunities for the whole family...crabbing, clam digging, boating, biking, beach combing, trail riding, swimming, wind surfing, deep sea fishing and year-around salmon and steelhead angling on the Rogue, a wild and scenic river.
Jot's offers luxurious rooms, deep sea charters, jet boat trips, and professional guides, lively entertainment and elegant dining.
RATE: Minimum winter $50, summer $90
DOG: allowed in pet rooms at nightly fee of $10 per night for cleaning.

HOOD RIVER
COLUMBIA GORGE HOTEL

4000 Westcliff Dr, Hood River 97031
800-345-1931, 541-386-5566

For scenery, hiking, fishing, surfing, skiing, and rafting, choose this hotel on the Columbia River Gorge. Offers 42 rooms, dining room. RATE: about $150 DOG: allowed. no charge. Take extra care to keep your dog from falling in this gorge area.

HOOD RIVER INN
(Best Western)

1108 East Marina Way, Hood River 97031 541-386-2200
800-828-7873

Here is a comfortable resort lodging in a prime outdoor playground ...the Columbia River Gorge and surrounding forests of Mt Hood with wonderful vistas. Activities include endless trails for walking, hiking, mountain biking, golf courses, ski trails, windsurfing, white water rafting. Visit Lost Lake where many partake in fishing, canoeing, and swimming. Offers 149 guest rooms and suites, private swimming beach, heated pool, hot tub.

RATE: summer minimum $79 DOG: allowed @ $12 cleaning fee per day.

• PORTLAND
BENSON HOTEL

309 SW Broadway, Portland 503-228-2000, 800-426-0670

Luxurious old world hotel with 290 rooms and suites, restaurant, health club. RATE: minimum $165 DOG: allowed, must be well-behaved and house trained.

THE SWEETBRIER INN

7125 SW Nyberg Road, Tualatin 800-551-9167, 503-692-5800

Lovely hotel 10 minutes from downtown Portland. 132 rooms and suites in a beautiful garden setting, swimming pool, exercise facility, restaurant RATE: minimum $60 DOG: allowed. $25 cleaning fee Good location to walk dog.

MALLORY HOTEL

729 SW 15 Ave, Portland 503-223-6311, 800-228-8657

Confortable and quiet hotel with 136 units, restaurant. Near golf. RATE: minimum $65 DOG: allowed

WARM SPRINGS
KAH-NEE-TA RESORT

P.O. Box K, Warm Springs 97761 800-554-4SUN, 503-553-1112
This resort is owned by the Confederated Tribes of Warm Springs. It is the centerpiece of their 600,000 acre reservation, complete with a working ranch and wild horses. The Lodge is bathed in sunshine over 300 days a year. It's contemporary design rises unexpectedly from the side of a bluff. Easy to locate when driving. Activities available include hiking, guided horseback riding, 18-hole golf course, tennis courts, fishing for trout, whitewater rafting, mountain biking, kayaking, swimming in pool, a fitness center, mineral baths, and a game room. There is an Indian salmon bake. Meals are tastefully served. Live entertainment in evenings.
RATE: minimum 1 bedrm cottage $105
DOG: allowed in cottages only. $8 per night charge. Must be on leash at all times and not allowed in patio area.

WALDPORT
EDGEWATER COTTAGES

3978 SW Pacific Coast Highway, Waldport 97394 541-563-2240
Hosts: Cathy Sorenson, Chuck Turpin, Edgewater Crew
" A good place for kids and dogs and well-behaved adults".
Resort is family owned and operated for 35 years. It is centrally located on the Oregon coast, along an 8 mile beach. There are numerous state and federal parks and forests, tidepools, agate hunting beaches, sea lion viewing areas, horse stables, the Oregon Dunes National Recreation Area, golf courses, Seal Rock, and clamming and crabbing areas in Waldport nearby.
Cabins have an ocean view, electric heat, a fully equipped kitchen, color cable TV, firewood and linens provided. Portable crib is available. Smoking outside only. RATE: 2-6 night minimum on reservations. Additional charge for stays of less than 6 nights. Mar-Oct, or 3 nights Nov-Feb. Rates start at $50-$150 for 2 people.
DOG: Dogs welcome by advance reservation only, providing they are totally housebroken, not allowed on furniture, not left unattended, and not disturbing other guests. Charge $5-$10 per pet per night. Management may limit number of pets.

WELCHES

OLD WELCHES INN, Bed & Breakfast

26401 East Welches Road, Welches 97067 503-622-3754

Host: Judi and Ted Mondun

This Inn is in the heart of the Hoodland Recreation Area. Complete winter activities at Mt Hood; spring and summer fishing, hiking, on mountains and wilderness areas; golf at the resort across the road. No smoking indoors. Social drinking permitted. Children over 12. RATE: cottage minimum $130

DOG: allowed in cottage only. Fenced yard. Dogs love to play in river on property. Dog must be fully house trained and very friendly. There is a resident dog also.

YACHATS

YACHATS INN on the Ocean

331 So Pacific Coast Highway 101, PO Box 307, Yachats 97498
541-547-3456

This is a small, quiet retreat nestled between a dense pine forest and the rocky Pacific Coast with spectacular ocean views, a river and tide pools close by.

Guests can fish, clam and crab, watch wales play and feed off shore as they migrate winter and spring. There are state parks with picnic facilities, hiking trails, 2 golf courses, and horseback riding nearby. This area has many sightseeing attractions.

There are 20 rooms at the Inn, an indoor heated pool, fully equipped kitchens and fireplaces in many units, a recreation room, free color cable TV, and easy access to many secluded beaches nearby. RATE: Summer range $59 dbl. Children under 3 free. Inquire about off-season rates. DOG: Housebroken and well-behaved pets are welcome at a rate of $3 per night. State in advance reservation you are bringing a dog.

PENNSYLVANIA

Pennsylvania boasts a 500,000 acre Allegheny National Forest and more than 100 state parks. Philadelphia and Pittsburgh are the major cities with historic buildings, museums, Independence Square, the Liberty Bell, a zoo. Attractions in the State include the Pennsylvania Dutch Amish farms and buggies., and Hershey area dominated by the chocolate manufacturer. The Poconos is the major resort recreational area with mountains and wilderness bordering the Delaware River. Lots of activities in area including swimming, golf, boating, horseback riding, and hiking.

CHALK HILL
LODGE AT CHALK HILL

Box 240, Rt 40 East, Chalk Hill 15421 800-833-4283, 412-438-8880

A mountain retreat, this Lodge is on 37 lush acres in beautiful Laurel Highlands. There are 60 garden units with private decks, a Lodge with large TV and fireplace and kitchen. Complimentary Continental breakfast served. Activities include catch and release fishing at Lake Lenore, volleyball, a 1/2 mile jogging trail, and childrens play area. The front desk will help guests with their arrangements for horseback riding, golf, tours, white water rafting, skiing, sleigh rides, and biking along trails. RATE: minimum weekdays $53.95 DOG: Dog welcome charge $5.

COOKSBURG
FOREST VIEW CABINS
Cook Forest State Park

Box 105, Cooksburg 16217 814-744-8413

Host: Pat Fitzgerald

Offers completely furnished cabins located on a hill overlooking the Clarion River. There are 40 miles of trails, pine and hemlock forest on approximately 8,000 acres. Roads are good. Recreational facilities include saddle horses, bicycling, swimming, golf, canoeing, dancing, fishing, and hunting. In winter, ski, ice skate, and more. RATE: 2 people per day $85. 2 people per week $390. Off season rates, inquire. DOG: Welcome. $5 per day or $25 per week, for cleaning.

GOULDSBORO
BIG BASS LAKE
on top of the Poconos

P.O. Box 225, Gouldsboro 18424 800-762-6669, 717-842-7600
Host: John R. Larsen Corp.

Big Bass Lake is a planned leisure community on top of the Poconos. Larsen Realty rents 135 private homes in the area for the owners for a weekend, month or season. The recreation center includes a heated indoor swimming pool, sauna, lounge, private ski slope and lift, three large private lakes and the Lehigh River for fishing. There are 6 tennis courts, a clubhouse with courts, an outdoor pool, and a wading pool. Bordering Big Bass Lake is the Gouldsboro State Park with over 7,000 acres of trails, streams, lakes, and picnic areas. RATES: minimum 1-bedrm/bath, max capacity 6, weekend $300. Week $485.

LANCASTER
EDEN RESORT INN (Best Western)

222 Eden Street, Lancaster 17601 717-560-8441, 800-528-1234

Situated in Pennsylvania Dutch Country, this resort offers 275 beautifully appointed guest rooms, TV, climate control. Residential lodgings include fully equipped kitchens with dining area and living room with fireplace. Friendly service. Two restaurants, 2 swimming pools...indoor and out, tennis, games, golf, spa. In Lancaster County you can ride in an Amish horse and buggy, explore historic sites, go to auctions, and shop. RATE: moderate DOG: allow dogs under 40 lbs. Many paths on Inn property which dogs enjoy.

MT POCONO
MEMORYTOWN
THE HERITAGE INN

Grange Road, Mt Pocono 18344 717-839-1680

This is a country-style Inn located in the heart of the beautiful Pocono Mountains. Offers an ideal setting for a relaxing or action-packed vacation. Rooms and cottages available, TV, fireplace, climate control. There is a dining room and a Tavern and country store to browse. Activities available include fishing, paddleboats, lakes, hiking trails, ice skating, games, children's play area. In nearby Pocono attractions include golf courses, horseback riding, boating and fishing. RATE: summer, midweek $80 dbl Packages available. DOG: welcome

READING
DUTCH COLONY INN

4635 Perkiomen Ave, Reading 19606
610-779-2345, 800-828-2830

This is a very pleasant Inn for a traveler with a dog. Quiet and friendly, it is located minutes from Reading and one hour from Philadelphia. Comfortable rooms, pool, landscaped grounds bar and restaurant. There is a large lawn and wooded area with trails. RATE: $60 DOG: allowed at $5 per night

SWIFTWATER
THE BRITANNIA COUNTRY INN

Upper Swiftwater Road, P.O. Box 8, Swiftwater 18370
717-839-7243 Host: Bob & Joan Steven

This Inn is "A Taste of England in the Heart of the Poconos" run by a warm British family. In a quiet country setting, the Inn has 12 acres with an outdoor pool. Rooms and various size cottages are available. All with private baths. The restaurant offers classic English dishes as well as traditional American favorites. Activities in the area include hiking, biking, white water rafting, swimming, lawn sports, golfing, horseback riding, and weekly bonfires.
In winter, enjoy 5 major ski areas nearby. Snowmobiling, cross-country skiing, ice skating, sledding all nearby. Pocono attractions also include shopping, Delaware Water Gap, Bushkill Falls, theater, Promised Land State Park, International Raceway, outlet stores.
RATE: minimum room $30 per person weekday, cottage $40.
DOG: Dogs welcome at fee of $20 per stay, per dog. Dog cannot be left alone unless in crate. Lots of fun to be had. The Pocono mountains is full of State Parks which offer fabulous hiking trails.

WHITE HAVEN
THE MOUNTAIN LAUREL RESORT
Conference Hotel and Golf Club

P.O. Box 126, White Haven 18661 800-458-5921, 717-443-8411
This is an elegant resort in a beautiful, unspoiled, private part of the Pocono Mountain range. Open all year. Get there by air or 2 hour drive from New York City. Shuttle service available. Remarkable collection of restaurants with world-class cuisine., nightclub. Activities include an 18-hole golf course, indoor and outdoor pools, health club, tennis center, games, winter ski trails, sledding, ice skating. Horseback riding 1/2 mile from resort. The resort is located on 300 wooded acres featuring numerous trails for hiking and biking. Northeastern Mts lie beyond the resort, and Hickory Run State Park has various recreational facilities, including fishing and rafting. There is a "Leave the Kids with Us" program...a summer day camp for age 6 and over. Others for younger children. There is a petting farm kids enjoy.
RATE: summer minimum $84 midweek, weekend $99
DOG: allowed

RHODE ISLAND

Visitors to this State visit the grand mansions of Newport, a haven for yachtsmen, and tour 400 miles of shoreline, through parks, forests, and beaches. Block Island is popular.

BLOCK ISLAND
1661 INN & GUEST HOUSE and HOTEL MANISSES

1 Spring Street, Block Island 02807 401-466-2421, 800-626-4773
Block Island is a secluded, lovely island with unspoiled beaches, and grassy cliffs and gentle hills. There is a variety of accommodations, but dog is allowed in the Guest Cottage only, not the hotel or Inn. Guests enjoy an animal farm and gardens, nature walks, buffet breakfast, and wine and nibble hour every afternoon.
RATE: minimum $75 DOG: allowed in Off-season only (after end of October) in the Guest Cottage only.

LEWIS FARM COTTAGES

Cooneymus Road, Block Island 02807 401-466-5093, 401-822-1435
Owner rents cottages by the week on this lovely island. RATE: inquire DOG: allowed. No charge.

NEWPORT/MIDDLETOWN

HOWARD JOHNSON LODGE
Newport

351 West Main Road, Middletown 401-849-2000, 800-654-2000
Offers 155 comfortable rooms outside Newport. swimming pool, tennis courts, restaurant, lounge. Adjacent to shopping center. Attractions in historic Newport include magnificent mansions along Cliff Walk, fine swimming beaches, fabulous shopping, and exciting festivals. RATE: summer minimum about $79
DOG: welcome in selected rooms.

PROVIDENCE

HOLIDAY INN, Providence Downtown

1-95 at Atwells Ave, Providence 02903 401-831-3900, 800-HOLIDAY
Offers 274 delux guest rooms, restaurant, pool, exercise room.
RATE: moderate DOG: allowed

PRIVIDENCE BILTMORE

Kennedy Plaza, Providence 02903 800-294-7709, 401-421-0700
Offers 214 rooms , fitness senter, restaurant. RATE: inquire
DOG: allowed

PROVIDENCE MARRIOTT

Charles & Orms Street, Providence 401-272-2400, 800-937-PROV
Offers 345 rooms, swimming pool, restaurant, lounge. Golf, tennis, boating, beaches nearby. RATE: inquire DOG: allowed at fee of $25.

SOUTH CAROLINA

Visitors here must see Charleston, with historic homes and buildings and churches. There are wonderful plantations and gardens as well as public parks. Along the coast, the Grand Strand is the top tourist area with 50 miles of beaches and recreation.

ANDERSON

CENTENNIAL PLANTATION Bed & Breakfast

1308 Old Williamston Road, Anderson 29621 864-225-4448
Host: Georgann and Ed Fontaine
This accommodation is a 100 year old farm on 10 acres, with horses, goats, and chickens roaming the pastures. Relaxed atmosphere. Three rooms available. Upcountry, Anderson is near a state park and Lake Hartwell. RATE: minimum $45 DOG: allowed. Has fenced outside kennel with dog house, or dog can sometimes stay inside with owner at host discretion. Dog must be well-behaved. Dog should be on leash when walked. Charge $15 per night.

CHARLESTON

SHERATON CHARLESTON

170 Lockwood Drive, Charleston 29403 803-723-3000
Offers 337 rooms, restaurant, tennis privileges. RATE: minimum $140. DOG: allowed, no charge.

TOWN and COUNTRY INN

2008 Savannah Hwy, Charleston 29407 803-571-1000,
800-334-6660
Offers 130 rooms, restaurant, swimming pool, sauna, fitness center, Golf and tennis in the area. RATE: minimum $59 DOG: allowed, no charge

EDISTO ISLAND

EDISTO ISLAND RENTALS

Edisto Sales & Rentals Realty

P.O. Box 8, 1405 Palmetto Blvd, Edisto Island 29438
800-868-5398, 803-869-2527
Edisto Island is 45 miles south of Charleston, SC. It is a non-commercialized, family style vacation beach. In addition to the beach, the island offers a state park, yacht basin, golf driving range, coves and creeks to explore, shops, restaurants, tennis courts, and a golf course. RATE: there are cottages, villas, and beach-front homes available. Rates vary. DOG: This company handles about 10 properties that will allow pets. Contact them for information. Edisto Beach has a leash law from Easter 'til October from 7am-10pm on beach. Otherwise voice command in effect.

• HILTON HEAD ISLAND
RED ROOF INN

Hwy 278, Hilton Head Island 29928 803-686-6808,800-843-7663
Moderate inn with comfortable accommodations.
RATE: minimum $38 DOG: allowed

HILTON HEAD ISLAND RENTALS
R.H. Realty & Rentals

6 Lagoon Road, Hilton Head 29928, 800-845-6802, 803-842-6212
Hilton Head Island is famous for its beautiful blue water, wide white beaches, fantastic accommodations, sporting events, unspoiled natural beauty, and excellent restaurants. You can reach the island by car or plane. There are golf courses, marinas, stables, excellent fishing, tennis courts, theaters, restaurants, and unique shopping. Various properties available...condos, villas, and homes.
RATES: variable DOG: Certain villas are available or special arrangements can be made to accommodate a guest with a dog. Must be advance arrangements. Inquire.

• MYRTLE BEACH
BEST WESTERN LANDMARK RESORT HOTEL

1501 S Ocean Blvd, Myrtle Beach 29577 800-845-0658
803-448-9441
Come for a complete Myrtle Beach vacation at this oceanfront setting, just steps from the beach, and minutes from amusements, shopping, dining, golf, and more. There are 327 oceanview rooms, a restaurant, lounge, and year 'round oceanside pool and sauna. Packages allow you to choose over 80 nearby golf courses, charter fishing, theaters. From Memorial Day to Labor Day, dogs not allowed on beach. Otherwise they are allowed on beach. RATE: about $100 in summer DOG: permit dogs under 25 lbs, who are well-behaved. $50 damage deposit required.

COMFORT INN

2801 S Kings Highway, Myrtle Beach 29577 800-868-1990,
803- 626-4444
Offers 151 rooms, continental breakfast, fitness center, pool.
RATE: summer minimum $75 DOG: allowed. no charge

DAYS INN, Waccamaw

3650 US 501 N., Myrtle Beach 29577
800-528-3875, 803-236-1950
Located on the highway. 159 rooms, swimming pool, restaurant, open all year. RATE: minimum summer $129 DOG: allowed @ $5 per day

FOUNTAINBLEU INN

701 N. Flagg St, Myrtle Beach 29577
803-448-8461 800-331-7300
Offers 61 rooms, swimming pool. RATE: minimum about $40
DOG: deposit required. Pet agreement must be signed for damages.

CASA DE ORO/STOKES

1610 S Ocean Blvd, North Myrtle Beach 29582 803-272-8184
Offers 28 apartments and rooms on oceanfront.
RATE: apartment in summer $600 per week (for 2 people)
DOG: allowed, no charge unless damage

SALEM

KEOWEE KEY RESORT

1-85 Exit 1 at SC 130 & 183, Salem 29676 864-944-1333
This is a 125 unit resort, swimming pool, restaurant, with 1-4 bedroom villas and townhouses located on a lake. Golf privileges.
RATE: minimum sgl $145 DOG: allowed in some units, no charge.

SOUTH DAKOTA

Visitors to this State explore Badlands and Black Hills National Forest, Custer State Park, Mt Rushmore, Deadwood, and Sioux Falls. and the prairies, rocky landscapes, and pine forests of this area.

CHAMBERLAIN

CEDAR SHORE RESORT (Radisson)

101 George S. Mickelson Shore Line Drive, Chamberlain 57325
605-734-6376, 800-333-3333
This is an exceptional resort hotel in an unspoiled area. It is nestled on lush banks of the Missouri River, surrounded by miles

of wild and beautiful shoreline and miles of water. Guest rooms have cable TV, private decks, bar, refrigerator, microwaves and coffee. There is a heated indoor swimming pool, exercise and game rooms, restaurant and lobby bar. Activities in this great area include: hiking, boating, swimming, horseback riding, jet skiing, mountain biking, golf, tennis, fishing, paddleboats, hunting, beach. A marina is nearby with boat rentals. RATE: minimum summer about $89 dbl. DOG: allowed. Pet charge $10

CUSTER STATE PARK RESORT, CO

HC 83 - Box 74, Custer 57730 800-658-3530, 605-255-4515
Closed in winter. Call for specific dates.
"Custer State Park is where bison roam free, where granite spires tower over pristine lakes, and where mountain streams flow through unspoiled forests...73,000 acres of natural beauty." Explore a scenic footpath, take a Safari Jeep Ride to scout bison or just look out your car window to see possible bison, elk, deer, goats, eagles, coyotes, bobcats and more. Scenic drives include Needles Highway through majestic granite spires, Iron Mountain Road to Mt Rushmore, or traverse the Wildlife Loop among hills. Swim, boat, hike, ride horseback, spend an evening at the Black Hills Playhouse. Trails are designated for hiking, horseback riding, and mountain biking. There are four beautiful lodges and resort settings. Sylvan Lake Resort, State Game Lodge Resort, Legion Lake Resort, and Blue Bell Lodge & Resort. All have cabins of various sizes.
RATE: minimum cabin rate (1-4 persons) $65 & up
DOG: allowed in cabins only @ $5 a day in any of the four resorts. No restrictions, however, dog must be controlled.

HERMOSA

J-D GUEST RANCH, Bed & Breakfast

HCR 89, Box 53, Hermosa 57744 800-261-3329
This B & B has a lodge and house with room accommodations. Located next to Custer State Park, there are lots of recreational facilities, including horses. RATE: Inquire DOG: allowed in kennel outside or inside with owner.

TENNESSEE

Visitors to this State may want to visit Memphis, the largest city and the financial and cultural center. It is also closely associated with the Blues and Rock and Roll music. Nashville is the country music capital, which has a lovely lake nearby, parks and recreational facilities. East Tennessee is a major recreation area with lots of recreation in the mountain areas of the Great Smokys.

CELINA
CEDAR HILL RESORT

2371 Cedar Hill Road, Celina 38551 615-243-3201

Host: R Roberts, manager

This is a full-service resort located on Dale Hollow Lake. The resort offers 1-2-3 bedroom cabins, modern houseboats, motel rooms, swimming pool, restaurant, and dock facilities. Dale Hollow Lake offers 620 miles of shoreline with lots of coves and islands. It's crystal clear water and wooded mountains make this lake the "most beautiful lake in the Southeastern United States". Favorite activities are fishing for Blue Gill, Striped Bass, Walleye, Small-mouth and Largemouth Bass, Muskie, Trout...waterskiing, skuba diving in this calm water makes a great vacation. There is lots of space to walk and run a dog.

RATE: Minimum summer cabin rate (2-bedrm, 4 people) minimum $88 daily, $445 weekly DOG: welcome at charge of $15 daily or $60 weekly. No restrictions.

CUMBERLAND GAP
HOLIDAY INN

P.O. Box 37, Cumberland Gap 37724 423-869-3631

800-HOLIDAY

Offers 147 in Cumberland Gap area, restaurant, swimming pool, golf. RATE: moderate DOG: allowed

GATLINBERG
HOLIDAY INN RESORT COMPLEX

520 Airport Road, Gatlinberg 37738 423-436-9201, 800-435-9201

Located at the entrance to Great Smoky Mts National Park. Offers 402 rooms, restaurant, lounge, swimming pool, exercise room, indoor recreation center. RATE: moderate DOG: allowed

WA-FLOY MOUNTAIN VILLAGE

3610 East Parkway, Gatlinburg 37738 423-436-5575
Host: Floy S. Bell
There is nature's therapy in getting away to a mountain. In this 100 acre mini-village, accommodations include 18 cottages, 8 group facilities, available for Christian retreats. There are 2 tennis courts, a swimming pool, fishing lakes, large play areas, and trails that lead into the Great Smoky Mountain National Park. Lovely acres are adorned by vegetation and flowers, streams, woods, and green fields. RATE: minimum cottage rate $45 per night
DOG: small dog allowed at nominal additonal charge

HAMPSHIRE

RIDGETOP Bed & Brkfst

Highway 412, Hampshire 38461 615-285-2777, 800-377-2770
A cottage and cxabin with fireplace on contemporary home property set on 170 wooded acres 4 miles from Natchez Trave, are available to guests with a dog. There are hiking trails, streams, and wild flowers. RATE: about $85 minimum DOG: no charge

KINGSPORT

SHADOWILDE MANOR,Bed & Brkfst

252 Ollis Bowers Hill Road, Kingsport 37664
423-323-4861, 423-288-9219 Host: Katherine, Elizabeth, and Charlene Grigsby
This bed and breakfast getaway is "southern charm graced by modern conveniences". Three cozy rooms available. Breakfast served poolside, in gazebo, porch, or dining room. Snacks in afternoon. Quiet country seclusion with trees, wildflowers, and rolling mountains. Property has 75 acres for dog to roam, including a trail along creek, plus cattle trails. RATE: minimum $69. Children over 14 allowed. Smoking outside. DOG: no charge, but dog not allowed inside house.

MEMPHIS

BROWNESTONE HOTEL

300 N Second, Memphis 38105 901-525-2511, 800-468-3515
Offers 243 rooms, restaurant, TV, lounge, swimming pool.
RATE $35 minimum DOG: allowed

COUNTRY SUITES BY CARLSON

4300 American Way, Memphis 38118 901-366-9333
800-456-4000
Offers 120 suites, kitchen, TV, exercise room, swimming pool.
RATE: moderate DOG: allowed

EMBASSY SUITES

1022 S Shady Grove Rd, Memphis 38120 901-684-1777
800-362-2779
Offers 220 suites, TV, exercise room, lounge, swimming pool, golf. RATE: inquire DOG: allowed

PIGEON FORGE
MOUNTAIN VALLEY PROPERTIES

513 Wears Valley Road, Suite 2, Pigeon Forge 37863
800-644-4859, 423-429-5205
Rents affordable luxury cabins and chalets, fully equipped. Hot tubs, fireplaces, decks, swimming, tennis. RATE: minimum $90
DOG: currently 8 properties will allow a pet dog

SPRINGVILLE
MANSARD ISLAND RESORT on Kentucky Lake

Rt 1, Box 261, Springville 38256 800-533-5590, 901-642-5590
This resort is 90 miles from Nashville, and 130 miles from Memphis. It is a perfect place for a quiet get-away or family vacation...laid back, fun, affordable. There is a swimming pool, tennis courts, playground, grocery store, and full-service marina with fishing needs and boat rentals. Nearby, areas offer Civil War history, sightseeing and antique shopping. Paris Landing State Park is 5 miles away with a top golf course. Available are cottages, townhouse apartments, mobile homes, and camping facilities.
RATE: minimum daily 2-bedrm cottage $60, weekly $300
DOG: allowed with $25 deposit per dog. no restrictions.

Texas boasts a number of interesting cities, Houston and Galveston, San Antonio, Dallas, Ft Worth. South Padre island is a resort area, as are Big Bend National Park and Davy Crockett National Forest.

AUSTIN
LAKE AUSTIN SPA RESORT

1705 Quinlan Park Road, Austin 78732 512-266-2444
This resort is in Texas Hill Country about 20 miles from Austin. Guests enjoy water views from lakeside cottages, lush gardens, and numerous recreational facilities. Spa emphasis is on relaxation and wholesome food and healthy movement. Fitness classes, walking, hikes, line dancing, tennis, swimming pool, steam rooms, mountain bikes and paddle boats available. Also aerobics and yoga.
RATE: variety of packages. 3-night sampler package is $835.
DOG: allowed if under 30 lbs. with $100 refundable deposit. Not allowed in resort buildings except in guest room. Guest must clean-up after pet. Dogs can enjoy walking, hiking, and swimming.

BANDERA
COOL WATER ACRES, Bed & Brkfst

Rt 1, Box 785, Bandera 78003 210-796-4866
Offers rooms and cabins on 50 acres overlooking 7 acre lake, hills and horses. Swimming, fishing, hiking, golf nearby. There are farm animals and a country farm atmosphere. RATE: minimum $50
DOG: allowed. must be well-behaved or kept on leash. Lots of farm animals of all kinds. No charge.

CENTER POINT
MARIANNE'S Bed & Bkfst

Rt 1, Box 527, Center Point 78010 210-634-7489
Host: Marianne & Dave Zuercher
This is a lovely, large brick home on a hill on 18 acres, located near Kerrville. Guests can relax in giant hot tub, walk the many trails, fish , relax on patio. There are sheep, lambs, deer and other wildlife on the ranch. Available are 2 rooms in the house and a separate cottage. Gourmet breakfast with a German touch is always enjoyed. Nearby Kerrville has restaurants, golf, parks, arts and crafts. RATE: cottage $85, bedroom in house $75. DOG: must be housebroken. Large fenced yard available. Walk trails on leash.

CONROE
HOLIDAY INN CONROE

1601 1-45, South Conroe 77301 409-756-8941
Lake Conroe resort area. Offers 136 rooms with continental breakfast, swimming pool, restaurant; golf nearby. RATE: $67 DOG: dog allowed, no charge

CORPUS CHRISTI
HOLIDAY INN AT NO PADRE ISLAND

15202 Windward Drive, Corpus Christi 78418 512-949-8041
This is a full service hotel directly on the shores of the Gulf of Mexico at North Padre Island. There are 148 guest rooms, some oceanfront. Amenities include cable TV and HBO, coffee makers, a restaurant, live entertainment, and outdoor swimming pool. There is golf, tennis, sailing, wind surfing, and shopping nearby. Fishing and deep sea fishing are popular. RATE: minimum $70 DOG: An Inn representative says "Dogs and their people visiting our area love to run along the beach or the seawall...about one mile long in front of the hotel" The Gulf is warm enough to enjoy swimming. Charge $10 per visit with $50 refundable deposit for cash paying guests. No restrictions.

DALLAS
CRESCENT COURT

400 Crescent Court, Dallas 214-871-3200, 800-654-6541
Upscale hotel offering 190 rooms and 28 suites. Offers luxury, style and excellent service. Courtyard, shops, fountain, swimming pool, spa, free shuttle service. RATE: expensive, inquire
DOG: allowed with $50 deposit, refundable at checkout.

MANSION ON TURTLE CREEK

2821 Turtle Creek Blvd, Dallas 75219 800-527-5432
214-559-2100
The Mansion on Turtle Creek has taken top honors among all American hotels for everything...service, restaurants, other facilities, and rooms. It is one of the finest in the world...a classis hotel where you experience the ultimate sensation of quality, style, and elegance. Offers 128 luxurious guest rooms and 14 suites with

butler-style service. Cuisine is Southwest, International, and American dishes. Swimming pool, golf nearby. The hotel is nestled on a 4 1/2 acre estate overlooking Turtle Creek. The delightful Lee Park is nearby, as are cultural facilities and shopping.
RATE; minimum sgl $255 DOG: Dog under 50 lbs allowed with a $50 non-refundable fee. over 50 lbs $100 deposit, damage waiver

RADISSON HOTEL DALLAS

1893 West Mockingbird, Dallas 75235 800-333-3333
214-634-8850
Offers 305 rooms, restaurant, swimming pool, workout facilities, cocktail lounge. RATE: minimum $89 DOG: $25 non-refundable fee

• HOUSTON

DOUBLETREE HOTEL

15747 John F Kennedy Blvd, Houston 77032 800-810-8001, 713-442-8000
Offers 309 units, restaurant swimming pool, workout facilities, golf nearby. RATE: $95 DOG: allowed

WESTIN OAKS

5011 Westheimer, Houston 77056 800-228-3000, 713-960-8100
Offers 406 attractive rooms, restaurant, tennis courts, pool, golf nearby, free parking, shopping. RATE: $165 DOG: accepts small well-trained dog

• GALVESTON

THE TREMONT HOUSE

2300 Ship's Mechanic Row, Galveston 77550
800-874-2300, 409-763-0300
Offers 117 units in the Galveston area, restaurant, golf nearby.
RATE: $130 DOG: allowed, no charge

• GRANITE SHOALS

TROPICAL HIDEAWAY

Beach Resort & Marina on Lake LBJ

604 Highcrest Drive, Granite Shoals 78654
800-662-4431, 210-598-9896

This resort is described as a truly tropical beach resort on magnificent Lake LBJ. It is 10 acres overlooking a private beach and Tiki Village with sun decks, huts, and waterfalls. Traditional Hawaiian luaus offered. There is a full marina with sailing craft, boat and jet ski rentals, 2 private pools, lighted tennis facilities, unique children's playground, and 4 challenging golf courses nearby.
RATE: Resort offers 1-2 bedroom suites w/living area.
1 bedrm suites $125 per night, 2 bedrm suites $175 per night.
Special packages available.
DOG: allowed at resort, but not allowed on beach area.

• HOUSTON
FOUR SEASONS HOTEL, HOUSTON CENTER

1300 Lamar Street, Houston 77010 713-650-1300
With 399 guest rooms and 12 suites, elegantly appointed, this hotel is ideal for a Houston get-away. Wortham Theater Center, Kones Hall, and the Alley Theater are within a pleasant walk. Climate-controlled walkways connect you directly to corporate offices and Houston's cosmopolitan shops. There is a swimming pool, sauna, and games room. The Houston Center Athletic Club is available with complete facilities, including racquet courts and paddeed padded jogging track. Also, fine dining facilities. RATE: minimum $185 DOG: all dogs accepted. The hotel concierge will walk your dog if you wish.

• KERRVILLE
Y.O. RANCH HOTEL, Holiday Inn

2033 Sidney Baker, Kerrville 78028 210-257-4440
This is a 200 room western hotel located in the heart of Texas Hill country. There are a variety of casually elegant rooms, a swimming pool with swim-up bar, a jacuzzi, game room, lighted tennis courts, basketball court, and access to 2 quality golf courses. There is a Saloon. This hotel "lives the Texas legend". Nearby you will find festivals, shopping, tours, art and museums, parks, recreation including bird watching, horseback riding, hunting, camera safari, an exotic game ranch, play golf, and visit and hike the parks. RATE: Minimum $85 DOG: allowed. No charge.

• KINGSVILLE
B BAR B RANCH INN

R.R. 1, Box 457, Kingsville 78363 512-296-3331

A unique South Texas B & B, this restored lodge was once a part of the historic King Ranch, and is completely surrounded by a 220 acre working ranch. Fresh air, green lawns, swimming pool, hay rides, fresh water pond, with Baffin Bay nearby for fishing . Golf also nearby. Tours of the legendary King Ranch are available. House has 6 bedrooms/baths and a pool house with more beds, TV. RATE: minimum $75 DOG: must be kept in kennel on property, not inside, but can be taken out during the day. Lots of space to run and play on property.

• LEAKEY
WHISKEY MOUNTAIN INN

HCR 1, Box 555, Leakey 78873 210-232-6797

Host: Darrell & Judy Adams

This Inn offers bed and breakfast and 3 housekeeping cabins. A German farmhouse, it was built in 1869 and has a 50' porch and a tin roof. This is a scenic rustic getaway...relax in wicker rockers and watch the abundant wildlife...deer, rabbits, birds, racoon, and even an occasional bobcat. Located near State parks, museums, shopping, hiking, fishing, hunting, cycling. Hiking trails on property. RATE: 3 cabins. minimum $50 DOG: welcome. Trails can be enjoyed on property and can swim in river.

• MABANK
HEAVENLY ACRES, Bed & Bkfst/ Guest Ranch

Rt 3, Box 470, Mabank 75147

located 12 mi southwest of Canton off Hwy #198

800-283-0341, 903-887-3016 Host: Vickie J and Marshall E Ragle

This country get-away is on an East Texas Ranch of 100 acres, 12 miles southwest of Canton,. There are 6 accommodations. Four individual cabins (1-4 people), one for up to 9 guests, the other up to 20 people., with TV, kitchens, and all comforts of home. Dining Hall seats up to 50. Each cabin overlooks one of two private spring fed lakes, fully stocked. Small fishing or paddle boats provided. This is a beautiful country spread, with warm and hospitable hosts. Lovely meadows and walking paths around each lake for hiking, and a large outdoor gamefield. There is also a petting zoo, the "Critter Corral" and a variety of domestic and exotic animals. RATE: $95 per night (dbl) Ask about discounts. Children welcome in specified cabins. DOG: Welcome with prior approval for certain cabins. No charge. Dog can run, play, and swim here. A "Great Escape" for city dog and owner.

PORT ARANSAS on Mustang Island
BEACHGATE CONDOMINIUMS

1922 On the Beach, PO Box 890, Port Aransas 78373
512-749-5900
Accommodations on Mustang Island, adjoins Padre Island, for those interested in beach, surfing, swimming. Offers 5 units that sleep 6 in each unit. Kitchens, patios. 2-day minimum stay.
RATE: inquire DOG: allowed, small fee

ROCKPORT
LAGUNA REEF HOTEL

1021 Water Street, Rockport 78382 800-248-1057, 512-729-1742
Hotel located on the coast. Offers 70 rooms, swimming pool, golf nearby. RATE: $60 minimum DOG: allowed with $40 deposit, refundable, plus $5 per day.

SAN ANTONIO
HOLIDAY INN RIVERWALK

217 North St Marys St, San Antonio 78205 210-224-2500
Offers 313 rooms, restaurant, workout facilities, swimming pool.
RATE: $125 DOG: allowed

SAN ANTONIO MARRIOTT RIVERWALK

711 E. Riverwalk, San Antonio 78205 800-648-4462
Offers 500 rooms, restaurant, workout facility, golf nearby.
RATE: $149 DOG: allowed

SEVEN OAKS HOTEL

1400 Austin Hgh, San Antinio 78209 800-346-5866, 210-824-5371
Offers 189 rooms with resort-type activities. Restaurant, 3 tennis

courts, work-out facilities, golf on premises, outdoor pool, volleyball, sand court. RATE: $50 DOG: $100 deposit against damages, refundable on checkout.

SOUTH PADRE ISLAND
RADISSON RESORT on So Padre Island

500 Padre Blvd, South Padre Island 78597 800-333-3333, 210-761-6511

This 10-acre beachfront resort has just completed a multi-million dollar renovation, with upgraded facilities and tropical atmosphere. It is located on the southern tip of the Texas coast, surrounded by the Gulf of Mexico and Laguna Madre Bay. There are 2 swimming pools, 3 jacuzzis, 4 lighted tennis courts. Beachfront water sports include parasailing, jet skiing, deep sea fishing, and sailing. The sand is pure white and sun-drenched. Shopping, dining. RATE: Minimum May-Sept $135. DOG: small dog allowed. $100 refundable deposit if no damage.

WIMBERLEY
THE HOMESTEAD Bed & Brkst

PO Box 1034, Ranch Road 12 at Country Road 316, Wimberley 78676 800-918-8788

Offers 17 units including 8 cottages with bath. Continental breakfast, 1,000' of swimmable Cypress Creek, decks, fireplaces, TV. Children welcome. Minimum 2-ngt stay, 3-ngts on holiday. RATE: $85 minimum DOG: allowed @$10 per ngt. Lots of property for walking dog.

UTAH

This State is known for Salt Lake City, plus five national parks and 44 state parks in interesting and dramatic country.

BEAVER
ELK MEADOWS SKI & SUMMER RESORT

PO Box 511, Beaver 84713 800-248-7669, 801-438-5433

This is an all-season resort located in Southwest Utah offering houses or condos for rent. Hiking, cycling, skiing, exercise equipment, restaurant. RATE: inquire DOG: in certain house or cabins Inquire.

BRYCE
PINK CLIFFS VILLAGE

13500 East Highway 12, PO Box 640006, Bryce 84764
801-834-5351, 800-834-0043

This motel, in Bryce Canyon country's most scenic and convenient location has recently been remodeled and redecorated. Rooms are comfortable. There is an indoor swimming pool, and restaurant. Location ideal for those interested in Bryce Canyon with thousands of miles of beauty; 2 miles from Bryce Canyon National Park, with high mountain lakes and streams with trails, green pines and blue spruce. In vicinity there are 2 national parks, 3 state parks, a giant national recreational area, wild animals, peaceful farms and ghost towns. Scenic attractions unmatched.
RATE: summer minimum sgl $76.30 DOG: $5 per dog in room.

GARDEN CITY
HARBOR VILLAGE RESORT

900 North Bear Lake Blvd, PO Box 201, Garden City 84028
801-946-3448, 800-324-6840

Offers 45 rooms near beautiful Bear Lake. Beaches, boating, and jogging trail. RATE: moderate DOG: no charge. must be controlled.

MOAB
PACK CREEK RANCH

La Sal Pass Road, P.O. Box 1270, Moab 84532 801-259-5505
Host: Ken & Jane Sleight

You'll find a warm welcome and a unique western experience located in the beautiful foothills of the La Sal Mts. The ranch is secluded, near Canyonlands National Park. Cabins offered are rustic and cozy, varying in size up to accommodations for 15 people. Enjoy scrumptious meals in the evening, a hot breakfast and luch buffet. Evenings are simple. Horseback riding is central with gentler horses and experienced wranglers...a safe and scenic way to see the high country. Also lots of wilderness hiking. Outdoor pool, hot tub, sauna, massage. Nearby, white water rafting, tours of Lake Powell, biking, jeep tours, and skiing. RATE: Summer cabin $125 per person, winter (Nov-Mar) $56.50, Trail rides from ranch 1 hour $15., 2 hrs $25. DOG: allowed on leash only. Owner is liable for damages.

SALT LAKE CITY

SALT LAKE HILTON HOTEL

150 W. 500 South, Salt Lake City 801-532-3344, 800-421-7602
Offers 350 rooms and suites, outdoor pool, sauna, restaurant.
RATE: moderate DOG: allowed

SALT LAKE MARRIOTT HOTEL

75 South West Temple, Salt Lake City 801-531-0800, 800-345-4754
Offers 515 rooms, swimming pool, saunas, restaurant.
RATE: moderate DOG: allowed

SPRINGDALE

CLIFFROSE LODGE

281 Zion Park Blvd, PO Box 510, Springdale 84767
800-243-8824, 801-772-3234
Offers 36 rooms near gateway to Zion National Park. Swimming pool. RATE: moderate DOG: $10 1 x fee. Dog cannot be left alone in the room.

VERMONT

A lovely vacation area, Vermont has many small towns, 300,000 acres of Green Mountain National Forest, numerous state parks, Resorts offer trails, swimming, fishing, and skiing. Popular towns to explore are Montpelier, Bennington, Manchester, Woodstock and Stowe.

ARLINGTON

HILL FARM INN

RR 2, Box 2015, Arlington 05250 800-882-2545, 802-375-2269
Host: George & Joanne Hardy
Historic Hill Farm is one of Vermont's first country inns, operating since 1905. It is surrounded by 50 acres of farmland with a mile of frontage on the Battenkill River. There are spectacular views. Offers warm country hospitality, homemade breds and cookies, cozy cabins with open porches. Very relaxed and friendly.
Activities include:
In spring, fish or canoe the Battenkill, shop, hunt for antiques.

In summer, hike mountain and forest trails, bike country roads, swim in lakes, streams, and the old quarry, and enjoy summer theater. In fall, capture the beauty of fall foliage on film or canvas, drive up Mt Equinox Skyline Drive, jog the back roads. In winter, downhill or crose-country ski, or just read a good book by the fire. RATE: Minimum cabin from $75 dbl, includes full hot country breakfast and afternoon snacks. DOG: Dog welcome in cabins only @ $5 per day, per pet. NOTE: smoking permitted only on porches and grounds.

AVERILL
QUIMBY COUNTRY LODGE & COTTAGES

Rte 114, Forest Lake Road, Averill 05901 802-822-5533
Offers quaint cottages on 700 acres, secluded lake. Swimming, hiking, tennis, fishing, canoes, sailboats, maid service. RATE: $83 min. DOG: welcome. no charge

BOLTON VALLEY

BOLTON VALLEY SKI AREA has trailside condos that are open in the summer as a resort. Call 802-434-2769 for information and reservations. Dog allowed.

BRISTOL
FIREFLY RANCH

PO Box 152, Bristol 05443 802-453-2223
Pleasant ranch offers contermporary country rooms, delectable gourmet cuisine, fly fishing, hiking, swimming pond, biking, skiing in area, and horses to ride along tree-lined trails in Green Mt foothills. English and Western. German apoken RATE: special equestrian bed and bkfst, and other packages. About $152 per day. Bed & bkfst sgl $65. DOG: small dog allowed with approval.

CAMBRIDGE
4 PAUSE B & B

Box 765 Pleasant Valley Rd, Cambridge 05444 802-899-3927
Two rooms in small, friendly B & B in foothills of Mt Mansfield on 28 acres. Nearby hiking, biking, skiing, restaurants. RATE: $50 DOG: allow small friendly dogs. Owner has 2 cats. Good space to run and play on property.

CRAFTSBURY COMMON
INN ON THE COMMON

Main Street, Craftsbury Common 05827 800-521-2233, 802-586-9619

Luxurious rooms, fabulous food, swimming pool, tennis, croquet, gardens, and comfortable accomodations. Nearby, golf, canoeing, skiing. RATE: $190 DOG: allowed with prior notice; $15 1 x fee.

CRAFTSBURY CENTER RESORT

Box 31-VTGB, Craftsbury Common 05827
800-729-7751, 802-586-7767

Full service 140 acre resort on Lake Hosmer, with miles of trails, biking, horseback riding, swimming, canoeing, sailing, fishing, skiing. RATE: minimum $52.50 DOG: allowed in 3 cabins. No charge.

FAIRLEE
LAKE MOREY INN RESORT

Fairlee 800-423-1211

Affordable 4-season family resort. Offers 166 delux guest rooms, cottages, lakeside dining. On site 18-hole golf course, 600 acre lake, childrens programs, sail, canoe, swim, fish, hike, bike, tennis, health club, dancing. RATES: minimum $93 DOG: resort prefers not to have a dog, but will accept in cottages only in summer. No charge.

JAFFREY
WOODBOUND INN

Jaffrey 03451 800-688-7770, 603-532-8341

This is a 200 acre, self-contained service country resort on the shores of 2 1/2 mile Lake Contoocook. Woodland, sandy beaches, and meadows feature an abundance of leisurely and recreational on-site activities including swimming, boating, fishing, hiking, skiing, ice skating, tobogganing, picnicking, golf, putting, tennis, biking, games. In the area, guests are interested in Mt Monadnock with its easy well-marked trails and views. Also, Cathedral in the Pines, Friendlt Farm petting zoo, historic homes, villages, antiques.

There are more than 200 lakes and ponds, forests and trails... all away from public roads. RATE: 1 bedrm cottage $125 sgl. $135 dbl. includes hearty country bkfst. Inquire about extended stay rates. Also, modified American Plan available.
DOG; Welcome at lake front cabins. Must be with owner outside cabin. Not allowed in Main Inn.

KILLINGTON
CORTINA INN

Route 4 HC 34, Box 33, Killington 800-451-6108, 802-773-3331
Host: Ted Bridges, manager
This Inn blends the hospitality and cozy charm of a country inn with amenities of a resort hotel. Provides comfortable, relaxing place, plus an indoor pool, health club, and gourmet restaurant. There are 8 tennis courts and miles of hiking and biking trails. Well -trained staff. Nearby, several challenging golf courses. When snow falls a shuttle bus carries skiers to slopes of nearby Killington and Pico ski areas. There is snowmobiling, ice skating, sleigh rides and snow shoeing on premise. Local antique shops, art galleries, and country stores and discount outlets nearby.
RATE: minimum sgl $108, dbl $150 per ngt, Includes hearty Vermont buffet bkfst. Children under 12 free.
DOG: welcome at $5 per ngt, per pet. Cannot be left alone in guest room. He should use an outside door to your room to enter Inn, and must be fed on tiled bathroom floor or outside.

LONDONDERRY
WHITE PINE LODGE

Route 11, Londonderry 05148 802-824-3909
Fully furnished cozy and confortable 4 and 5 room suites, fire-places, kitchens, on 15 acres adjacent to National Forest. Hiking, swimming, fishing, x-country skiing. 5 minutes to Bromley.
RATE: minimum $45. discount on longer stays. DOG: well-behaved dog welcome @ $7 per day. Lots of space to run and play.

MENDON
RED CLOVER INN

Woodward Road, Mendon 05701 800-752-0571, 802-775-2290
A cozy inviting Inn on 13 acres in beautiful Green Mts. Offers

12 rooms, some whirlpools, fireplaces, jacuzzis, game room. Guests relax, swim, bike, hike. RATE: minimum $130 DOG: dog allowed in some rooms in Carriage house with outside entrances.

ORLEANS
GREEN ACRES CABINS

R.R. #2, Box 424, Orleans 05860 802-525-3722
Offers five charming 2-bedrm housekeeping cottages, large lawn, sandy private beach, dock, canoe. RATE: inquire, DOG: allowed with a small fee

PUTNEY
TAILS UP INN

Dusty Ridge Road, Putney 05346 802-387-2297
Host: Honey Loring, Director; Mary Quinn, manager
This is a colonial farmhouse guest house with rental rooms dedicated to dogs and their humans, run by personnel from Camp Gone to the Dogs. (see special section). Offers dog beds, dog biscuits, dog books, and 7 fenced acres of woods and fields, a pond, and paths to explore. Your dog can run free. You can enjoy the luxury of doing nothing. Nearby, horseback riding, restaurant, and shops in Putney. RATE: minimum sgl $40. This is also the site of weekend training retreats for dogs and owners. Rate $275 weekend training. Call for additional information.

STOWE
GOLDEN EAGLE RESORT

Rt 108, Mountain Road, PO Box 1090, Stowe 05672
802-253-4811, 800-626-1010
Offers rooms, efficiencies, mountain and pool views, some fireplaces. Swimming pool, fitness center, tennis, fishing, nature trails, dining, children's programs. Village 1/2 mile. RATE: min. $79 DOG: allowed in 2 rooms in older style hotel rooms of resort across street. No charge or deposit.

TEN ACRES LODGE

14 Barrows Road, Stowe 05672 802-253-7638, 800-327-7357
1840 farmhouse country inn. Individually furnished guest rooms.

some fireplaces, hot tub, restaurant, swimming pool, tennis. Has 2 cottages and 18 rooms. RATE: $50 DOG: well-behaved dog in cottages only.

THE MOUNTAIN ROAD RESORT

P.O. Box 8, Stowe 05672 802-253-4566, 800-367-6873
Host Bill Mintzer
This mini-resort has ultra-delux and luxury accommodations, with world class amenities, an Aqua-center pool and spa, a mini-gym, and is just minutes from terrific downhill and cross-country skiing. At the resort is a new large heated pool, whirlpool, tennis, and games on 7 acres of landscaped grounds and gardens. There are bicycles, grills, and lawn games. Adjacent is a 5 1/2 mile Stowe recreational area and an 18-hole golf course. Stowe's newest AAA 4 Diamond award winner. RATE: minimum dbl in summer $89, Suite minimum $195 DOG: One dog allowed in room or suite. Owner must sign statement responsible for damage. Plus 1 x cleaning fee os $15-$25. There is a dog walking area on property.

TOPNOTCH RESORT & SPA at Stowe

4000 Mountain Road, Stowe 05672 800-451-8686, 802-253-8585
This is an internationally acclaimed 120 acre resort and spa that takes its inspiration directly from the glory of its surroundings. Walls of glass open onto mountain landscapes and the timeless beauty of New England. It combines European charm and service with New England warmth and excellent cuisine. There is endless activity. Play tennis, hike to the summit of Mount Mansfield, explore nature trails, bike or walk on Stowe's 6 mile recreational path, swim in indoor and outdoor pools. Horseback ride and play golf at an 18-hole course 5 minutes away. In winter, Stowe is the "ski capital" of the East with lessons available. There is an internationally acclaimed spa with professional services available. RATE: Minimum sgl $113 off season. Children under 12 free. Special packages available. DOG: Small dogs only in rooms. Check with reservations if in doubt. No fee or restrictions.

VERGENNES
BASIN HARBOR CLUB

Vergennes 05491 802-475-2311, 800-622-4000
Host: the Beach family

This is an exceptional 700 acre family resort paradise on the 600 mile shoreline of Lake Champlain. Offers 77 cottages and rooms in 2 lodges. Lakeside dining. There are 5 tennis courts, a pool, rental boats, an 18-hole golf course, and an airstrip. There is fishing, lake or pool swimming, jogging, biking trails, nature strolls. Views of the Green Mountains and Adirondacks. A children's program frees parents to pursue their own interests. Open May-October.
RATE: example: Fall special. 3 nights $540 per couple per cottage.
DOG: smaller, well- trained dog allowed @$5 per day in cottage only. Dog must be leashed on resort property and kept away from waterfront. Owner responsible for any damage.
You can reach this resort by car, boat, private or commercial plane.

WARREN
POWDERHOUND LODGE

Route 100, Sugarbush Valley, Warren 800-548-4022, 802-496-5100

This is a charming New England Inn for dining and socializing and adjacent modern accommodations. In warmer months, hike, bike, canoe, golf, and shop for antiques. There is a swimming pool, clay tennis court, lawn games, and a hot tub. In winter, enjoy some of the finest skiing in the East at 3 major ski areas, i.e. Sugarbush North and South, and Mad River Glen. Two room suites feature a living room with cable TV, phone, bath, kitchen, and bedroom, for up to 4 persons. RATE: minimum dbl about $65
DOG: welcome. Fee $10 for short stay, or $20 for a week or more.

WOODSTOCK
KEDRON VALLEY INN

Route 106, South Woodstock 05071 800-836-1193
Host: Max and Merrily Comins

This charming country Inn has been rated in the top 10 by travel writers and has been featured in national magazines. The restaurant is tied for honors in Vermont, has top wine list. Located on 15 acres in a valley of the Green Mts, it has a large spring-fed swimming lake flanked by 2 white-sand beaches. There are miles of hiking trails, perfect for romps with a dog. There is a 50 horse stable and 5 ski areas, plus fishing, canoeing,golf, and a large fitness center. Right on the property, a beautiful stream can provide your dog with a dip, after jogging and frisbee fun. In Woodstock, there is an art gallery which specializes in canine effigies, which dogs can visit and will be offered doggie treats. RATE: Minimum $120 per night for 2, incl breakfast. Discounts and special packages mid-week non-peak. DOG: Well-behaved dogs are welcome. Must be on leash at all times. Must be quiet when left alone. Not allowed in dining room, on beach, or in lake. Owner responsible for any damage.

• VIRGINIA

Spectacular scenery as you drive Blue Ridge Parkway, Skyline Drive. There are national forests and Shenandoah National park, as well as 35 State parks. Northern Virginia relates more closely to Washington DC. Visitors and vacationers go to the Richmond, Tidewater area which boasts historic Williamsburg, Norfolk, Virginia Beach, the Shenandoah Valley.

• CABINS IN VIRGINIA STATE PARKS

Dept of Conservation and Recreation, Commonwealth of Virginia
203 Governor St, Richmond 23219 804-786-2121, 800-933-PARK
Virginia State parks provide 140 rustic cabins, and 1500 campsites, in which dogs are permitted. Cabins are located in Claytor Lake, Douthat, Fairy Stone, Hungry Mother, Seashore, Staunton River, and Westmoreland. Hiking trails, bridal trails, bicycle trails, swimming, boat rentals, fishing, restaurants and picnic areas available at various parks. Call for further information .
RATE: minimum cabin about $205 weekly, plus pet fee.
DOG: allowed in cabins. Charge is $3 per night per dog. They must be kept in cabin, tent, or vehicle at night and on leash no longer than 6' at all times.

BASYE
SKY CHALET MOUNTAIN LODGE

P.O. Box 300, Basye 22810 540-856-2147

This 1937 lodge brings the feeling of "Switzerland" to the beautiful Shenasndoah Valley. Mountain lovers paradise, offers comfortable lodging, good food, rustic atmosphere, fireplace. Area offers hiking, skiing on snow or grass, golf, horseback riding, tennis, swimming, in pool or lake, fishing, antique and flea market shopping. Located near Skyline Drive and George Washington National Forest. Children welcome. RATE: minimum about $35 DOG: allowed in some rooms with advance notice.

CLIFTON FORGE
LONGDALE INN, Bed & Bkfst

6209 Longdale Furnace Road, Clifton Forge 24422
800-862-0386, 540-862-0892 Host: Bob & Kate Cormier

Victorian mansion located on 12 acres in the Allegheny Mts, minutes from Shenandoah Valley, in historic district. Lots of nature, culture. Hiking on trails. RATE: $120 dbl approximate
DOG: allowed in 1st floor suite only, which has outside entrance. Lots of space to run and play. No charge.

FORT HAYWOOD
THE INN AT TABB'S CREEK LANDING, Bed & Bkfst

P.O. Box 219, Fort Haywood 23138 804-725-5136
Host: Cabell & Catherine Venable

This Inn on 30 acres was originally the antebellum home of sea captain Billups in 1820's. There are many country lanes with virtually no traffic, plus canoeing and fishing. There is a swimming pool on the grounds, screened porches, shade trees, magnolias, and 100 rose bushes. Offers bedrooms in the house and 2 suites in a cottage. Breakfast provided. Dinners can be arranged. Several nice restaurants in area. RATE: minimum bedrm $99 DOG: welcome, additional charge $20.

FREDERICKSBURG

BEST WESTERN JOHNNY APPLESEED

543 Warrenton Road, Fredericksburg 22405 540-373-0000
Offers 88 rooms in family oriented hotel near battlefields. Swimming pool, playground, extensive nature trails good for walking your dog. RATE: Minimum $38 DOG: $5 per pet 1 x charge

SHERATON INN

P.O. Box 618, Frederisksburg 22404 703-786-8321, 800-682-1049
This Inn in historic Fredericksburg offers 200 guest rooms and suites, dining room and lounge, an out-door pool, tennis and basketball courts and a fitness center. RATE: minimum $119, DOG: small dog allowed, not over 20 lbs.

GORDONSVILLE

NORFIELDS FARM, Bed & Bkfst

1982 James Madison Hwy, Gordonsville 22942
800-754-0105, 540-832-2952 Host: Teresa T. Norton
Has 500 acre working dairy farm. Farmhouse offers 2 rooms and 1 suite, 2 private baths. Full country breakfast. Fresh air, long walks, animals, and quiet. RATE: minimum $75 DOG: allowed in room with owner. no charge. Lots of space to exercise.

SLEEPY HOLLOW FARM Bed & Bkfst

16280 Blue Ridge Turnpike, Gordonsville 22942
540-832-5555, 800-215-4804 Host: Beverley Allison & Dorsey A. Comer.
Farm with 2 cottages with fireplaces and whirlpool. Pond with gazebo for swimming and fishing. Nearby horseback riding. Near Skyline Drive, Montpelier, and Monticello, 90 minutes drom Wash. DC. There is a children's play area. Golf, hiking, croquet lawn available. Delicious country breakfast. Beautiful gardens and long grassy lawn. RATE: minimum rate cottage $95-$125 DOG: allowed in cotttage only at $10 per night. Dog can swim in pond on property but must behave with resident ducks.

HILLSVILLE

DOE RUN LODGE

RT 2, Box 338, Hillsville 24343 540-398-2212

Offers chalets and villas in the Blue Ridge Highlands. Recreation includes tennis, golf, fishing, bird watching, hunting, hiking, and touring. RATE: inquire DOG: $45 fee for 2-nights.

IRVINGTON
THE TIDES LODGE and Marina

P.O. Box 309, Orvington 22480 800-248-4337, 804-438-6000
Host: owner/mgr E.A. Stephens, Jr
Open mid-March- December
This Lodge is a small resort that emphasizes luxury in an informal setting. It is located on its own 75 acre peninsula a few miles from Chesapeake Bay. Among the varied activities are 45 holes of golf, 3 tennis courts, sauna, a salt water and heated fresh water pool, yacht cruises, small boats, bikes, fishing, an exercise room. The Royal Stewart Dining Room has innovative cuisine. Moonlight cruises on a private yacht are popular, as are dancing, tennis or putting. RATE: Range of rates and packages. Inquire. Example: Min. rate waterside cottage with 2 bedrms, kitchen, liv/din, private deck European Plan $230. No charge children under 18. DOG: one small dog welcome at $10 daily. Kennels available. No restrictions.

LOCUST DALE
INN AT MEANDER PLANTATION

HC 5, Box 460, Locust Dale 22948 540-672-4912, 800-385-4936
Host: Suzanne Thomas and Bob Blanchard
Historic colonial country estate in lovely elegant, restful surroundings. Thomas Jefferson was a frequent guest. Has rooms and cottage-type "dependency buildings" outside house. RATE: $105 in outside buildings. DOG: allowed in outside bldgs. Lots of space. No charge.

LURAY
DEERLANE COTTAGES & CABINS

PO Box 188, Luray 22835 301-567-3036, 800-696-3337
Offers a variety of private comfortable 1-3 bedroom cottages and cabins, some riverfront, some in beautiful wooded area. Fireplaces, decks, kitchens. Nearby horseback riding. hiking, fishing, golf, shops. RATE: min. $100 DOG: welcome @ $10 per day

NATURAL BRIDGE
NATURAL BRIDGE OF VIRGINIA HOTEL

P.O. Box 57, Natural Bridge 24578 800-533-1410, 540-291-2121
"One of the seven natural wonders of the world" Natural Bridge is part of Virginia history. Surveyed by George Washington and owner by Thomas Jefferson. Hotel offers luxurious accommodations, fine restaurants, and a special brand of hospitality. You can explore underground caverns, see history in the wax museum, play tennis, golf, swim, and hike mountain trails. Offer hotel, annex, and cottage.
RATE: in cottage $35 DOG: allowed in cottage onl y. $5 charge per ngt. Owner must clean-up after dog. There are many hiking paths, streams in area that dogs and owners enjoy.

NORFOLK
LAKE WRIGHT RESORT (Quality Inn)

6280 Northampton Blvd, Norfolk 23502 800-228-5157, 804-461-6251
Resort offers 305 guest rooms, suites, apartments, restaurant, 18-hole golf course, outdoor pool, tennis, jogging, on 135 beautiful acres. Located minutes from Norfolk and Virginia Beach.
RATE: summer dbl $59 DOG: allowed $25 1 x charge.

NORFOLK MARRIOTT WATERSIDE

235 E. Main St, Norfolk 23510 800-228-9290, 804-627-4200
At an ideal location in popular resort area. Virginia Beach east, colonial Williamsburg west. Offers health club, pool, sun deck.
RATE: inquire DOG: under 35 lbs allowed with $35 non-refundable fee

SCOTTSVILLE
HIGH MEADOWS INN, Bed & Bkfst

High Meadows Lane, Scottsville 24590 804-286-2218, 800-232-1832
Host: Peter Sushka & Mary Abbit
Offers 12 rooms on 50 acres in classic European Auberge, located 15 mi south of Charlottesville. Gourmet bkfst. Candlelight dining, fireplaces. Relaxed and romantic. RATE: min $95 DOG: allowed in certain rooms. Lots of space to run and play. $20 1x charge.

STAUNTON
INGLESIDE RESORT

1410 Commerce Road, Staunton 24401 540-248-1201
Resort in beautiful Virginia hills offers 18-hole golf course, 2 large swimming pools., tennis courts, 3 restaurants. Special golf pkgs. RATE: min. about $49 DOG: allowed in certain rooms. $5 charge.

SYRIA
GRAVES MOUNTAIN LODGE

Route 670, Syria 22743 703-923-4231 Host: Jim Graves
Open Mar 14-Nov 30.
A family owned and operated rustic mountain retreat deep in the foothills of Blue Ridge Mts. Known for hospitality and home-cooked food, surrounded by natural beauty and wide range of activities. Hike, fish, golf nearby, tennis on 3 courts, swim in olympic pool, or just "porch sit". There is a central lodge and various accommodations. Hikers have a wealth of trails, easy to challenging. Guides available. An 8,000 Rapidan Wildlife Area open to public for hunting and fishing. State game regulations apply. Historic areas, antique shops, auctions near. Horseback riding popular. RATE: min. about $65 DOG: allowed in some cottages. No charge.

VIRGINIA BEACH
FOUNDERS INN

5641 Indian River Road, Virginia Beach 23464 800-926-4466
4-diamond resort-type hotel encircled by beaches, waterfront, wildlife preserves, golf courses, and mfgs outlets on 26 acres with lake and English gardens. 249 rooms, restaurants, tennis, pool, fitness. RATE: inquire DOG: allowed according to room availability and dates. Inquire directly with hotel reservations personnel. Must be well behaved.

OCEAN HOLIDAY HOTEL

25 St & Oceanfront, Virginia Beach 23451 800-345-SAND
Offers 105 air conditioned oceanfront rooms, balconies, TV, sun deck, indoor heated pool, exercise room. Activities include golf, fishing, walks. Near new oceanfront park. RATE: summer $95 min. DOG: small dog welcome at $10 per day

WILLIAMSBURG
HERITAGE INN

1324 Richmond Road, Williamsburg 23185 800-782-3800
804-229-6220

Inn with colonial ambiance, warmth, and charm, located close to the restored district, major shopping outlets, and College of Wm & Mary. Traditional rooms, TV, swimming pool, terrace, spacious front lawn.
RATE: summer $72 DOG: allowed. can be walked on lawns.

WASHINGTON

Visitors see Seattle, Mt. St Helens, Olympic National Park, No Cascades National Park, and Whidbey and San Juan Islands, among others. State is a natural vacation land for guests with dogs.

ANACORTES
OLD BROOK INN , Bed & Bkfst

530 Old Brook Lane, Anacortes 98221 360-293-4768
Host: Dick Ash

Lovely Inn set in orchard planted in 1868. Pick your own berries in season. Continental breakfast served. This is a quiet setting with 10 acres of cleared farm and forest land with walking trails, a pond stocked with bass, an 18-hole golf course 1 mi. away.
RATE: min. $70 DOG: allowed. no charge. Good setting for walking

ASHFORD
MT RAINIER COUNTRY CABINS
entrance Mt Rainier National Pk

38624 S.R. 706 East, Ashford 98304 206-569-2355
Host: Norma & Gordon Babo

Offers cabins located 900 ft from Mt Rainier Nat Pk Nisqually entrance. Cozy cedar cabins with electric heat, fireplaces, housekeeping units, set off highway in park-like setting. Large lawn for picnic or play. Activities include watching wildlife, waterfalls, photography, hiking to Indian Henry's Hunting Ground, fish in Mineral Lake, ride scenic railroad, hike Wonderland Trail, snowshoe, ski.
RATE: 2 people small unit $55-$65. Kitchen with fireplace, $60-$75. DOG: charge $10 per ngt. Cannot be left alone in cabins. Outside must be leashed due to wildlife.

- BAINBRIDGE ISLAND

MONARCH MANOR ESTATES, Bed & Bkfst

7656 Yeomalt Pt, Dr. Bainbridge Isld 98110 206-780-0112
Host: T.W. Smith
B & B and private house rentals available, TV, kitchen, all linens, washer, hot tub. Private beach and walking trails are a delight. Children allowed. RATE: min. $95. DOG: allowed with $50 deposit.

- BLAINE

INN AT SEMI-AH-MOO

9565 Semi-ah-moo Pkway, Blaine 98230 800-770-7992
360-371-2000
4-star resort has 18-hole golf course, tennis, health club, kids program, bike and walking trails, sand beaches, pool, sailing, jet skii, parasail, and more. Offers 198 guest rooms, fireplaces, restaurant, library. Located on scenic peninsula surrounded by Puget Sound., 2 hrs from Seattle. RATE: inquire DOG: $50 non-refundable deposit

- CHELAN

KELLY'S RESORT

R.R. 1, Box 119, Chelan 98816 509-687-3220
Small family resort on 20 acres on Lake Chelan. Offer 10 cottages spaced in woods and 4 on lake, fireplaces, decks, kitchen. No dog in lakeside units. There is lake swimming, docks, boat moorage, woodland walking trails, yard with games. No jet skiis. RATE: min. cottage summer abt $110. DOG: allowed in cottages $20 per pet, per week or $10, 3 days or less. Dogs enjoy wooded trails and can swim in lake.

- COULEE CITY

COULEE LODGE RESORT on Blue Lake

33017 Park Lake Rd,, Coulee City 99115 509-632-5565
Host: Keith & Louise Granacki
Beautiful Blue Lake 3 1/2 mi long, located in the scenic "little grand canyon" of Washington State is a firherman's delight. Vacationers also enjoy swimming and water skiing. Nearby, Grand Coulee Dam, horseback riding, and 9-hole golf. Resort offers housekeeping cabins on lake, a lawn, sandy beach, jet ski, bikes, games, protected marina, store. RATE: min. cabin $45. DOG: welcome

However, leash law strictly enforced. Dog may not be tied outside unattended. Charge $5 per night in cabins. There are areas to walk dogs without a leash, and places on shore for dog to swim.

FORKS

KALALOCH LODGE by the sea in Olympic National Pk

157151 Hwy 101, Forks 98331 360-962-2271

An all-inclusive resort in Olympic National Park; charming with all modern conveniences. Activities include hiking, biking, fishing, beachcombing. Explore rain forests of Pacific Northwest. Scenic trails. Full dining, lounge. RATE: Minimum cabin $101 dbl. Children under 5 yrs free. DOG: small dogs on leash allowed in cabin area only. Pet fee $12.50 per pet, per ngt.

GLACIER

MT BAKER CHALET

P,O. Box 5009, Glacier 98244 360-599-2405 Host: Dorothy Copp

This is a rental agency for a large selection of delux to rustic vacation chalets, cabins, A-frame, condos. Open all year. Located in Mt Baker area, the last village at edge of national forest. All are privately owned; many allow dogs. Wooded locations, some near creek, linens provided. Near golf courses, hiking trails, fishing, boating, safe bike areas, restaurants. RATE: summer minimum $75, $50 midweek, winter rates a little higher. DOG: welcome at no extra charge. Dog will enjoy hiking spectacular mt trails, beautiful forests, and swimming in river or creek. Rural area ideal for dog "walkies".

GLACIER CREEK MOTEL AND CABINS

PO Box 5008, Glacier 98244 206-599-2991

Host: Cathy & Tom Miron

The entrance to Mt Baker National Forest is located at Glacier, with many walking paths, hiking trails, climbs, views, waterfalls. Fishing and hiking excellent. During winter, Mt Baker claims longest ski season in No America. Guests also view wildlife, treasure hunt, in abondoned towns, river raft, pick berries, and pan for gold. Accommodation offers 11 cabins, 9 motel type rooms, a main building with hot tub, coffee bar. Four restaurants nearby. RATE: min. cabin $60 (dbl) DOG: allowed in designated cabins only. Must advise if bringing a dog. Cannot leave dog unattended, must clean up after dog, and is responsible for damages.

EASTSOUND, on Orcas Island, Gem of the San Juans
GIBSON'S NORTH BEACH INN, INC.

Gibson, Hatten, & Seagrave, PO Box 80, Eastsound 98245
360-376-2660 Open all yr except 12/1- 2/14

These North Beach Inn housekeeping cottages consist of 11 cottages in a wooded setting along 1/3 mi pebble beach There are 90 acres of woods, fields, views, and sunsets. All cotttages have fireplaces, electric heat, and are completely furnished. RATE: Off season: Studio 2-3 days (dbl) $70, weekly $425.
2-bedrm 2-3 days (4 people) $100, weekly $550. Summer rates slightly higher. Inquire. DOG: Charge $10 per dog, per day. Inn allows 2 dogs per cottage with understanding that owners responsible for their behavior. Dog can run free on beach if aren't people around. However, dog must be controlled. One neighbor with llamas who doesn't want dogs on their property.

WEST BEACH RESORT

Route 1, Box 510, Eastsound 98245 360-376-2240

Located on Orcas Island, this resort is directly on water on sand/ pebble beachfront. 15 cabins have a view, kitchens, deck, linens at waters edge or among fir trees. No maid service. No smoking in most cabins. RATE: 1 bedrm cabin (max 4) summer $125 per ngt. DOG: allowed by arrangement in certain cabins $10 per pet per day. Also, signed pet agreement with a $50 pet damage deposit; refundable.

MAZAMA
LOST RIVER RESORT

672 Lost River Rd, Mazama 98833 509-996-2537, 800-996-2537
Host: Jim & Sharon Sandon

Resort offers rustic cabins, fully furnished with kitchens, for year around recreation. Surrounded by National Forest, close to Pasayten Wilderness. Ideal for hiking, back-packing, fishing, mt biking, cross-country and back-country skiing for all skill levsls. Historic is about 21 mi away. Harts Pass, state's highest point is 10 mi from resort. RATE: Min. sgl unit $50 couple per ngt, $10 each addtl person. 7th day free. Children under 5 free. DOG: no charge Dogs welcome. Your host, the Sandon's enjoy having guests bring dogs. Their own dog Lennon makes friends and likes to play. Dogs can run free here. Numerous hiking trails.

MOSES LAKE
SHILO INN

1819 E. Kittleson, Moses Lake 98837
800-222-2244, 509-765-9317
Moses Lake is state's second largest lake. Numerous parks and campgrounds in area make it a wonderful recreational spot to visit. Fishing and boating are popular. Many attractions and events in area. In offers indoor pool and spa, sauna, and fitness room.
RATE: min. $68 DOG: allowed at fee of $7.

MOCLIPS
HI-TIDE OCEAN BEACH RESORT

P.O. Box 308, Moclips 98562 800-MOCLIPS 206-276-4142
This 33 unit resort offers spectacular views of the magnificent Washington coastline and blue Pacific...a perfect get-away.
Fly your kite, hike the beach, swim, dig clams, kayak the ocean and river, and visit the Olympic Rain Forest nearby.
Accommodations feature completely equipped kitchens, comfortable living rooms, bedrooms, fireplaces, TV, lanai. Several good restaurants nearby. RATE: about $85 (dbl) DOG: Guests with dog have special units. Dog must be approved in advance. Owner responsible for damage. $10 charge per dog per ngt. Leash required. Dog towel provided.

PACKWOOD
TATOOSH MEADOWS
offers rental vacation homes by TMC Properties

P.O. Box 487, Packwood 98361 800-294-2311
Various sized vacation homes available for rent near Packwood... a gateway to Mt Rainier. Proximity to national park entrances provides fine hiking, skiing, fishing, scenic drives, guided horseback riding along river. RATE: min cottage $135 DOG: pet fee $25 per visit. Lots of space for fun. Your hosts, the Lerchens, live in River House with their Newfoundland dogs.

PORT ANGELES
LAKE CRESCENT LODGE

416 Lake Crescent Road, Port Angeles 98362 360-928-3211
Offers a lodge, small cabins, a restaurant, fishing and boating,

overlooking beautiful blue Lake Crescent. RATE: moderate DOG: allowed.

SOL DUC Hot Springs

P.O. Box 2169, Port Angeles 98362 360-327-3583

This is a hot springs resort located in Olympic National Park. Good initial base for a vacation trip in car. To the east lies Hurricane Ridge and Port Townsend. To the west is rugged coast, a beach combers paradise. To the north Lake Crescent. To the south Olympic National Pk. Resort offers cabins, swimming, mineral pools, bar and restaurant. No phones, radios, or TV in cabins. RATE: min $83 DOG: Fee per day $2. NOTE: Park service requires dogs to be on leash. Not allowed on park trails, in public bldgs, or to be left unattended.

• QUINAULT
LAKE QUINAULT LODGE

P.O. Box 7, 345 South Shore Rd, Quinault 98575
800-562-6672, 206-288-2900 open all year

Located in Olympic National Forest, this Lodge offers a fine dining room, indoor pool, sauna, jacuzzi, games, hunting, fishing, rain-forest hiking trails, canoes, paddle boats. This beautiful area has towering firs, rugged shores and sandy beaches. Excellent fishing. RATE: Annex rates: peak season min $90; winter $49. Children 5 and under free. DOG: allowed in annex rooms. The Forest Service allows dogs on 6' leash on their trails.

• SAN JUAN ISLAND
INNS AT FRIDAY HARBOR SUITES

680 Spring St, Friday Harbor, San Juan Island 98250
800-752-5752 360-378-4000

Two beautiful Inns offer a selection of 72 rooms and mini-suites. Golf, tennis, water sports, whale watching, large indoor pool and spa, exercise room. Inn offers delightful tours of island on unique dbl-decker bus. Restaurant, game room. Many opportunities for dogs to enjoy the beaches as well as hiking trails, with owners. RATE: min about $60 DOG: allowed in designated "pet rooms"

• SEATTLE

ALEXIS HOTEL

1007 First Ave, Seattle 98104 206-624-4844, 800-426-7033
Elegant 109 room hotel with fine services, spa, fitness center.
RATE: minimum $175 DOG: allowed

FOUR SEASONS HOTEL

411 University St, Seattle 98101 206-621-1700, 800-821-8106
Offers 450 rooms, elegant building, health Club, solarium, boutiques, restaurant, near city attractions. RATE: min $220, ask about packages DOG: allowed. Require pet damage waiver signed.

SEATTLE MARRIOTT

3201 S 176 St, Seattle 98188 206-241-2000
Offers 459 comfortable rooms, restaurant, swimming pool, fitness.
RATE: min. $79 DOG: allowed

• UNION

ALDERBROOK RESORT

E. 7101 Highway 106, Union 98502 800-622-9370
360-898-2200
This is a lovely resort, golf, and conference center located on the picturesque Hood Canal in the midst of 525 wooded acres. It offers fine accommodations and unlimited recreation. Includes waterfront activities, top golf course, tennis, biking, heated pool, games, hiking through miles of forests. Offers spacious rooms and cozy cottages, restaurant with waterfront dining, entertainment, dancing.
RATE: summer cottage about $129. golf packages.
DOG: allowed at charge of $8 and a refundable damage deposit of $25. Dogs enjoy beach access and the extensive wooded areas.

• WHIDBEY ISLAND

HARBOR PLAZA (Best Western)

5691 State Hwy 20, Oak Harbor, Whidbey Island 98277
360-679-4561, 800-927-5478
Ideal lodging to explore Whidbey Isld and San Juan Islds. Has comfortable rooms, continental bkfst, fitness center, heated pool, restaurants. Area has little towns, parks, grren forests, lakes, gardens. Hike, bike, horseback ride. RATE: min $63 DOG: al lowed.

Charleston is the center of commerce, while the north has farms and the east mountains and wilderness. Hiking is popular in the Monongahila, Elkins, and George Washington national forests with very large number of acres. State parks number 35. Favorite ski areas are Canaan Valley and Timberline. Potomac Highlands is a good general recreational area.

• CANAAN VALLEY
DEERFIELD VILLAGE RESORT

Rt 1, Box 152, Canaan Valley 26260
800-342-3217, 304-866-4698 open all year
This fine private resort is nestled in the center of the Appalachian Mountains. It offers the best in luxury accommodations for a relaxing mountain get-away.
There are luxurious townhouses with wood burning fireplaces after a long day outside skiing. Swim at the outdoor pool, play golf or tennis, stroll through two nearby parks. Try whitewater rafting, canoeing, horseback riding, bicycling, fish, hike, visit the nearby parks. RATE: minimum 1 bedrm $125 daily. Special pkgs. DOG: allowed in selected units. Lots of area for them to enjoy. $35 fee.

• DANIELS
GLADE SPRINGS RESORT

3000 Lake Drive, Daniels 25832 800-634-5233, 304-763-2000
Nestled in the Appalachian Mountains of southern West Virginia lies this beautiful and spacious 4,100 acre resort estate, with spectacular scenery and cool mountain air providing the perfect environment for a wide variety of vacation activities, such as: an 18-hole golf course, tennis center, equestrian center, outdoor olympic size pool, fishing, hiking on forest trails and paths, white water rafing nearby. Golf and ski packages available. Lodging in villas and suites. RATE: Summer minimum sgl suite $88. No charge for children under 12. DOG: $50 deposit against damage. No restrictions.

CREEKSIDE

P.O. Box 111, Greenville 24945 800-691-6420
Host: the Sandell's

Creekside is a family-run resort in the heart of the Appalachian Highlands. Situated beside beautiful Indian Creek, its 200 acres of scenic hiking and biking trails are a perfect environment for canine guests. Country roads, covered bridges, old barns, small country stores and the absence of TV and telephone, create a perfect atmosphere to relax and unwind. Offers 8 cottages of various sizes with fully equipped kitchens and bath. Most have fireplaces and jacuzzis. There is a picnic grounds, playground area, outdoor grills, and fishing. Nearby are white water, cave tours, and other historic and cultural attractions. RATE: 2-ngt minimum stay @ $135. DOG: welcome at $10 per night.

• LEWISBURG

GENERAL LEWIS INN

301 E. Washington St, Lewisburg 24901 800-628-4454
304-645-2600 Host: Mary Noel & Jim Morgan
This is a magnificent mansion with columns and green lawn, antiques, and good meals. RATE: Inquire DOG: dog allowed on the first floor. Extra charge for dog $10 per day per dog.

• WHEELING

OGLEBAY RESORT

Wilson Lodge and Cabins

Wheeling 26003 800-624-6988
This is a top family resort on a 1,500 acre municipal park. Offers golf, tennis, swimming pools, jacuzzi, paddle boating, fishing, 4 1/2 miles of walking and jogging trails, playgrounds, picnic areas, gardens, restaurants and shops. Offers lodge rooms and about 40 cabins. Dog allowed in all cabins at no charge.
RATE: moderate, inquire DOG: no restrictions stated, but bring your leash.

Milwaukee, on the shores of Lake Michigan, is the largest city with with good shopping, restaurants. A Municipal park, Whitnall Park, has 660 acres and is one of the largest municipal parks in the nation. Lots of recreation, and botanical gardens. Visitors also visit rock formations in Wisconsin Dells and Lake Delton, plus Lake Superior's 22 Apostle Islands.

BOULDER JUNCTION
ZASTROW'S LYNX LAKE LODGE

P.O. Box 277M, Boulder Junction 54512
715-686-2249, 800-882-5969

This is a good resort for families with children. There is a lodge and nicely spaced individual cabins with lots of nature and privacy. Cabins are from 1-5 bedrooms with TV and refrig. Maid service provided. Lodge offers American Plan option with delicious and plentiful food. Activities include: hiking on marked nature trails, safe sandy swimming beach, playground, boating and canoeing, games, fishing boats. RATE: abt $275 per week DOG: allowed

CABLE
LAKEWOODS RESORT & LODGE

HC 73, Box 715, Cable 54821 800-255-5937, 715-794-2561
Host: Phil and Kathy Rasmussen

Located in Wisconsin's northern forest on the shore of Lake Namakagon, this is a complete lodging, restaurant, bar, and recreation facility. Rooms are comfortable to luxurious 1-3 bedrm condos. There are also lodge rooms and cottages. There is an indoor pool, sauna, excellent food graciously served. Activities include an 18-hole golf course. Guests can fish, swim, water ski, sail, play tennis, and hike and bike in the beautiful Northwoods.

In winter, enjoy 500 miles of snowmobile trails, or ski, ice skate and sled. RATE: minimum 2-bedrm cottage (for 4) about $135. Minimum sgl $40. DOG: Allowed by prior arrangement only. All dogs must be leashed on resort property. Charge $25 .

HAYWARD WISCONSIN

ROSS' TEAL LAKE LODGE and Teal Wing Golf Club

Route 7, Ross Road, Hayward 54843 715-462-3631
Host: Prudence and Tim Ross OPEN: late May-mid-October resort.
All year, self-contained private guest homes.
Deep in the one million acres of Chequamegon National Forest, this northwoods "un-roughing-it" resort offers luxury accommodations, superb food, excellent service, and old fashioned hospitality. "This is a lodge where everything is done right".
There is a main lodge with dining room, indoor recreation center, modernized holiday homes spaced along 1/2 mi of private shoreline Complete kitchens, fireplaces, linens, TV, and daily maid service. Activities include fishing in Teal Lake and Lost Land Lake, canoeing, paddleboating, swimming in lake or heated pool, golf at Teal Wing Golf Club, tennis, shuffleboard, bike, hike on miles of trails, hunting in Fall, and more. Known by Audubon Intl for environmental sensitivity and awareness. Nearby are state and national parks, rivers, golf facilities, water skiing, and horseback riding.
RATE: Min. 1-bedrm (dbl) offseason $100. There are 1-2-3 bedrm guest homes, sleep up to 12 people. DOG: well-behaved dogs welcome. Maximum 2 dogs per cabin. Must be leashed in center of resort and around guests. Charge $5 per pet, per day.

EAGLE RIVER

GYPSY VILLA RESORT on Cranberry Lake

950 Circle Drive, Eagle River 54521
715-479-8644 (let phone ring at least 10 x's)
414-782-7652 (office) Open all year
This is one of the top favorite cottage resorts in the midwest, located on Cranberry Lake...part of the largest chain of lakes in the world. This resort is different. The main part is on Cranberry Island (100 acres), the lakefront vacation island villas each have 200' of their own waterfront with a private dock, boat, and swimming at your front door. Each villa includes screened porch, lv rm, fireplace, kitchen, bath, hot water, heat, electric, phone, TV, some linens. Guests can do aerobics, games, campfires, fish, tennis, children's games, cookouts, golf. Service rentals include sail boats, ski boats. Horseback riding and golf courses nearby RATE: example, summer, Min $564 for 4-2 bedrm. Inquire. DOG: under 40 lbs accepted at $40 per week. Owner must pick-up after dog,

Dog must be kept on leash on resort property, and not left alone.

IRON RIVER
DELTA LODGE

Rte 2, Box 161, Iron River 54847 715-372-4299
Host: Marilyn & Andy Einspanier
This Lodge is a wilderness playground located in the heart of the Chequamegon National Forest. The Lodge is a central recreation area with restaurant and games. There are 11 cabins of various sizes around the property. Each unit has deck and porch. No phones but you can bring your own TV or TV provided. Largest cabin is a 3-bedrm. There is a sand beach and 70' swimming dock on Lake Everett. Some boats available. In area you can fish with a guide, horseback ride, mountain bike, tour Apostle Islands, and shop. RATE: summer 1-bedrm cabin weekly $395; call for details on variable rates and meal plans available. DOG: welcome at $30 per pet charge. Keep leashed on lodge property, out of swimming area and off furniture.

LAC DU FLAMBEAU
DILLMAN'S SAND LAKE LODGE

3305 Sand Lake Ln, Lac Du Flambeau 54538 715-588-3143
Host: Mrs Dillman, the Loars and Robertsons Open: May 15-Oct 15
A highly rated family vacation destination, this Lodge offers rooms and cabins and an endless list of activities such as: waterskiing, canoeing, fishing, tennis, sailing, ball games, kayak races, cook-out and picnics, nature studies, biking, hiking, scuba diving, and the enjoyment of the solitude of the majestic Northwoods pine forests. There are fun activities from toddlers to teens, fully supervised. Lakeside dining offers Northwoods delicacies and more traditional cuisine. Nearby guests find many fine golf courses. Horseback riding is available. Numerous other attractions include waterfalls, summer theater, Chequamegon National Forest, and more.
RATE: min. room daily $55, weekly $400.
Minimum cabin (dbl) daily $127.20, weekly $840.
DOG: Guests can bring dog but must consider the rights of others. Dog not permitted on beaches and shound be on leash when outdoors. Also, cannot be left unattended in units.

TY-BACH, Bed & Bkfst

3104 Simpson Lane, Lac Du Flambeau 54538 715-588-7851
Host: Janet & Kermit Bekkum
A unique bed & breakfast. Offers a modern home on the shore of a tranquil northwoods lake, located on a Chippewa Indian reservation. Area has 49 acre lake, 80 acres of woods with walking trails, "logging roads", a native American cultural center, Pow-Wows, casino and a recreated Ojibue Village, state and national forersts, Activities available include swimming, fishing, boating, hiking, cross-country skiing. RATE: $70 1-bdrm
DOG: dog allowed with advance arrangements required. Owners have three quiet, well-behaved pets.

PHELPS
AFTERGLOW LAKE RESORT

5050 Sugar Maple Road, P.O. Box 5, Phelps 54554 715-545-2560
This resort is located in the North woods of Vilas County. It has 240 wooded acres with hiking trails, and beyond this, Nicolet National Forest. There are 3 tennis courts, 3 sailboats, canoes, photography, mountain bikes, or bring your own wind surfing equipment. There is an exercise center and recreation room. There is a children's playground with swings, jungle gym etc. Hunting in season. Sightseeing trips nearby. RATE: off·season cottage minimum abt $400 (2 bedrm) per week for 2 adults. Partial week prorated. DOG: dog allowed all year except NOT in summer. Otherwise specific permission required prior to arrival. Fee is $30 per week per dog.

RHINELANDER
HOLIDAY ACRES RESORT on Lake Thompson

4060 S. Shore Dr., Rhinelander 54501 715-369-1500, 800-261-1500
Resort located in Northwoods of Wisconsin. The grounds encompass over a thousand acres of beautiful deep woods, a long, lovely Lake Thompson shoreline, tennis courts, anc children's playground. Nearby are golod courses, riding stables, and thousands of lakes. Rhinelander, only 4 mi away, has shopping, theaters, more. Resort is

family managed and continues to reflect the best in resort life in friendly service. Has restaurant and cocktail lounge. Activities include a heated pool, game room, boating, 3 tennis courts , lake sports, hiking, nature and bike trails, swimming beach, winter sports in season. Nearby, golf, stables, a farm, and more. RATE: 28 lodge rooms and 28 cottages available. min. sgl $79, cottage about $80. packages available, weekly rates. DOG: allowed in lodge or cabin at $5 per night. Must be leashed for control in resort area.

WYOMING

Among the treasures of Wyoming is Yellowstone, which provides access to treasures such as the Grand Canyon. Grand Teton National Park is popular. Recreation areas list Jackson Hole as a top interest of visitors.

CHEYENNE-LARAMIE

A. DRUMMOND'S RANCH, Bed & Bkfst

399 Happy Jack Road, Cheyenne-Laramie 82007
Host: Tadie & Kent Drummond 307-634-6042

A quiet, gracious retreat, featured in several magazines, is set on 120 acres by a national forest and state park. Offers a carriage house loft and "55,000 acres of outdoor adventure at absolutely no charge." Activities include hiking, llama packing, mt biking, rock climbing, camping, golf, dinner theater, back country tour, fish. You can bring your own horse. RATE: min. room $60, carriage house loft $125. Your horse can be boarded at $15 per night. Vacation with your horse and dog. (They do not provide horses). DOG: charge $10 per night. Must be kenneled in inside facility on property. Not allowed in rooms. Can hike with owners. There is a county leash law.

CENTENNIAL

SNOWY MOUNTAIN LODGE

P.O. Box 151, 3474 Snowy Range Road, Centennial 82055
307-742-7669

Wilderness cabins located in Medicine Bow Routt National Forest, 6 miles west of Centennial. Birds, elk, deer squirels and bear abound. Accommodations offered are several heated cabins for 2-4 people, 2 cabins for 5-8 people, a bunk house for 25 people. The Lodge has a restaurant, lounge, and dance floor. Ski, snowmobile, hike, fish, bike, hunt, birdwatch, pick berries. RATE: cabin minimum $35 DOG: allowed

JACKSON HOLE
SNOW KING RESORT

400 East Snow King Avenue, PO Box SKI, Jackson Hole 83001
800-522-KING, 307-733-5200
This is a beautifully designed 204 room hotel and condos located at the base of Snow King Mountain in Jackson Hole, set in "America's most beautiful outdoors" and most elegant rustic indoors. Amenities include 2 restaurants, a saloon, indoor ice rink, game room, sauna, outdoor heated swimming pool, Alpine slide, miniature golf, and stables (summer only), skiing,..downhill, cross-country, and night skiing, and shops. Grand Teton National Park is just 4 miles, and Yellowstone National Park 55 miles from resort. RATE: Offseason minimum (Sept-Dec, April-May) $90 May-Sept $160 Children under 12 free. DOG: allowed with a $50 non-refundable deposit.

MORAN
SIGNAL MOUNTAIN LODGE

Grand Teton National Park, P.O. BOx 50, Moran 83013
307-543-2831 Open May 7 through Mid-October
This is the only resort located on Jackson Lake inside Grand Teton National Park. The views are incredible. The Teton Mountains, sparkling Jackson Lake, and nearby Yellowstone National Park is only 25 miles away...all are magnificent. The variety of accommodations tions include cozy log cabins, lakefront retreats, country rooms and family bungalow. Memorable dining at Aspens restaurant. Store and gift shop. Backcountry scenery can be enjoyed on a tranquil scenic float or thrilling whitewater ride on Snake River. On the lake, a wide variety of boats available. Fishing excellent. There are hundreds of miles of trails and mountain climbs. Horses available. RATE: min. cabin $67 DOG: leashed, housebroken, not left alone.

• YELLOWSTONE
YELLOWSTONE NATIONAL PARK ACCOMMODATIONS

AMFAC Park & Resort, Yellowstone National Park 82190
303-297-2757, 307-344-7311

Open May 5–October 22, and Dec. 15 -March 12

There are 9 convenient locations for lodging throughout Yellowstone, a favorite visitor destination among the national parks. Eight of these allow a pet dog, they are:

Mammoth Hot Springs Hotel and Cabins
Roosevelt Lodge and Cabins
Yellowstone Canyon Village, Lodge and Cabins
Lake Lodge Cabins
Grant Village
Old Faithful Lodge Cabins
Old Faithful Snow Lodge and Cabins

Almost all have cabins with bath. There are 5 dining rooms.

Park activiities include:
horseback riding, stagecoach rides, cookouts,
sightseeing motor tours,
boat rentals, fishing,
skiing, snowmobiling in winter.

RATE: Minimum cabin rate about $35. Children under 11 free.

DOG: dogs permitted in all cabins. Must be housebroken and quiet. Must not be left unattended.

CAMPING

PARK, FOREST. WILDERNESS

If your resort is near a forest or park, you will want to read the dog regulations that follow, for a possible day trip. Further inquiry with rangers at the local park level is also helpful to get maximum safe freedom for your dog, especially off-season when regulations about where dogs can go and the leash law may be more relaxed.

As a primary vacation destination, camping out in our magnificent federal and state forests, parks, and wilderness is the least expensive way to vacation and can be most rewarding if you enjoy camping outdoors. Many recreational opportunities are offered in various parts of the country. Phone the areas that interest you and get direct information and information sheets.

This guide does not cover private RV camp sites. You can get this information from state tourism offices.

CAMPING IN A NATIONAL FOREST

There are 155 National Forests located throughout America. You can hike, fish, camp, and ski and more. Guests especially enjoy the forest surroundings. There are over 100,000 miles of trails and 10,000 recreation sites awaiting visitors. The best way to get specific information about the forest you may want to visit, and how to make reservations for camp sites, is to contact the regional office of the Forest Service service listed below. For national information contact: US Forest Service, Dept. of Agriculture, 201 W 14 Street, SW Washington, DC 20250

NORTHERN REGION. Federal Bldg, 200 East Broadway St., PO Box 7669, Missoula, Montana 59807 406-329-3511
Whether you are looking for the rigors of a wilderness trek or an easy drive along a scenic byway, you'll find it here.

ROCKY MOUNTAIN REGION 11177 West Eighth Ave, PO Box 25127 Lakewood, Colorado 80225 303-275-5350
Challenge yourself on some of the world's finest ski slopes or hike through rugged mountains or on well-maintained trails.

SOUTHWESTERN REGION Federal Building, 517 Gold Ave, SW, Albuquerque, New Mexico 87102 505-842-3292
Magnificent mountains, colorful desert, canyons and mesas are yours in this region.

INTERMOUNTAIN REGION Federal Bldg, 324 25 Street, Ogden, Utah 84401 801-625-5352
This is a land of contrasts, from deep red canyons to tall mountains wrapped in pine and fir. Opportunities for sightseeing, camping, and whitewater rafting.

PACIFIC SOUTHWEST REGION 630 Sansome Street, San Francisco California 94111 415-705-2874
See coastal redwoods, mountain meadows, and rushing streams. Camp near the Sierra Nevada Mountains, or climb sleeping volcano, Mount Shasta.

PACIFIC NORTHWEST REGION 319 SW Pine Street, PO Box 3623 Portland, Oregon 97208 503-326-3651
Float the Snake River, drive around snow-capped Mount Hood, or explore a rain forest.

SOUTHERN REGION 1720 Peachtree Road NW, Atlanta, Georgia 30367 404-347-2384
From cypress swamps to mountain meadows and forests, this region offers exotic beauty or hiking challenges shuch as that of the Appalachian Trail.

EASTERN REGION 310 West Wisconsin Ave, Room 500 Milwaukee, WI 53203 414-297-3646
In the fall, drive among the blazing autumn colors of a hardwood forest, hike, and ski in winter in this lovely area.

ALASKA REGION Federal Office Bldg, 709 West 9th St, PO Box 21628, Juneau, Alaska 99802 907-586-8863
Evergreen forests, rugged snow-capped mountains, rushing streams with salmon, caves and gold rush trails all await visitors.

RATES: camping rates will be part of the information provided. Even though rates may be raised in the near future, they are still nominal.

DOG: Keep in mind that dog regulations help keep your pet safe, as well as protecting the environment. Dog must always be restrained or on a leash while in developed recreation sites . They are not allowed in swimming areas. In most cases this means that THEY ARE ALLOWED on hiking trails, roads and paths, and in some rivers and streams. Check with your local District Ranger for specific information about where your dog can go and what he can do. The season of the year and the number of people in the park may influence the policy.

CAMPING IN A NATIONAL PARK

For national information contact the National Park Service, U.S. Department of the Interior, Washington DC 20240

There are about 308 national parks in America. Those that are also national recreation areas provide a wide variety of possible activities such as: hiking, camping, hunting, four-wheel driving, kayaking, canoeing, whitewater rafting, horseback riding, swimming, scuba, road and mountain biking, rock climbing, expoloring, more.

Overview information about the parks, where they are located, and what they provide can be obtained by writing to the address above. For specific information about specific parks, contact the Regional Office. Among the better known parks with camping facilities that take reservations are:

ACADIA, PO Box 177, Bar Harbor, Maine 04609. Charge $10 daily 207-288-3338

ASSATEAGUE ISLAND Route 611, 7206 National Seashore Lane, Berlin, Maryland 21811 Charge $10 daily 410-641-3030

GRAND CANYON Mather, Box 129, Grand Canyon, Arizona 86023 602-638-7888 Charge $10 daily

GREAT SMOKY MOUNTAINS, Gatlinburg, Tennessee 37738 615-436-1231 Charge $7

OZARK RIVERWAYS PO Box 490, Van Buren, Missouri 63965 314 323-4236 Charge $7

ROCKY MOUNTAIN Estes Park, Colorado 80517 303-586-1206, 303-386-1333 Charge $10

SEQUOIA & KINGS CANYON Three Rivers, California 93271 209-565-3774 Charge $10

SHENANDOAH Route 4, Box 348, Luray, Virginia 22835 703-999-2266 Charge $12

YELLOWSTONE PO Box 168, Yellowstone, Wyoming 82190 307-344-7381 Charge $10

YOSEMITE PO Box 577, Yosemite, California 95389 209-372-0200 Charge $12

DOG : In a national park, dog must be on leash, length varies in different parks. Dog must not be left unattended in campground. Owner must clean-up after pet. Owner responsible for keeping dog quiet. Parks differ somewhat in regulations about dogs. Once you have determined the park you are interested in camping in, it is important to ask exactly where the dog can go on leash. Some parks permit dogs on hiking trails, others do not, but they can go on roads and paved areas. Some parks permit dogs in backcountry, others don't. Most parks prohibit dogs in public buildings. In some cases dog must have current proof of rabies innoculation and have an identification tag with owner name and asddress. This is a good idea anyway. All dogs that travel should have "papers" with owner and an identification tag in case pet gets lost.

CAMPING IN A STATE PARK

If a camping vacation with your family and dog is your goal, don't overlook the parks of the 50 States. Some are extensive and offer recreation, education, and relaxation in a beautiful setting at low cost. For example, in the State of California, there are 275 state parks, with a land area of 1.4 million acres. There are plant and animal species, activities such as swimming, sailing, touring, hiking, horseback riding on more than 1,500 mi of trails throughout the parks. This system has more than 17,500 campsites for visitors and groups. Each State has regulations about the use of the parks. Contact the department in charge of Parks in the state you may want to visit. In some cases it is the Dept. of Parks and Recreation, or the Department of Conservation, or the Department of Fish, Wildlife.
DOG: In general, most parks permit dogs at the camp sites on leash or in a vehicle. Nominal fee per dog. Dog may not be allowed on trails or beaches. Check with each park individually.
RATES are variable but minimal.

NOTE: We have noted in the "resorts" section of this book some unusually good federal or state recreation lands where cabins are available that will allow dogs.

NOTE:

Drives through forests, parks, and wilderness areas can be very interesting. However, one word of caution...be sure your dog is under control even if you do not plan to get out of the automobile. Bears and other wildlife often come up to the car windows since tourists often feed them. If you camp out, it is essential to keep your dog controlled, for his own safety...as well as protection of animals.

CITIES

A big city vacation is still the best vacation for many people who want to see theater, museums, shop, eat at famous restaurants, and more, that only as big city offers.

These vactions need not mean leaving your dog at home. With the proper planning and the right hotel... located near a park...everyone can have fun .

First choose a "walkers city". The five cities described here are all "walkers cities". They are delightful to tour on foot...of course, with your dog on leash beside you. Most important, they have park recreational facilities available for your pet and owners to enjoy.

Consider vacations in Boston, Chicago, New York City, San Francisco, and Washington, D.C.

MASSACHUSETTS

BOSTON

Boston is a picturesque, dynamic, culturally aware city, which is steeped in history and attracts many visitors. It has many institutions of higher education in the area that add to its dynamic qualities, such as Boston University, Harvard, Tufts, and others. Places to visit include museums, a planetarium, and an aquarium. The Boston Symphony performs, as well as the Boston Ballet. Theater is active in Boston, with many plays moving to Broadway in New York, after tryouts in Boston. The Boston Pops performs from May to mid-July and gives some free outdoor concerts at the Hatch Memorial Shell. For shoppers, there are large department stores, such as Filene's basement, which will interest those seeking real values.

The best sightseeing should be done on foot. Well-behaved dogs can walk along to historical areas...the Freedom Trail which begins at the Boston Common, Beacon Hill with cobblestone streets, through flower-filled Boston Public Garden, past chic shops on Newbury Street and up to Hancock Tower. The Cambridge area, across the river, a higher education mecca, is also worth a visit. Dogs can be taken on leash also to the Boston Common, and along the Charles River Basin near central Boston. The best times to visit Boston are late spring, summer and early fall. Winter is very cold.

DINING in Boston for that special dinner. Try:
L'ESPALIER, 30 Gloucester St, Boston 617-262-3023 This is a contemporary French restaurant in a Back Bay townhouse with several dining rooms.
CHART HOUSE, 60 Long Wharf, Boston 617-227-1576 Located on the waterfront, it specializes in steak and seafood.
BAY TOWER ROOM, 60 State Street, Boston 617-723-1666. In a high rise tower with a view, this is an elegant dining room with a variety of special cuisine.
JASPER'S, 240 Commercial Street, Boston 617-523-1126
A fine restaurant with nationally known cuisine. Try the New England boiled dinner.

HOTELS in Boston that allow dogs with guests include:

BOSTON HARBOR HOTEL, 70 Rowes Wharf, Boston 02110
617-439-7000. 800-752-7077 A fine hotel at harbor location.
RATE: minimum $195 DOG: allowed

FOUR SEASONS, 200 Boylston Street, Boston 02116
617-338-4400 800-332-3442 Multilingual staff. Large pool.
Jog or walk along the Charles River. RATE: min. $210
DOG: under 30 lbs allowed.

HOWARD JOHNSON HOTEL, KENMORE, 575 Commonwealth Ave,
Boston 02215 617-267-3100 800-654-2000 Comfortable hotel.
RATE: min. $135 DOG: allowed, no restrictions stated

RITZ CARLTON, 15 Arlington Street, Boston 02117
617-536-5700, 800-241-3333 Luxury hotel in Back Bay.
RATE: $245 DOG: allowed with $75 deposit, $50 returnable.
cannot leave dog alone in room.

SHERATON BOSTON HOTEL & TOWERS, 39 Dalton Street, Boston
02199 617-236-2000, 800-325-3535
RATE: min. $165 DOG: allowed. no restrictions stated.

WESTIN HOTEL, COPLEY PLAZA 10 Huntington Ave, Boston 02116
800-228-3000, 617-262-9600 Lovely hotel.
RATE: min. 617-262-9600, 800-228-3000

NOTE: have your travel agent get you the best rate on hotel.

When you leave Boston, consider taking an additional mini-vacation up toward Maine with its breath-taking forests and coast, or travel to Cape Cod with its 300 miles of shoreline, open for public recreation, plus lighthouses, museums, and other attractions.

CHICAGO

Chicago is a midwest city that is fun to visit and quite easy to take your dog. Be sure your hotel is within a very short distance from the scenic walkways that trace the Lake Michigan shoreline. There is grass and trees that your pet will enjoy, and you can walk or jog for miles of exercise. Also explore Grant Park.

For walking in the city itself, stroll the downtown area with the Magnificent Mile and the Loop. There is lots of art, architecture of interest, many unusual shops, and good restaurants available. Department stores should not be missed if you like to shop. There are evening theater and concerts. Fall and spring are the best times to visit with your dog, since summer is hot and winter is cold with a brisk breeze from Lake Michigan. Hotels often have week-end or get-away packages which would lower the rates.

DINING in Chicago for that special dinner. Try:
ART INSTITUTE RESTAURANT IN THE PARK, Columbus Drive, 312-443-3543. This fine restaurant is open to the public. It has a stylish dining room and very good food. Overlooks Grant Park.
EVEREST, 440 S La Salle St, Chicago 312-663-8920
Located in a financial center skyscraper. Serves conpemporary French cuisine.
PRINTER'S ROW, 550 S Dearborn Street, Chicago 312-461-0780
Serves delicious food in several dining areas.
SPAIGGIA, 980 N. Michigan Ave, Chicago 312-280-2750
Offers elaborate Italian dining.

HOTELS in Chicago that allow dogs with guests include:
BLACKSTONE HOTEL, 636 S Michigan Ave, Chicago 60605
800-622-6330,312-427-4300 Offers rooms, suites, restaurant.
RATE: minimum $109, DOG: allowed
CLARIDGE HOTEL, 1244 N. Dearborn Pkwy, Chicago 60610
312-787-4980, 800-245-1258 Offers, rooms, suites, restaurant.
RATE: RATE: min. $109, DOG: smaller dog allowed

ESSEX INN, 800 S. Michigan Ave, Chicago 60605
312-939-2800, 800-621-6906 Offers pool, restaurant, rooms. RATE: minimum $89 DOG: must sign waiver and use service elevator

FOUR SEASONS HOTEL, 120 E Delaware, Chicago 60611
800-332-3442 312-280-8800 Luxury hotel, restaurant, fitness, indoor pool. RATE: min. $305 DOG: Cannot leave alone

RAPHAEL HOTEL, 201 E Delaware Place, Chicago 60611
800-821-5343, 312-943-5000 In Gold Coast near Magnificent Mile, restaurant, lounge with piano player RATE: minimum $130, weekend packages. DOG: allowed

REGAL KNICKERBOCKER HOTEL, 163 E. Walton Pl, Chicago 60611
312-751-8100, 800-621-8140 300 rms near Lake Michigan jogging trail and Oak Street Beach & Health Club.
RATE: minimum $125 DOG: allowed

MARRIOTT HOTEL , DOWNTOWN 540 N Michigan Ave, Chicago 60611 312-836-0100, 800-228-9290 Rooms, pool, restaurant
RATE: minimum $139 DOG: under 20 lbs only

TREMONT HOTEL 100 E. Chestnut St., Chicago 60611
800-621-8133, 312-751-1900. In the heart of the Gold Coast, near the Magnificent Mile. Excellent location for shopping, dining, and nightlife. RATE: $220 minimum DOG: allowed

WESTIN HOTEL, 909 N Michigan Ave, Chicago 60611
800-228-3000, 312-943-7200 Has renovated delux rooms, restaurant, health club. RATE: minimum: $195 DOG: allowed

NEW YORK CITY

The "Big Apple" is our nation's most populous city and the capital of finance, business, communications, and theater. With an amazing diversity in every area, it remains unrivaled as a place to visit. To enjoy a family vacation in New York City with a dog, choose a centrally located hotel within easy walking distance of Central Park. Since city travel is always a problem, a central hotel will put you near good restaurants, museums, midtown shopping, and self-guided walking tours around town, on which you can take your dog. There are many, many dogs in New York City, which is fond of them.

Although you should not walk your dog in Central Park after dark for safety reasons, early morning is delightful and you will see many dog owners jogging and exercising their pets. There is a leash law and "pooper scooper" regulation here. Come prepared. Central Park is located between 59th Street and 110 Street, between Fifth Avenue and Central Park West. It has 840 acres containing a lake, zoo, boat rentals, rink, outdoor theater, restaurants, a castle garden, bridle path and nearby horse rentals, and miles of walking and jogging paths. There are free concerts in the park during the summer, and various other entertainment. Dog owners often sit on the lawn on the fringes to enjoy concerts on warm summer evenings. Sidewalk vendors sell hot dogs, ice cream and pretzels from stands.

In the city itself, cultural activities range from traditional Broadway to off-Broadway avant-guarde in plays, dance and theater. There are many historic areas from Wall Street financial districts downtown, to artistic Greenwich Village, and a large Chinatown. For shopping, enjoy Fifth Avenue shops and department stores and see famous churches. Many museums are located near the central part of the city, such as the Guggenheim Museum at 88 St & Fifth Ave, the American Museum of Natural History at 79th and Central Park West, and the Metropolitan Museum of Art at 82 Street. The Lincoln Center is located at Broadway and 64 Street. There is a real diversity of restaurants in New York City, with ethnic specialties such as Little Italy for Italian food and Chinatown for Chinese foods. The best times to visit New York are spring, early summer, and fall.

DINING in New York City for that special dinner, try:

CHIN CHIN 216 E 49 St, NYC 212-888-4555 This restaurant offers excellent chinese dishes in a central location, in three dining rooms.

FOUR SEASONS 99 East 52 St, NYC 212-754-9494. Try the Grill Room for lunch or the Pool Room for dinner. Generally excellent foods with especially memorable desserts.

LUTECE 249 East 50 Street, NYC 212-752-2225 Fine restaurant with French food. Try a sample of combination dishes.

TAVERN ON THE GREEN Central Park West & 67 Street, NYC 212-873-3200 Lovely location in the park. Beautiful dining and good food.

HOTELS in New York City that allow dogs with guests include:

CHATWAL INNS 234 W.48 St 800-621-4667

Owns a number of hotels in central area that have low-moderate rates and accept a small or medium dog with guests with a $100 deposit against damage. Among them are:

Best Western Woodward, 210 W. 55 St

Chatwal Inn on Park 429 Park Ave S.

President Hotel 234 W 48 St

Quality Inn 157 W. 47 St. and more. Phone above number.

THE CARLYLE, Madison Avenue & 76 St, NY 10021
800-227-5737, 212-744-1600 5-star hotel on upper east side near Central Park. 1-7 rm apartments. RATE: min. $300
DOG: small dog allowed $10 charge

ESSEX HOUSE/ Hotel Nikko 160 Central Park South, NYC 10019
800-NIKKOUS, 212-247-0300 Grand hotel in excellent location.
RATE: min. $275 DOG: small dog only with $100 deposit

THE LOWELL 28 E. 63 St, NYC 10021 212-838-1400,
800-221-4444 RATE: min. $295 DOG: small and medium accepted. Sign waiver. No charge.

MAYFLOWER HOTEL ON THE PARK 15 Central Park West, NYC 10023 800-223-4164, 212-265-0060 Excellent hotel in very good location. RATE: min. $155 DOG: allowed

NOVATEL 226 West 52 Street, NYC 10019 800-221-3185
RATE: $115 is the travel agent rate. DOG: allowed. guest is responsible for damages. No charge.

SAN FRANCISCO

San Francisco is an international city, with a Barbary Coast history, natural beauty, unique architecture, and great appeal. Tourism is the most important industry, but the economy also has other bases such as a role as a shipping mecca, a world communications center, finance center, manufacturing, and publishing center and others.

The city is a walker's paradise for owners and their dog. The Golden Gate National Recreation Area, which is the largest urban park in the world, has a federally protected shoreline through much of San Francisco and some of Marin coast. There are many beaches, 100 miles of hiking trails, and a bridle path. There is also a 3 1/2 mi footpath through the Presidio and Fort Mason Park. Golden Gate Park includes 1,077 acres and is highly worth visiting with your dog almost daily. Leash laws apply.

San Francisco boasts performing arts, symphony, opera, theater, and ballet. There is a wide variety of nightlife. There arew famous restaurants at major hotels, and at Chinatown and Fisherman's Wharf. The Wharf also has outdoor vendors and seafood stands convenient for dog owners who cannot take pet into a restaurant. To shop, be sure to visit the Ghirardelli Chocolate Factory, Pier 39, and the Cannery. For a drive, try the 49 mile scenic drive marked with signs around the City.

DINING in San Francisco for that special dinner, try:
HAYES STREET GRILL 320 Hayes Street, SF 415-863-5545
Offers a wide variety of superb fish dishes you will enjoy.
MASA'S at the Vintage Court Hotel 648 Bush Street, SF 415-989-7154 French cuisine elegantly presented. Jacket and tie required.
POSTRIO at the Prescott Hotel 545 Post Street, SF 415-776-7825
Offers California dishes with fresh ingrediants. Emphasis on pastas, breads, grilled seafood, and salads.

HOTELS in San Francisco that allow dogs with guests include:

BERESFORD HOTEL 635 Sutter St, S.F. 94102 800-533-6533
RATE: minimum abt $80 DOG: allowed at no charge. Call first to inquire.

CAMPTON PLACE HOTEL 340 Stockton St, S.F.
800-235-4300, 415-781-5555 RATE: $165. special DOG: @$25 per stay for cleaning.

CHANCELLOR HOTEL 433 Powell St, S.F. 94102
415-362-2004, 800-428-4748 RATE: $69 DOG: allowed

FOUR SEASONS CLIFT HOTEL 495 Heary St, S.F. 94102
800-332-3442, 415-775-4700 Elegant world-class hotel. RATE: minimum $205 DOG: small dog welcome. No charge. Dog given own package of treats. Can be walked by hotel staff if desired.

SIR FRANCIS DRAKE 450 Powell St, S.F. 94102
800-227-5480, 415-392-7755 In the heart of Union Square, restaurant, dancing. RATE: minimum $110 DOG: $75 refundable fee.

WESTIN ST FRANCIS Union Square, 335 Powell St, S.F. 94102
415-397-7000, 800-228-3000 On historic Union Sq. RATE: $195 DOG: no charge.

WASHINGTON, D.C.

More than 20 million tourists come to this national, and indeed international, capital city each year. Tourism ranks with government as a major industry. But in spite of all the activity, the general atmosdphere is still gracious, hospitable, and very southern. Washington DC is another "walk-about" town. For visitors there are many, many interesting places to visit, most with no admission charge. There are museums, memorials, libraries and the Kennedy Center for the Performing Arts. Just walking around on foot can be fun and your dog on leash beside you. He will not, however, be allowed inside buildings.

A major park to enjoy is Rock Creek Park, 1,750 acres within the city, with trails for walking, biking, and jogging, lawns and playing fields. There is also a National Zoological Park. You will need a car or taxi to get there from midtown.

While walking, investigate the numerous cafes and boutiques that line the streets, stroll along the Potomac River, visit Potomac Park, and stroll along the Mall. The Cherry Blossom Festival is late March or early April. Georgetown House and Garden Tours are held in April. In summer there are free concerts. Other "must see" areas are Embassy Row, Foggy Bottom, and Chinatown. Georgetown is a favorite destination with unique shops, major department stores and an atrium at Georgetown Park. In a more outlying area, Wolf Trap Farm Park for the performing arts in Vienna, Virginia gives performances throughout the year. It is 15 miles from Washington, DC and has 100 lovely wooded acres with paths to stroll with your pet.

DINING in Washington DC for that special dinner, try:
GALILEO 1110 21 Street, NW 202-293-7191 This is an excellent Italian restaurant.
LE LION d'OR 1150 Connecticut Ave NW 202-296-7972
Offers delightful French cuisine. Jacket and tie requested.
MAISON BLANCHE 1725 F Street NW 202-842-0070 For a "power lunch" try this French dining room near the White House.
SAM & HARRY'S 1200 19 Street NW 202-296-4333
A fine steak house. Jacket and tie requested.

HOTELS in Washington DC that allow a dog with guests include:

ANA HOTEL 2401 M St. NW Wash, DC 20037 202-429-2400 Near Georgetown. Multilingual staff, restaurant, pool, fitness ctr RATE: minimum $129 DOG: small and medium alllowed

CARLYLE SUITES HOTEL 1731 New Hampshire Ave NW, Wash DC 20009 202-234-3200 800-964-0377 Near Embassy Row. Kitchens, TV, health club. RATE: min. $69 DOG: trained allowed

DOUBLETREE GUEST SUITES 2500 Pennsylvania Ave NW, Wash DC 20037 800-424-2900, 202-333-8060 Located in fashionable West End neighborhood, near Kennedy Center & Georgetown. RATE: min. $99 DOG: allowed at $12 per day

FOUR SEASONS HOTEL 2800 Pennsylvania Ave NW Wash DC 20007 202-342-0444 Close to Georgetown. Pool restaurant, fitness club, night club. RATE: min. $230 DOG: allowed

GEORGETOWN INN 1310 Wisconsin Ave NW, Wash DC 20007 202-333-8900, 800-424-2979 Located in the heart of Georgetown. restaurant, fitness. RATE: inquire, packages DOG: allowed with a $150 non-refundable deposit, plus $25 per day.

GEORGETOWN SUITES 1111 30 St, NW, Wash DC 20007 202-298-7800 800-348-7203 Located in heart of Georgetown, health club. RATE: min $145 DOG: allowed $200 deposit which is refundable, plus $6 per day cleaning fee.

HOTEL WASHINGTON 515 15 St NW, Wash DC 20004 202-638-5900, 800-424-9540 Historic hotel near White House, Smithsonian; restaurant, fitness ctr. RATE: Inquire DOG: small dog allowed.

HILTON HOTEL 1001 16 St, NW Wash DC 20036 202-393-1000 Elegant hotel 2 blocks from White House. 70 VIP tower suites. Multilingual staff, restaurant, fitness. RATE: min. $130 DOG: allowed on signed agreement for damages. No charge.

SHERATON WASHINGTON 2660 Woodley Rd, NW Wash DC 20008 202-328-2000, 800-325-3535 1505 rms and suites in a park-like setting, rerstaurants, pools, fitness RATE: $89 DOG: small dog allowed

LINCOLN SUITES DOWNTOWN 1823 L St, NW, Wash DC 20036 202-223-4320, 800-424-2970 Good location. Offers 98 suites with with full kitchen, restaurant, health club. RATE: min. $109 DOG: allowed $10 per day charge

ADDITIONAL ORDER INFORMATION

To order extra copies of this book for family, friends or employees with a dog, send $19.95 per book, plus $2.75 1st class postage/handling to:

MARTIN MANAGEMENT BOOKS
2108 Kahekili Highway, Wailuku, Hawaii 96793

(808)244-4187

ALSO

Readers may be interested in:
GREAT VACATIONS FOR YOU & YOUR DOG, ABROAD

Call the above number for further information.